Islay Voices

Islay Voices

Edited by

Jenni Minto and Les Wilson

Dear Pam.

With best wishes

Jenni Minto

Les Wilson

EDINBURGH

First published in 2016 by Birlinn Ltd
West Newington House
10 Newington Road
Edinburgh
EH9 1QS
www.birlinn.co.uk

ISBN: 978 1 78027 291 7

British Library Cataloguing in Publication Data

A catalogue record for this book is available from the British Library

Typeset in Bembo with headings in ITC Benguiat at Birlinn

Printed and bound by
Gutenberg Press Ltd, Malta

Contents

Illustrations

Introduction

For thousands of years the island of Islay has drawn migrants, invaders and inquisitive wanderers to its shores. They have often come as lonesome travellers, but sometimes in great numbers like migrating geese. For many, their visits were inspired by innate human curiosity, while others came seeking a land that would sustain them. A few were washed up, half-dead, on Islay's shores. One such saved soul, seventeen-year-old Private David Roberts of the US Army, wrote to his mother of the 'Scots lads' who had dragged him ashore and to miraculous safety after his troopship sank off Islay in a terrible storm in 1918.

Among the most revealing accounts of journeys to Islay are those of the Skye-born traveller and writer, Martin Martin; the Edinburgh-born naturalist and clergyman, John Walker; the Welsh naturalist and antiquarian, Thomas Pennant; and the distinguished English scientist, Joseph Banks. These serious-minded and perceptive men subjected Islay to the same kind of scrutiny as Banks had employed when he visited Tahiti with Captain Cook. Viewed from London or Edinburgh, eighteenth-century Islay seemed almost as exotic as Tahiti.

The people of Islay – the Ileachs – too have written of the place. Islay has made an enormous contribution to Gaelic literature and song through the work of its bards, including William Livingston, the brothers Charles and Duncan MacNiven, and Duncan Johnston.

John Francis Campbell – known as *Iain Òg Ìle* (Young John of Islay) – was a renowned folklorist and Celtic scholar whose bilingual work, *Popular Tales of the West Highlands*, revealed the richness of Gaelic tradition to an international audience. Folklorists, many from Edinburgh University's School of Scottish Studies, have continued to draw from Islay's deep well of tradition; and local enthusiast Peggy Earl was a zealous recorder of stories.

John Murdoch, the campaigning journalist and passionate agitator for crofters' rights, never forgot that he was an Islay man. His testimony to the 1884 Napier Commission into the plight of poor Highland cottars and crofters reveals the hardscrabble lives led by most Ileachs in these times. Murdoch's accounts of landlordism, clearance and emigration make compelling reading.

ISLAY VOICES

A sense of medieval Islay can be gained from a unique land charter signed by a Lord of the Isles; a member of the Beaton medical dynasty left us good advice on health and welfare; and local clergymen penned revealing descriptions of island life for Scotland's first *Statistical Account*, compiled between 1791 and 1799. The 'tacksmen and gentlemen' of the Stent Committee, Islay's eighteenth-century (strictly undemocratic) 'parliament', left records of their endeavours. Landowners and law officers too had their say.

The late nineteenth and early twentieth centuries saw the arrival of a new species on Islay – the tourist. The growing demand for lively and illuminating guide books to the island was met by some highly gifted and well informed local writers, including the Rev. John G. MacNeil and the Port Ellen-born future Member of Parliament and biographer of Ramsay MacDonald, Lachlan MacNeill Weir.

Last but not least were the 'non-professional' writers of Islay – the men and women whose diaries and letters shed an intensely personal light on island life and contribute immensely to understanding the 'people's history' of Islay. Gossip about a mutual friend with a fondness for 'mountain dew' and an eye for the ladies, the business of planting crops and raising chickens, the trauma of shipwreck, and the experience of men fighting in two world wars are all to be found in letters preserved in the Museum of Islay Life.

While much of the material is organised chronologically, this is no history book. We have fleshed out the bare bones of history by plunging deeply into the well of myth, legend, superstition, fiction, poetry and song that Islay has inspired.

The writing about – and from – Islay is rich and rewarding. This anthology is, necessarily, brim-full of omissions, and could have been much longer. Our attempt to distil the essence of Islay is simply a very personal selection. We've chosen material that vividly describes, for us, the fascinating island that we love. The tone of the writing varies from the profound to the downright quirky, but we believe that all of it is revealing about aspects of Islay and its people, past and present.

There is wide discrepancy in the spelling used by different generations of writers. For example, Islay sometimes appears as *Ila*, *Ile* or *Isla*, Rhinns as *Rinns*, Lochindaal as *Lochindaul* or *Lochin-dàla*, and Kintyre as *Cantire*. It is a nightmare for proof-readers, but we've kept the original spellings in the passages we've included, as we believe that it reinforces for readers the antiquity of the writing. Gaelic spellings too may differ from modern usage.

The illustrations contained in this book are all from the collection of the Museum of Islay Life, and we are indebted to the Museum's trustees for permission to reproduce them.

In Islay Gaelic, 'thank you' is never expressed as *Tapadh leat*, only sometimes as *Moran Taing*, but usually as *Gun robh math agad*. A heartfelt *Gun robh math agad* is due to to all the quoted writers who have committed their experiences of Islay, and their thoughts and feelings about it, to paper. Any mistakes and omissions are ours.

What's in a Name?

In his biography of St Columba, written in the seventh century, Adomnán, who was the ninth Abbot of Iona, wrote of a place he called *Ilea insula* – the island of Islay. The name is a puzzle, and has been interpreted in several different ways. One eminent Celtic scholar has even deciphered the ancient name as meaning 'big-buttocked island'.

> Ilea insula corresponds to our modern *Eilean Ìleach*, *Ilea* being an adjective formed from *Ile*. The name, anglicised as Islay, occurs often in Irish records and literature, usually as *Ile*, sometimes as *Ila*; the modern Gaelic form is *Ìle* . . . If the name is Celtic, it might be compared with Gaulish *Ilio-marus*, a man's name, in which *Ilio-* may be some part of the body, like Latin *ilium*, *ilia*, the flanks of a man or animal: *Ilio-maros* would thus mean 'big-flanked or perhaps big-buttocked'. The Welsh verb *ilio*, 'ferment', may be compared: the root notion is 'swell'. The peculiar shape of the island lends itself to such an origin for its name.
>
> William J. Watson, *The History of the Celtic Place Names of Scotland*, 1926

Fortunately, there are more romantic explanations for the name Islay.

> The burial ground of Kildalton is marked by two large rudely-sculptured stone crosses. Of more ancient interest is the tomb of Yla, or Eila, a Danish princess, who has bequeathed her name to the island, and also to some of its daughters. A high conical green hill above the Bay of Knock, seemed a fitting tumulus of nature's own building, so here the Danish lady was buried, and the spot is marked by two great upright stones, called "The Stones of Islay".
>
> C. F. Gordon Cumming, *In the Hebrides*, 1901

There has been considerable diversity of opinion as to the real derivation of the name "Islay" – some tracing its origin to "Ila" (easily convertible by some Saxon sage to Islay), the daughter of a Norwegian

Viceroy who resided there when the Island was possessed by the Danes; and from the fact, that the grave of this Lady is still being pointed out in a lonely spot near to the beautiful wooded policies of Ardemersay . . .

The grave is on a beautiful green spot, the whole length of which is almost required – the head stone being 30 feet distant from the stone at the foot of the grave – the Princess was not an insignificant pigmy.

Robert Oliphant, *The Tourist's Guide to Islay, The Queen of the Hebrides*, 1881

Tradition says that the island of Islay derives its name from Ile, a Scandinavian princess, who went to bathe in a loch there, and sticking in the soft mud, was drowned. The head and footstones of her grave are some distance from each other, and of three persons, who successfully attempted to open the grave to see what the bones were like, each died mad! Their action in opening a grave, to satisfy an idle curiosity, was in keeping with a morbid character, and they only died as they lived.

John Gregorson Campbell, *Witchcraft and Second Sight in the Highlands and Islands of Scotland*, 1902

One collector has a creation myth for a whole string of islands, involving a princess from Lochlann, an ancient Celtic name for Scandinavia.

A Danish Princess, called Iula, left Lochlann with an apron full of stones of different sizes. As she proceeded on her journey some of the stones fell out.

One of these became Ireland, another Rathlin and another Texa. She made for Loch a' Cnoic (Loch Knock) and as she went along, the remainder of the stones fell out and became the string of islands from Ardbeg to Kildalton and beyond. At last she reached the shore, tired and exhausted, only to sink in the soft sand. She did not have the strength to save herself, and when the tide came in she perished. Her body was taken to Seonaid Hill above Loch Knock and buried there. Her grave is marked by two small standing stones in a hollow copse on the left hand side as one proceeds up country. There is a fair distance between the two stones, and local tradition has it that she had to be cut off at the knees so that her body could be got out of the sand. She must have been of great height, a giantess in fact.

Peggy Earl, *Tales of Islay*, 1980

A more probable derivation (because supported by the structure of the word and the history of the place) is here offered. It is well known that *I*, in Gaelic, signifies Island. It is equally true that the great Mac-Donald, Lord of the Isles, or his predecessors the Norwegian Lord Lieutenant of Islay, established a council there of fourteen of the heads of the principal families of the Island: and that the said fourteen judges of *Armuinn* assisted their Lord with advice in his deliberations, and administered the Law among his subjects. Hence the seat of Judgement – this centre of wisdom, came to be called *"J-lagh"*, that is the Island of Law, Jurisprudence, or Legislation – *lagh* being the Gaelic for law – but convenience and refinement eased the guttural *agh* to give place to the vowel sound which now terminates the word *Ila*.

William MacDonald, *Sketches of Islay*, 1850

A poetical genius, now dead, suggested the signification "I-lagh", the Island of halves, from the fact, that Lochindaal nearly cuts it in two – an idea, not at all improbable, but a very likely circumstance . . .

Robert Oliphant, *The Tourist's Guide to Islay, The Queen of the Hebrides*, 1881

Various attempts have been made to give the true etymology of Islay. Mr. Alexander MacBain, M.A., one of our most competent authorities says that "Islay is one of those bottom names in our to-pography that we *cannot* make out. It shares with *Eire* or *Eireann* the peculiarity of applying to isles and rivers. The name *Ila* is common as a river name in Scotland, spelt *Isla* usually, and there is also the island of Islay so named. The root *eil*, *íl*, means 'move, swell, hasten, go,' and is very applicable to a river, but an island? Anyway the name is either Pictish or non–Celtic. Pictish is Celtic of Brittonic stock." Stokes suggests the German root *eilen*, to go. Skene thinks the name is pre-Celtic, and says that *Il* enters largely into Basque place-names. Captain Thomas draws attention to the fact that "the ancient Pictish or Gaelic names of the Hebrides are descriptive, and there can be little doubt that Islay would be in Welsh *Y-lédd*, and *I-leithe* in Gaelic, *i.e.* the parted or divided Island, in Gruineart." An allusion to its being nearly cut in two by the opposite estuaries of Lochindaal and Loch Gruineart, *I-lagh*, and *I-eile* i.e., the Isle of Law, and the Other Island, has been suggested.

J. G. MacNeill, *Islay*, 1899

First Impressions

The keenly observant and well-informed Welsh traveller, Thomas Pennant, first saw Islay from his 785-metre high perch atop the mountain of gold, Beinn-an-Òir, the highest of the three Paps of Jura.

> We gain the top, and find our fatigues fully recompensed by the grandeur of the prospect from this sublime spot: Jura itself afforded a stupendous scene of rock, varied with little lakes innumerable. From the west side of the hill ran a narrow stripe of rock, terminating in the sea, called, the Side of the Old Hag. To the south appeared Islay, extended like a map beneath us; and beyond that the north of Ireland; to the west, Gigha and Cava, Cantyre and Arran, and the Firth of Clyde, bounded by Ayrshire; an amazing tract of mountains to the north-east, as far as Ben Lomond; Scarba finished the northern view; and over the western coast were scattered Colonsay and Oransay, Mull, Iona and its neighbouring group of isles; and still further the long extents of Tirey and Col just apparent.
>
> Thomas Pennant, *A Tour in Scotland and Voyage to the Hebrides*, 1772

In the same year that Pennant was touring the Hebrides, the English natural-ist Joseph Banks fetched up at Lochindaal. He had not long returned from a voyage to Brazil, Tahiti, Australia and New Zealand with Captain Cook,

> At day break this morn we anchored in Loch Indaal and went ashore immediately. The town of Bowmore we found to consist of but few houses among them however were two publick ones these could supply us with victuals but by no means with lodging or even a room to eat in so it became necessary to pitch our tents which was finished about 4 o'clock in the midst of an immense crowd of people who had been brought together on account of preparation for the Sacrament which is here administered only once a year and seems to be received with much more respect and much more generally than in England.

The evening proved rainy so we were obliged to amuse ourselves with a plentiful Highland dinner composed of various legs of mutton and puddings which showed the plentifullness of this country and that luxury had yet made few advances in it. Some gentlemen of the country dined with us and after dinner introduced us to some of the Ladies who gave us tea and thus we at once commenced an acquaintance in this country.

Being Sunday an immense concourse of people came to receive the Sacraments so many that the three Clergymen officiated by turns the Communicants passed and repassed till after six o'clock this whole day it rained immoderately to which circumstance chiefly we owe the preservation of our characters for had we done any kind of work even walked out on a day held so sacred in this country this black deed would have been irreversibly sat upon us.

Joseph Banks's Diary, 1st August 1772

The isle of Ilay, Isla, or, as it is called in Erse, Ile, is of a square form, deeply indented on the south by the great bay of Loch-an-Daal, divided from Jura, in the north-east, by the sound, which is near fourteen miles long, and about one broad. The tides most violent and rapid; the channel clear, excepting the south entrance, where there are some rocks on the Jura side.

Thomas Pennant, *A Tour in Scotland and Voyage to the Hebrides,* 1772

From the celebrated poem of Dargo by Ossian, we learn that the Fingalians had to take shelter in Islay when on their way to Ireland to assist the king of Innisfail against the Scandinavian invaders. Ossian thus speaks: "The night is stormy and dark: but the Isle of bays is nigh. It spreads its arms like a bow when bent; and its bosom, like the breast of my love, is calm. There let us spend the night – gladsome place of the pleasant dreams." Everyone who has studied the geography of the western isles knows that Islay is the only one of them which agrees with the description given by the Fingalian bard.

William MacDonald, *Sketches of Islay,* 1850

The fierce tides that rip and roar round Islay leave an unforgettable impression on many visitors.

The tides are known to run through the Sound of Islay with the strength and rapidity of an enormous river, and an ordinary sailing vessel can no more make way against them, than an antelope can withdraw its slender limbs from the crushing coils of a boa-constrictor. A steamer alone can oppose that rushing current with any chance of success. We beat across and across again, and then, as if "Dragging at each remove a lengthening chain," we found ourselves nearly where we were:– so we went below to dinner, while the cutter kept off and on as she best could, till the tide should turn. The Maid of Islay steamer passed us ere long, with the accustomed successful pertinacity of these paddlers, but our Princess Royal made a great start the moment the flow was with us, and we were speedily abreast of Portaskaig.

There are few places of more picturesque appearance than this little station, with its quay and fishing boats, a few small houses assembled near a rocky creek, and a finely wooded glen retiring backwards towards the "hill country". We merely landed with our letters, and also gave notice to the country people, that we would willingly afford a passage to anyone bound like ourselves to Colonsay. A poor woman and a sick child (mother and daughter), who had been as far as Greenock to consult the doctors, were all who needed to avail themselves of our proposed kindness, so we pursued our way northwards with a head wind. However, the tide was still with us, and we speedily cleared the remaining portion of the Sound, of which the northern opening also presents several fine features.

James Wilson, *A Voyage Round the Coast of Scotland*, 1842

The Sound of Islay is in the centre about a mile in width, and is lined by abrupt but not very high cliffs. It is remarkable for the close correspondence of the opposing shores and the great rapidity of its tides, and the navigation is rather dangerous. On entering the Sound, a strong current is perceptible, which in a spring tide, if it happens to be adverse, with any considerable strength of wind also ahead, will impede very considerably even the power of steam, while the cross and short sea, raised by the current, may even create alarm to an indifferent sailor. The island of Islay now becoming 'tangible to sight', presents no very interesting or promising appearance. The coast seems bleak and bluff, without rising into the dignity of real hill or mountain, and presenting little else than the stunted and healthy vegetation of Alpine scenery.

> George Anderson and Peter Anderson, *Guide to the Highlands and Western Islands of Scotland*, 1863

On sailing through the Sound of Jura that "Queen of the Hebrides" the beautiful and ever verdant island of Islay was seen lying quietly resting on the bosom of the deep, away from the rush and bustle of work-a-day world. . . . Someone says that sailing into Port Ellen Bay, when the sun is setting behind the hill of Oa, is like entering a bit of Fairyland, the sky being bathed in all the varied shades of light; but if Islay is not Fairyland it is certainly a very fair and beauteous island, and a land of "*much speerit*" (because there are eighteen distilleries there), which often make, not only those on the island, but outside of it, *bow-more* than is pleasant or necessary.

> Robert Thomson, *A Cruise in the Western Hebrides or a Week on Board the SS* Hebridean, 1891

Islay stands out in the bright morning light, the headland of the Mull of Oa in bold tracery. Its coast-line, though rugged, is not repelling, its green fields rising to moorland and rounded hill-tops behind Mac-Arthur's Head grow more prominent. It is with a feeling of surprise we find that green Islay can boast such bold hillsides, steep cliffs and lofty uplands, for the summits behind MacArthur's Head rise to a height of 1,500 feet.

Across the Sound we look on the lower slopes of Jura, wide sweeping moorland rising to the three summits, the Paps of Jura, the landmarks of the Southern Hebrides.

Though the entrance to the Sound of Islay looks broad and safe as MacArthur's Head lighthouse passes abeam, to port, it is perhaps one of the most treacherous stretches of water in the Southern Hebrides. For many years I never passed this place without seeing some solitary mast rising out of its calm waters – the mast the only mark of the watery grave of some trawler. A considerable reef stretches from the Jura shore towards MacArthur's Head, and its cruel teeth have torn the plates from the hulls of several trawlers when a sleepy steersman has misjudged his distance from MacArthur's Head or fog and storm have hidden the light. Deep water on either side of the reef has been the resting-place of these ships, for here in fog, with the fast outflowing current of the Sound, lurks treachery and danger to the navigator.

As we glide up the silent narrowing Sound we soon realise the strength of the current flowing through it by the relatively slow progress of our ship. On the still surface of the Sound ugly boils of water erupt as if from the base of some devil's cauldron, until at places, with these eruptions and swirls of the current, one wonders if the Sound resents the progress of our ship.

A pleasant surprise awaits us as we pass a small point midway up the Sound, and we find our ship slowing and turning to come alongside the little jetty at Portaskaig.

Iain F. Anderson, *Across Hebridean Seas*, 1937

Let us imagine an aeroplanist following a truant eagle across Scotland to his eyrie in the Western Isles . . .

Careering in the wake of his winged pilot, he tilts upward to supernavigate Arran. From the airy altitude of cloud-land he sees it shaped like a Celtic shield and embossed with peaks like a buckler.

Past the beaconed headland of Kintyre he comes to the rim of the Western Ocean.

> "Where loud the northern main
> Howls through the fractured Caledonian Isles."

Northwards as far as the eye can see are islands, and islands, and islands, – a rosary of islands – stretching up and out to where St Kilda lies "looking through a cloud of gannets to the polar night." In the midst of this sea of a hundred islands, he comes to "green grassy Islay" – an island of a hundred lakes.

As he glides earthward, to alight on one of the lonely peaks beside Proaig, he notes the great bights of Lochindaal and Loch Gruineart, which almost bisect the island.

L. MacNeill Weir, *Guide to Islay*, 1911

Lachlan MacNeill Weir's vision of the 'aeroplanist' following an eagle to Islay was an up-to-the-minute one in an era when flight was in its infancy. What is interesting is that he has the eagle landing on Islay, not the aeroplane. It would be another seventeen years before that feat was attempted.

What is understood to be the first aeroplane flight to Islay with a landing on the island took place on Sunday. A two-seater Avro, carrying

Captain Stirling as pilot and Mr Robert Paul, Mount Vernon, as passenger, flew from Renfrew Aerodrome to Islay in an hour and twenty minutes. By train and steamer the journey occupies about eight hours. On descending on the island Captain Stirling and Mr Paul were met by Mr Duncan McIntyre, proprietor of Machrie Estate and hotel, with whom they had lunch.

The return journey to Renfrew was performed in 53 minutes. The round journey, including one hour spent in Islay, occupied three hours and fifteen minutes . . .

While this is the first actual landing on Islay, Captain Kingwell of the Renfrew Aerodrome, has done the same flight without attempting a landing.

The Campbeltown Courier, 21 July 1928

At first I told myself that I might have been in Knapdale for all the difference I noticed. Then, suddenly, I passed a low white croft and the smell of peat smoke hit me. As I drove on, the smell of peat established itself firmly in my reaction to Islay, because of all smells it makes me feel most lyrical. For the first time that day I began to feel cheerful; I persuaded myself that even if I spent two days on the island with nothing better to do than smell peat I should not have come in vain. As I drew near to the middle of the island I noticed that the houses looked neat and prosperous. Bridgend, with its trees and bridges, was trim and neat and almost pretty. I smelt money as well as peat.

James Bramwell, *Highland View*, 1939

Like Thomas Pennant atop Beinn-an-Òir on Jura, the modern writer, Andrew Jefford, gives us a memorable 'on-high' image of Islay.

It has been said before, but in its overall outline, Islay resembles a witch. The witch has a fierce, long and resolute chin which juts out into the Atlantic; she has a small nose, a thin neck and a small, peaked cap. Her back is inevitably humped, though this hump culminates in a point. She is stout-bodied, but her hands have been gathered together to form a little fist, and her short legs seem to have been bundled into a sack. Should you wish for a naming of parts, here they are. The chin culminates at Portnahaven; the nose is at Coull; and the peaked cap at Ardnave. The lighthouse at Rhuvaal marks the pointed summit of her hump, while her fists are gathered together at Laggan Point. Those short, stumpy legs are hidden away in the sack called the Oa. Kildalton and Ardtalla mark her unspeakable nether regions. And thus, cat-less and with no sign of a broomstick, she is crouching for eternity, ready to meet the Atlantic and face whatever the jaunty hateful sea cares to throw at her.

Andrew Jefford, *Peat Smoke and Spirit*, 2004

The Ileachs

Travellers have not been reticent about reporting what they thought of the Ileachs they met.

> The genuine Islaymen are to this day remarkable for the size and goodliness of person.
>
> George Anderson and Peter Anderson, *Guide to the Highlands and Western Islands of Scotland*, 1863

> No objection can be made against their natural parts and abilities, which are subtle and ingenious. They are fond of their own country and are not much addicted to enlisting in the army or navy. They marry young, and are generally connected by intermarriage, which must always be the case with insular situations; and yet they are very kind to all strangers, who come to reside among them, or visit them. They are in general as contented with their situation as most people, as they have the comforts and conveniences of life in a reasonable degree. The Gaelic is the general language of the common people; yet English is pretty well understood and taught in all our schools.
>
> The dance and the song, with shinty and putting the stone, are their chief amusements. Numbers of them play well on the violin and the bagpipe. They have a natural ease and gracefulness of motion in the dance, which is particular to themselves. The gentlemen, once a year, treat the ladies with a ball, where cheerfulness and propriety of conduct, always presides; and more elegance of manners are to be seen, than could well be expected in so remote a situation.
>
> *Statistical Account, 1791–1799*
> Parish of Kilchoman, The Rev. Mr. John M'Liesh, Minister

New Year day was called *Làth nollaig* in Islay. Formerly there were two Nollaig days. One was on the 25th December, and was called the *Nollaig Mhòr*. It was not much observed by the people. The other was on the 13th January, and was called *Nollaig Bheag*. This was the popular New Year day among the people generally. It commenced with twelve o'clock of the night before. First-footing was largely in-dulged in, and as it was considered an honour to be the first visitor to a friend's house in the New Year, there was a great rush immediately after midnight by the first-footers. Of course they generally did not know each other's plans, and several parties often enough met at the same house. The first-footer brought a Bottle of Whisky with him, and where accompanied with a friend, or it might be two, or even three, each might have a bottle. The inmates had to be treated to the contents of each Bottle, of course, and they returned the compliment in a "dram from my bottle", accompanied with bread and cheese . . .

After breakfast, shinty players began to gather on the various places where shinty games were in the habit of being played. Balinaby Machair was one of the most famous of these shinty fields. On this field there were vast crowds of players usually, cheered on by six or seven pipers, who played on the field the whole day, and the pres-ence of Mr Campbell of Islay, and the Laird of Balinaby, both in full Highland dress. Balinaby's men played against Shawfield's men, and the contest was often keen and carried on with great spirit. DD remembers to have seen two men, one, McNiven, and the other, McLaughlain take part in one of these contests. They were both old and grey-haired at the time, but were recognised as distinguished players. So keen was the contest on the occasion that they divested themselves of nearly every article of clothing, their feet were bare, and they had napkins tied round their head, while they were wet with perspiration. While the shinty play was going on, others amused themselves in groups dancing to the music of the pipes. In the even-ing Balls were held. Men and lads clubbed, each paying 6d which admitted himself and a partner.

. . . A good shinty [stick] was very important and men went some-times great distances for a good one. DD and a companion went with moonlight, after their day's work, across Lochguirm from Balinaby to Foreland wood in quest of shinties.

School of Scottish Studies Archives, University of Edinburgh, from Donald Dewar, labourer, Port Charlotte, Islay. Published in *Tocher* 24, 1976

One wonders if it was the thought of an Islay man, bold with the spirit of one of the island distilleries, that gave rise to the expression "If the Islay men come to the mainland, good-bye to the peace of the mainland".

I have no doubt that the men of Islay are doughty fighters: they were in the past. Their spirit of determination is still evident in the number of them who today have climbed the ladder of success in commerce and in other spheres. I know them only as hosts, and as such they are perfect. I know no island where one can find the inherent sense of hospitality of the Islesmen more marked today than in the natives of the charming southmost isle of the Hebrides.

Iain F. Anderson, *Across Hebridean Seas*, 1937

An old proverb, recorded on Islay by Gilbert Clark, the boatbuilder of Port Charlotte, takes a more critical view of Islay men, and of their near neighbours on Mull.

> Muileach is Ìleach is deamhan
> An triùir as miosa an domhain
> 'S miosa am Muileach na 'n t-Ìleach
> 'S miosa an t-Ìleach na 'n deamhan
>
> A Mull man, an Islay man and a devil
> The three worst in creation
> The Mull man is worse than the Islay man
> The Islay man is worse than the devil

Seanchas Ìle, Oral History Project, 1988

The author of the next extract published his book anonomously, under the name of 'Gowrie' – presumably in case he met natives of the island at a future date. We are happy to 'out' Gowrie as one W.A. Smith.

I have always found the men sturdy, intelligent, and hospitable, and ready to give their assistance kindly and good-humouredly; but a total disregard for the truth, a "plentiful lack" of knowledge regarding everything except whisky and potatoes, and the most degrading filth, these are the principal characteristics of the mass of natives.

While the men of Islay had strengths as well as faults, Smith despaired of the women of Islay.

Not until the women of the island have some higher standard of excellence and cleanliness brought constantly before them; not until the ladies of the lairds visit the cottages of the poor, and exercise the benign influence which ever belongs to a virtuous woman; not until the women are taught by one of their own sex, that a neat wife and a bright clean fireside to welcome him at home are the best induce-ments to make a man work hard, and cut the public-house on his return; in fact, not until the dirty slatternly habits of the women are thoroughly revolutionised, can any real progress be anticipated.

W. A. Smith, *Off the Chain*, 1868

On the occasion of a funeral (in Isla) a fight took place, when a la-bourer of Mr. W. Campbell's was killed in a brutal manner, and on Mr. Campbell, who acts as magistrate, transporting the offenders, the people exclaimed that he could not be his father's son in thus committing one of his own people; and the witnesses from the island perjured themselves.

The operation of law is still much obstructed by the old clannish feelings of not betraying a relation or clansman, of protecting him if possible, and of uttering a falsehood, or committing perjury, rather than be the means of convicting him, mixed with much of the old prejudice interwoven with the illegal habits of people, of consider-ing the law as an infringement on their rights and legitimate sources of profit: on the other hand, there is no inducement to discover an offender; and a falsehood, in order to secure a person of the same name, is regarded as not only justifiable, but obligatory. An old woman once petitioned Mr. W. Campbell to release her from the penalties of violating the excise law, on the ground of her grandmother having been foster-mother to his grandfather.

Lord Teignmouth, *Reminiscences of Many Years*, 1878

Even today Islay has a very low crime rate, and in the past the honesty of its people was proverbial.

. . . two large vessels, belonging to Clyde, went ashore in the Island of Islay; one of them contained on board ten thousand pounds in specie.* As these vessels were not under management merely because of the sickness and lassitude of the crew, as often happens from a long voyage, although the weather was not tempestuous, the cargos were taken out, and placed along the shores in the best way they

---

*Money in coinage.

could. The vessels were then got off, and when the articles of the two cargos were collected together, there was not one thing missing, save one barrel of tar, which had probably been hove overboard, or lost through carelessness. But the most singular instance of the kind I met with was as follows. A vessel from Ireland, laden with linen yarn, was stranded in Islay. The weather happened to become easy, and the cargo was got out; but as it was drenched in salt water, it became necessary to have the whole washed in fresh water. This was done in a river that was near, and the yarn spread about along some extensive fields near the shore. Seven hundred persons were employed in this work for several weeks. Yarn is the staple manufacture of this island, so that the temptation for embezzlement was very great, as a discovery in these circumstances would have been very difficult. Yet when the whole was collected together, to the utter astonishment of the parties concerned, a very few hanks of the yarn, (about five or six to the best of my recollection,) value about two or three shillings, were wanting.

I gladly record these instances of honesty and friendly care of the unfortunate. How different I have been witness to on the coast of England and Ireland!

Major-General David Stewart, *Sketches of the Character, Manners and Present State of the Highlanders of Scotland*, 3rd edition, 1825

A century later, there were still Ileachs to be found with little regard for making a fast buck – even honestly. James Bramwell tells of a meeting with a man who knew the islanders well.

In Islay, he said, no automation could ever hope to succeed, since time and money were not matters of vital concern to the natives.

I was interested to hear this from a man who had spent years dealing with islanders, because it had seemed to me that the large summer tourist trade attracted by Machrie golf course and the daily air service to Campbeltown and Glasgow must have commercialised the natives to some extent. But he said, that they were totally uncorrupted, remaining as they had always been, frugal, clean, religious and content with what they had.

"Don't you ever get fed up?" he asked one farmer up in the Rhinns.

"Why should I?" the man asked in astonishment.

"Being so much alone."

The man smiled and shook his head. "I am never alone," he said. "I have always my own thoughts and God is always with me on the hill."

James Bramwell, *Highland View*, 1939

Under Our Feet

To the geologist . . . Islay presents a field of study of surpassing interest.

L. MacNeill Weir, *Guide to Islay*, 1911

The history of Islay and the lives of its people have been moulded by the very fabric of the island itself, especially its rocks and soil. The first geological reference to the island is found in a medieval Irish text. Although most of this source is in Irish, the Islay reference is in Latin.

Terre Motus in Ili ij.Id Aprilis
An earthquake in Islay on the second day before the Ides of April.

Annals of Ulster, 740

The depth of 'geological time' is so great that little has changed in a mere twelve centuries.

Islay was rudely awakened from its sleep yesterday morning by what was variously described as a big bang, a deep rumble like thunder, shaking of the house, and a combination of all three. Most folk concluded that it was thunder, or Concorde, or NATO exercises, or even Belfast blowing up. Mr Stewart, principal keeper at the Rhinns of Islay lighthouse, who was waiting to come off duty at 6.00 am, thought a ship had struck rocks nearby.

Mrs Elizabeth Cunningham of Neriby Farm was convinced, however, that the prolonged shaking of the house could only be caused by an earth tremor, and claims to have experienced the same alarming effects twice before during the winter.

When we contacted Dr Browitt of the Global Seismology Unit of the Institute of Geological Sciences, he confirmed that their seismograph at Eskdalemuir had recorded an earth tremor of magnitude 3.3 at 05.58 and 24 seconds, BST – a time corresponding exactly with the time given by one early bird in Bowmore.

The Ileach, 16 July 1976

ISLAY VOICES

On the reverse side of a 1773 map of Scotland, the Flemish cartographer, who is regarded as the 'father' of the modern atlas, wrote a note about the Hebrides.

> *Maxima omnium and nominatissima Ila est, frumenti ferax, and metalli dives*
> The greatest and most renowned is Ila, fertile for grain, and rich in minerals.
>
> Abraham Ortelius, 1527–1598

Many early visitors recognised that Islay had commercially exploitable minerals as well as rich farmland – among them Martin Martin, as he travelled the Port Askaig road.

> There's about one thousand little Hills on this Road, and all abound with Lime-stone; among which there is lately discovered a Lead Mine in three different Places, but it is not turn'd to any account as yet.
>
> Martin Martin, *A Description of the Western Islands of Scotland*, 2nd edition, 1716

By the time Thomas Pennant visited, Islay lead deposits had indeed been turned to some account.

> Return by the same road, cross the sound, and not finding the vessel arrived, am most hospitably received by Mr Freebairn, of Freeport, near Port Askaig, his residence on the southern side of the water, in the island of Islay. Walk into the interior parts: on the way see an abundance of rock and pit-marl, convertible in the best of manures. Visit the mines, carried on under the directions of Mr Freebairn, since the year 1763: the ore is of lead, much mixed with copper, which occasions expense and trouble in the separation: the veins rise to the surface, have been worked at intervals for ages, and probably in the times of the Norwegians, a nation of miners. The old adventurers worked by trenching, which is apparent everywhere: the trenches are not above six feet drop; and the veins which opened into them not above five or six inches thick; yet, by means of some instrument, unknown to us at the present, they picked or scooped out the ore with good success, following it in that narrow space to the length of four feet.
>
> The veins are of various thickness; the strings numerous, conducting to larger bodies, but quickly exhausted. The lead ore is good: the copper yields thirty-three pounds per hundred; and forty ounces of

silver from a ton of metal. The lead ore is smelted in an air furnace, near Freeport; and as much sold in the pig, as, since the first undertaking by this gentleman, has brought in six thousand pounds.

Thomas Pennant, *A Tour in Scotland and Voyage to the Hebrides*, 1772

Future travellers confirmed that Islay's mineral deposits were a well-worked and valuable resource.

The face of the country is hilly, but not extremely high. Several mines are here wrought with considerable profit. The lead-ore is very rich. It produces seventeen hundred weight of lead each ton, and no less than forty-two ounces of silver. The copper-ore yields about one third of its weight in metal. Amid vast strata of iron-stone, there is here found in abundance the peculiar sort called Emery. This substance pulverized is much used by artists in polishing stones and metals. Native quicksilver has also been met with in small quantities; but no discovery has been made from whence it came, nor has any native cinnabar been found in this country. Some small pieces of the mineral called Black-lead, have here been observed; but the mass from which these have been detached remains undiscovered. In this place, nature had provided immense stores of limestone, marl, and shellsand, on purpose, as it were, to manure the soil, which is for the most part very improvable.

Robert Heron, *Scotland Delineated, or a Geographical Description of Every Shire in Scotland*, 1799

The mineral products are also rich and varied. Lime abounds, and symptoms of tin occur in boulders. Copper, iron, and lead are well known, and different ornamental articles have been manufactured from the silver obtained from the latter ore . . .

Islay may indeed be regarded as the richest and most productive island of the Hebrides; and not withstanding all that has been done for it in recent years, its capabilities of improvement are still very far from being exhausted.

James Wilson, *A Voyage Round the Coast of Scotland*, 1842

Situated about a mile north from Ballygrant, we come to the lead mines of Islay, with their ponderous looking apparatus and ore-crushing machinery, propelled by steam and water power, standing a little way off the main road, bringing into view a scene of activity, and we trust of profit. Those mines are presently owned by an English company – a source of good employment, and considerable circulation of money in the district. The scenery in the immediate neighbourhood of the works, bears some resemblance to the Black Country of England.

Robert Oliphant, *The Tourist's Guide to Islay, The Queen of the Hebrides,* 1881

Lead-mining in Islay finally petered out towards the end of the nineteenth century.

In the district around the village of Ballygrant, between Bridgend and Port Askaig, veins of galena are frequent in the Islay limestone. At Mulreesh a large mine was formerly worked and appears to have been at one time a profitable undertaking; but a fall in the price of lead, coupled with increased cost of production, led to considerable loss, and the mine has been closed . . .

Robolls mine, in connection with the Mulreesh mine, was worked more recently and a fair sample of lead obtained, but not in sufficient quantities to be profitable.

S. B. Wilkinson, *The Geology of Islay, Memoirs of the Geological Survey,* 1907

Although Islay's mineral resources were much commented on, the island's saltmarsh, rock formations and fertile 'champaign' areas – broad expanses of level pasture – were also appreciated by early travellers.

In some places also the Land is so low, especially about Lochondaal and Loch Grunard, that it is overflowed by the Sea, at Spring Tides. This creates a great Extent of Salt Marsh, the most valuable Pasture that is known, both for black Cattle and Sheep . . .

Its Mountains consist of a Rock composed chiefly of a coarse debased Chrystal, of a white Colour, that their Summits which are mostly bare both of Earth and Herbage appear at Sea, as if covered with Snow.

The Champaign parts of the Island are Intersected with Dykes of a coarse whitestone. They are of various Degrees of thickness from 10 inches to 20 or 30 feet. In some places they are not above 100 Feet distant from one another and in others above a mile. In many places they are risen entire, several Feet above the Surface of the Grounds, and never intersect one another, running always parallel. In this way they look like the Foundations of old Walls and Buildings and give the face of the Country a very odd Appearance.

The Rev. John Walker, *Report on the Hebrides*, 1764

It is easy to recognise the bands of limestone which traverse the quartz-rock series. Their brighter colours stand out conspicuously in pleasing contrast to the dun-coloured heath of the surrounding hillsides. From the hill-top we may trace these ribbons of limestone for miles.

L. MacNeill Weir, *Guide to Islay*, 1911

Islay is at its most spectacular where the wild Atlantic Ocean has gnawed away at its coast.

All along the rocky coastline the sea has eaten into the land in many caves and numerous grotesque rock formations. At Bolsa, at Slochd Mhaol Doraidh, at Killean, at Sanaig, are geological phenomena which make these places resemble the playgrounds of some Titanic sculptor who has let his savage imagination run riot, and carved the coast into mysterious subterranean chambers, whimsical images, and fantastic shapes.

L. MacNeill Weir, *Guide to Islay*, 1911

For what people didn't understand about the geological forces that formed Islay, they had storytellers to make up likely explanations. Here's one about Loch Corr, a little hill loch in the north-west of Islay. The loch has an island on it, on which are the remains of a crannog.

Loch Coar is a small loch on the farm of Braico in the parish of Kilchoman, Islay. In the centre of the loch there is a small island, on which there is a large number of loose stones. The reciter says that he used to hear old people saying that they are the ruins of a house that was there long ago, in which a priest lived, At that time there was no loch there, and what is now the island was just a little piece of ground on which the Priest's house had been built. It was a little higher than the rest of the ground round about it. The way the loch came to be there was this. The Priest had a well which he kept always locked; but one time when he was from home, his servant forgot to lock the well, and the consequence was that the water sprung up, and poured over, and before the Priest had come back, all the land round about his house was covered with water. He was only in time to save his house, and prevent the water from spreading further. Had he been later in coming home, the loch would have been bigger than it is. The narrator says that this story was believed by many, and in confirmation of it, it was pointed out that no water comes in, and none goes out, and still the loch remains, just as it was on the day on which it was formed – a warning of what may happen through the carelessness of a servant.

School of Scottish Studies Archives, University of Edinburgh, recorded from Mr A. Maclachlan, Braico, Islay, in about 1893, published in *Tocher* 28, 1978

The mysteries of the earth are a challenge for the scientist as well as for the storyteller. Islay contains some of the oldest, and some of the youngest, rocks in the British Isles, and this complex mosaic has made the island a mystery, and a magnet, for generations of geologists. Students still come to the island every summer to carry out fieldwork as part of their geology degree courses. But it was not always so. Even though the 'father of modern geology' was the Scot, James Hutton, it was a long time before the ringing of rock hammers was heard regularly on Islay.

There are few parts of Scotland where we know so little of the geological features as those of the Island of Islay.

James Thomson, *Transactions of the Geological Society of Glasgow*, 1875

James Thomson was one of the first scientifically minded men to come to Islay to gaze into the abyss of time. His account is thorough, scientific and rather dry. But there is one section in which a sense of excitement about what he was discovering somehow intrudes into his prose. Near Port Askaig, Thomson was confronted with evidence of the vastness and power of the ice sheet that once covered Islay.

On the north side of Little-Free Port bay, blocks were recently being quarried to build a new pier at Port Askaig, which exposed a section about 100 feet deep, and showing numerous imbedded fragments and boulders of transported rocks. At its base there is a dull bluish grey arenacous schist, shading, as it passes upwards, into a light brownish grey. In the earlier stages of the deposits the matrix had been soft and plastic, into which the transported fragments and boulders had been dropped, with subsequently a great influx of arenacous matter. It then passed with almost imperceptible graduations from a stiff blue talcose mass in the interior, to a gritty sandstone in the superior deposit. There is, therefore, evidence of great physical changes throughout. The contained pebbles and boulders are frequently well water worn, others subangular, whilst others again are angular. They chiefly consist of granite, quartzite, and rarely gneiss.

. . . The granite fragments largely predominate, and vary in size from the smallest pieces possible to boulders as large as 4 feet 10 inches in diameter . . . After a careful examination of the shore, and of the blocks embedded in the matrix, I am satisfied that these erratics could not be traced as belonging to any part of the island. Similar rocks do not occur *in situ* nearer than forty miles to the north, in the island of Mull, with a deep sea intervening, while some of the varieties only exist at a considerably greater distance. The entire absence of stratification in one part of the section, which in another shows signs of regular deposition, and the occurrence of far transported rocks of the character already stated, indicate that the mass had been transported and dropped from melting ice in a shallow tranquil sea, the bottom consisting of mud and sand. The absence of stratification in one part of the section may be accounted for by the disturbing action of icebergs, which moved to and fro, grounding as they went before they were finally stranded.

James Thomson's pioneering work was admired by a geologist who later made a lengthy and systematic geological survey of Islay.

Mr Thomson was the first to pronounce definitely as to the Laurentian (Lewisian) age of the gneiss of the Rinns of Islay. He lays stress on the difference in age between these rocks and those of the central part of the island, and points out their close lithological resemblance to the fundamental gneiss of Sutherland and the Outer Hebrides.

S. B. Wilkinson, *The Geology of Islay, Memoirs of the Geological Survey,* 1907

And here is Thomson's revelation about the immense age of the rocks of the Rhinns.

The metamorphic rocks on the western extremity of the island, and skirting the shore of Lochin-dàla and dipping S.S.W., are of Laurentian age . . . If, however, we glance at the topographical aspects of the Highlands and islands, and compare the boulders with the granites throughout the Highlands, we feel the necessity of tracing them to another source. And we hope we do not overstep the bounds of prudent speculation in suggesting that these erratics are the re-assorted material of some great Northern Continent which has yielded to the ceaseless gnawing tooth of time, leaving those scattered fragments as the wreckage of its former greatness; and that the materials of which the mass is composed, have been transported by the agency of ice. The mineral characters of these boulders differ so widely from the granites at present found *in situ* throughout the Highlands, that a much higher antiquity for those found in Islay is suggested, while the finding of the glaciated rock at the base of the mass stamps their true character, and points to a period of time deeper than we have hitherto suspected; when glaciers and icebergs planed the hardest rocks, and transported matter, as they still do, obedient to one great law.

James Thomson, *Transactions of the Geological Society of Glasgow*, 1875

Sydney Berdòe Wilkinson was a Montreal-born professional geologist who, from 1890 to 1898, surveyed Islay for the one-inch series of geological maps of Scotland. The 'memoir' he wrote is a not only a classic description of Islay's complex geology, but one brimming with appreciation of the beauty of the place.

Between Port Ellen and Ardtalla, in the south-east of the island, the scenery is very striking. The white gleaming summits and slopes of the quartzite range rise conspicuously in the background, flanked by dark igneous rocks that weather out into the picturesque jagged ridges clothed with the indigenous tree growth of the country. These nearer features combine with the brilliant colouring of the sea, the blue line of the distant hills of Knapdale, and the peaks of Arran beyond Cantyre, to invest this portion of the West Highlands with remarkable beauty.

Wilkinson also confirms what many visitors suspect, as soon as they see the low wetlands between Loch Gruinart and Loch Indaal.

The island is divided into two distinct areas, which at an earlier period, indicated by a 50-feet raised beach, evidently formed two separate islands, but are now connected by the strip of marine and freshwater alluvium that lies between Loch Indaal and the head of the tidal estuary of Gruinart.

No description of the geology of Islay would be complete without reference to that vital ingredient of whisky, peat – a slowly accumulated blanket of partially decayed vegetation that covers much of Islay.

The peat deposits over the island are of vast extent and practically inexhaustible. Although peat is in general use for fuel all over the island, and is used in large quantities by numerous distilleries to give the spirit the correct amount of "reeky" flavour which is the feature of the excellent whisky of Islay, the amount that has been "cut" is trifling as compared with what remains.

S. B. Wilkinson, *The Geology of Islay, Memoirs of the Geological Survey*, 1907

Fans of Islay whisky should brace themselves for a stormy future. We've got our hands on some research that will strike terror into the hearts of peat heads: peat on Islay will run out by 2021.

During a recent environmental impact survey, conducted for a company investigating the feasibility of building a new distillery on Islay, information was literally dug up that showed that the peat reserves on the island are significantly less plentiful than expected.

Flawed survey procedures in the 1980s led to a vast overestimation of the amount of peat on Islay.

The report wasn't looking into the state of peat on the island, instead focusing on the water table at the site of the new distillery, but test cores and a geophysics survey revealed more than the surveyors expected. The last in-depth analysis of Islay's peat beds was back in the 1980s, and it seems that mistakes were made. The 1980s' reports made assumptions about the distribution of peat across the island, extrapolating from a few core samples. Unfortunately, this led to serious overestimation, thanks to until-now-undetected structures beneath the peat beds to the north of Port Ellen.

The new survey showed that much of the material identified as peat during the earlier surveys is – instead – coal. Islay lies on the Loch Gruinart Fault, an extension of the Great Glen Fault that divides

Scotland along Loch Ness, and while this usually only shows itself in minor earth tremors, underneath the surface there has been more going on. As the fault has moved over the millennia, layers of coal have slowly pushed themselves upwards into the peat bogs, and due to the similar structure of peat and coal when examined by ground-penetrating radar, this was not detected in the original 1980s surveys.

We've worked with the geology team at the Heriot-Watt University to put together a more accurate map of peat distribution across Islay, and have found that instead of reserves of thousands of years being present, at current usage rates the island will run out within the next decade.

The Whisky Exchange blog, 1 April 2015

Readers should carefully note the date of the above article.

The First Ileachs

The last Ice Age – between 30,000 and 25,000 years ago – smothered Islay under more than 500 metres of ice that didn't disappear till about 15,000 years ago. Islay was colonised by plants, animals, and – finally – man.

In the Mesolithic period, Scotland once more became inhabitable after the northward retreat of the ice sheets that had covered and moulded the land during the Ice Age. By 10,000 BC most of the ice had melted, and the process of regeneration was underway. Soils were developing, vegetation was recolonising and animals were beginning to return. We know from ancient pollen deposits that this process was well advanced by 6,000 BC, when *birch* and *hazel* were already established throughout Scotland.

William Milliken and Sam Bridgewater, *Flora Celtica*, 2004

The hazel trees that grow wild on Islay are the descendants of specimens once harvested by the Mesolithic people.

Much of the carbonised material at a site of c.6,500 BC in Islay consisted of hazelnut shells. Hazelnuts were a widespread food resource in Europe at similar periods. Hazelnut kernels, which have a mild, farinaceous, oily taste, could even be formed into bread. They also produced oil which was nearly as good as oil of almonds. Hazel wands or rungs were, of course, used for a multitude of jobs. Hazel, therefore, was a valued resource.

Ten thousand years ago, hazelnuts could have served a number of purposes for early man in Scotland. They could be nibbled in a fresh state, stored, after drying, possibly in pits and in other containers, crushed into a kind of flour, after charring to ease the removal of the husks, perhaps for baking a kind of bread, and perhaps also for barter in the way of trade.

Alexander Fenton, *The Food of the Scots*, 2007

Archaeologist Steven Mithen has done groundbreaking work on the hunter-gatherers who first set foot on Islay not long after the end of the last Ice Age. His excavations have pushed back the earliest evidence of people on Islay by 2000 years to about 12,000 years ago. But Professor Mithen admits that the scant discoveries of Meslithic archaeology are 'ephemeral and unimpressive'.

> So why is it my passion? The simple answer is that hunting and gathering is the original state of all humankind and I can't think any of any archaeology topic more important to study.

Mithen believes that hunter-gatherers ranged over vast territories as they sought specific resources, like flint, or seasonal food plants and migrating animals. These first Ileachs would have been nomads with wide horizons.

> With Hannah in a back-pack, Sue and I climbed Beinn Tart a'Mhill on a fine clear day and were treated to a spectacular panorama. To the north we could see Oronsay and Colonsay, and possibly Tiree as a sliver on the distant horizon; to the north-east the rest of Islay was laid out before us and then the Paps of Jura and the Scottish Highlands, possibly Ben Nevis in the distance; swivelling around 180 degrees we could see the distant coast of Northern Ireland, and to the south-east we could look over Loch Indall towards the southern peninsula of Islay, the Oa.
>
> When I was standing on the summit of Beinn Tart a'Mhill the thought struck me that Mesolithic hunter-gatherers would have seen much the same from this summit 8,000 years ago, or whenever they first came to Islay. The sea level would have been a little higher and the landscape covered by woodland, but the basic topography of the land would have been much the same. I didn't doubt for a moment that they would also have climbed the hill for the view. This made me realise that my walking experiences on the islands might be as informative about the long-gone Mesolithic life as the artefacts we were extracting from the peat at Gleann Mor.

An excavation near Bolsay Farm, in the Rhinns, revealed evidence of what would have been a busy Mesolithic camp.

> I was pleased with the Bolsay site; the vast quantities of artefacts and the signs of structures suggested that the site could be a Meso-lithic base camp. This would be a location where several families based themselves for a whole season and from which parties left for

specialised tasks, such as to collect flint pebbles or to visit fishing and hunting camps. It seemed ideally situated for a base camp since it was adjacent to a spring and close to a lake, with resources from both woodland and the coast easily accessible. I imagined a wide range of activities must once have been undertaken at the site, and so expected to find a diverse range of tool types once analysis was complete. But I would also need a more extensive excavation, with a far larger team to confirm this interpretation. I felt sure that we would find further features and provide evidence for dwellings.

Steven Mithen, *To the Islands*, 2010

Nobody knows for certain what happened to Islay's Mesolithic folk. But we do know that around 6,000 years ago a new culture – a farming Neolithic culture – was present on Islay. These early agriculturalists came with domesticated animals and crops, like barley, that would be recognisable to local farmers today. Islay's mild climate and fertile soil made it a rich prize for land-hungry tribes.

It would appear that in prehistoric times the aborigines of Islay belonged to the Iberian race, the same type of people as the Basques who occupy the Basque Province at the Bases of the Pyrenees. Probably an intermixture of various races, such as the Basques, the Caledonians, and the Picts, constituted its population before the arrival of the Gaels and the Brythons who intermarried with the native race. Probably in the third and fourth centuries Gaelic settlements were made in Islay.

At the beginning of the sixth century the Dalriads or Scots from Ireland effected a fresh settlement on this delightful island, whose position in the path of the Gulf Stream renders its climate so mild, and its vegetation so rich and green

J. G. MacNeill, *Islay*, 1899

The earliest inhabitants of the Western Isles or Ebudes (corruptly, "Hebrides") were probably a portion of the Albanich, Caledonians, or Picts. In some of the southern islands, particularly Islay, this race must have been displaced or overrun by the Dalriads on their first settlement; so that, at the date of the Scottish conquest, the Isles, like the adjacent mainland, were divided between Picts and Scots.

Donald Gregory, *History of the Western Highlands and Islands of Scotland: 1493–1625*, 1881

The 'mists of time' are thick enough around Islay for myth and history to be easily mistaken for each other.

> The earliest direct references to the island of Islay are in the hazy narrative of the Irish chroniclers, where it appears, first, as part of the plunder of the mysterious Firbolg, and thereafter, in the 5th century, as the adopted home of a branch of the family of the great Erc, son of Eachach. The story of this settlement is too circumstantial to be altogether mythical, and it is not difficult to identify the names of the small colonies with those of districts on the modern map. Of the history of this community during the next four centuries there is nothing on record beyond a few picturesque glimpses in the pages of Adamnan; how St Cainneach by dint of prayer recovered his staff on Island Texa; how Lugne Mocumin was made prior of the northern islet Naomb; how Feredach, a rich man of Islay, treacherously murdered the noble Pict, Tarain, who had sought his protection by the advice of St Columba; and how the murderer died soon thereafter. Between this act of poetic justice and the coming of the Norse rovers we hear of nothing but the ominous earthquake which troubled the island in the spring of 740.
>
> Alexander Gray, *The History of Islay Placenames*, 1940

According to an eleventh-century Irish manuscript that claims to tell the history of that land from the dawn of time, the Fir Bolg were a people driven from Ireland to the islands of Arran, Islay and Rathlin by a more powerful tribe, the Tuatha De Danann.

> The Fir Bolg gave them (the Tuatha De Danann) battle upon Mag Tuired; they were a long time fighting that battle. At last it broke against the Fir Bolg, and the slaughter pressed northward, and a hundred thousand of them were slain westward to the strand of Eochaill. There was the king Eochu overtaken, and he fell at the hands of the three sons of Nemed. Yet the Tuatha De Danann suffered great loss in the battle, and they left the king on the field with his arm cut from him; the leeches were seven years healing him. The Fir Bolg fell in that battle all but a few, and they went out of Ireland in flight from the Tuatha De Danann into Ara, and Ila, and Rachra and other islands besides.
>
> *Lebor Gabála Érenn (The Book of the Taking of Ireland)*, edited and translated by R. A. Stewart Macalister, 1941

An intriguing text tells of the conquest of the Pictish lands of what is now Argyll in the early sixth century. Erc, a chieftain of the Dal Riada in Antrim, divided his new lands in Scotland between his followers. Areas of Argyll (*Earra-Ghàidheal,* or *Airer Goídel* – Border or Coast of the Gaels) became home to Gaelic-speaking 'kindreds' – all named after Eric's sons, brothers and grandsons: Cenél Loarn (who occupied present day Lorne), Cenél Gabran (Kintyre and mid-Argyll), Cenél Comgal (Cowal), and Cenél Óengus or 'Angus' (Islay and Jura).

The 'Senchus' is an extremely difficult and confusing document, but the great historian of Gaeldom, Dr John Bannerman, painstakingly translated and analysed it. Although the existing manuscript dates from the mid-fourteenth century, Dr Bannerman argues that the original was written in the seventh century, no later than 660.

> Erc had 12 sons, six of them took possession of Scotland: two Loarnds, Loarnd Bec and Loarn Mór; two Mac Nisses, Mac Nisse Bec and Mac Nisse Mór; two Ferguses, Fergues Bec and Fergues Mór. Six other in Ireland (including) Oengus, whose seed however is in Scotland – Enna, Bresal, Fiachra, Dubthach. Others say that this Erc had another son who was called Muredach.

With the tempting reward of new lands in Scotland, brotherly love was not universal among the sons of Erc.

> Fergus Bec, moreover, son of Erc, his brother killed him. He had one son, Sétna, from whom are the Cenél Conchride in Islay.

The document suggests that these were warlike times when power was measured in the strength to wield a sword or pull on an oar. Much of the *Miniugud Senchusa Fher n-Alban* is an inventory of the fighting strength of the various Cenél and the number of galleys they possessed.

> The expedition strength of the hostings of the Cenél Oengusa five hundred men.

John Bannerman argued that the document was translated in the tenth century for a political reason – to make a genealogical case for uniting the different Cenél who ruled the western islands and seaboard of Scotland behind the Kings of Alba. What is clear is that the Gaelic-speaking people of Dal Riada were a warlike tribe.

A hundred and fifty men, the ship expedition, went forth with the sons of Erc, the third fifty was Corpri and his people.

This is the Cenél nGabráin, five hundred and sixty houses, Kintyre and Crich Chomgaill with its islands, two seven-benchers every twenty houses in a sea expedition.

Cenél nOengusa has four hundred and thirty houses, two seven-benchers every twenty houses in a sea expedition.

Cenél Loairnd has four hundred and twenty houses, two seven-benchers in every twenty houses in a sea expedition.

It is thus throughout the three thirds of the Dál Riadda

Míniugud Senchusa Fher n-Alban (Explanation of the History of the Men of Scotland), seventh century, translated by John Bannerman, *Studies in the History of Dalriada*, 1974

The Gaels of Dal Riada were known to the Romans as the *Scotti*, and around 312 AD featured on list of tribes hostile to the empire. By the fifth century the Scotti were firmly settled in the land now named after them. They brought a powerful new magic from Ireland with them – the Christianity of Columba.

About the middle of the sixth century, the famed Callum Cille, or St Columba instituted Culdeeism in Islay and in the rest of the Hebrides . . .

William MacDonald, *Sketches of Islay*, 1850

A written reference to the island of Islay – *Ilea insula* – appeared in the seventh century, in a tale about a prediction – or perhaps a curse – made by Saint Columba.

Columba's biography was written by Adomnan, an Abbot of Iona who, after his death in 704, himself became a saint. Written in Latin, Adomnán's *Vita Columbae* is a masterpiece of the Celtic Church. Adomnán paints a vivid and spellbinding picture of Gaelic-speaking Argyll in the seventh century. Sadly, the first Ileach to appear in literature was a murderous villain, whose just punishment was to be 'blotted out of the book of life'.

. . . the holy man specially recommended a certain exile, of noble race among the Picts, named Tarain, to the care of one Feradach, a rich man, who lived in the Ilean island (Isla), that he might be received in his retinue for some months as one of his friends. After he had accepted the person thus highly recommended at the hand of the holy man, he in a few days acted treacherously, and cruelly ordered him to be put to death.

When the news of this horrid crime was carried by travellers to the saint, he replied by the following prediction: "That unhappy wretch hath not lied unto me, but unto God, and his name shall be blotted out of the book of life. We are speaking these words now in the middle of summer, but in autumn, before he shall eat of swine's flesh that hath been fattened on the fruits of the trees, he shall be seized by a sudden death, and carried off to the infernal regions."

When the miserable man was told this prophecy of the saint, he scorned and laughed at him; and when some days of the autumn months had passed, he ordered a sow that had been fattened on the kernels of nuts to be killed, none of his other swine having yet been slaughtered: he ordered also, that its entrails should be immediately taken out and a piece quickly roasted for him on the spit, so that by hurrying and eating of it thus early, he might falsify the prediction of the blessed man.

As soon as it was roasted he asked for a very small morsel to taste it, but before the hand which he stretched out to take it had reached his mouth he expired, and fell down on his back a corpse. And all who saw or heard it were greatly astonished and terrified; and they honoured and glorified Christ in his holy prophet.

Adomnán's Life of St Columba, edited by William Reeves, 1857

The treacherous Feradach, according to one source, lived at Island Farm, the 'island' being on the River Laggan a couple of miles south of Bowmore.

Its local designation is *Eilean na Muice duibhe*, Island of the Black Pig. It is related in *The Life of Columba* that towards the close of the sixth century there lived on this farm a rich man called Feredach, who was cut off by sudden death.

L. MacNeill Weir, *Guide to Islay*, 1911

Weir retells Adomnán's story, then writes of another possible reason for the farm's Gaelic name.

Another tradition says that this farm was infested with snakes, and that with a view to getting rid of the poisonous pests, the farmer let loose upon it a big, black, hungry pig, with her numerous litter, which quickly devoured this live food. Hence the name of the farm.

There is an Islay tradition that Columba, who had been exiled from Ireland, first landed on Islay – but sailed on to Iona because he could see his native land from Islay's shores. Why else, believe proud Ileachs, would he not have settled on beautiful Islay? We may never know if the saint actually set foot on Islay, but he has stamped his mark on local tradition.

Tradition says that Calum-cille one day saw a man fishing in the river of Saligo, and asked him to give him the first fish he caught. In a short time the man hooked a salmon, but greed made him keep it for himself. He again cast his line and baited hook in the river and forthwith landed another salmon, which he also put into his own basket. Having now put a fresh worm on his hook he threw it a third time into the stream and in a minute or two pulled up a frog which he offered to the saint. "Henceforth," says Columba, "let there be no salmon in this brook." In Gaelic: "*Aghaidh gach bradan a mach 's gun gin idir a stigh.*" The story goes that ever since no salmon has been caught in this river.

L. MacNeill Weir, *Guide to Islay*, 1911

Not very long ago, in a newspaper article Islay was called 'The Pagan Island'. Far from being called 'The Pagan Island' it should be called 'The Island of Saints', for there is no island of its size which has so many chapels dedicated to such a variety of saints. There are at least thirty-three named chapels, and others whose names are lost forever.

Peggy Earl, *Tales of Islay*, 1980

The late Peggy Earl's little book goes on to list many of the chapels, and the saints they were named for. Here a few extracts:

Kilchoman . . . The chapel of Kilchoman was dedicated to St Comman, born in Ireland, who was supposed to be buried in Kilchoman and so gave the parish its name. He had two brothers who were priests or monks, and his uncle was Abbot of Iona.

Comman, being influenced by this, went to Iona which had a college for training young men for the monastic life, and became a monk. He was then sent as a missionary to Islay.

Kilchiaran . . . It was dedicated to Kiaran mac an t-Saoir, who was the Abbot of Clonmachaois, in Ireland. He was said to be the tutor of St Columba, and died in 548 AD aged only 33 years . . .

He must be buried in Islay, for on one occasion when Columba visited the island he had taken some earth from Kiaran's grave. On his way back to Iona he got caught in the eddy and swirl of Coirebhreacan and was in danger of being swamped, when he remembered the earth from the holy man's grave. Something urged him to throw the earth into the vortex of the whirlpool. Miraculously, the turbulence subsided and he was saved.

Kildalton . . . The present chapel of Kildalton, about eight miles from Port Ellen, probably dates from the thirteenth century. There are indications of an ancient settlement and there is a small harbour called Port Mor which the monks are said to have used when going to and from Kildalton and Iona.

Peggy Earl, *Tales of Islay*, 1980

The tourist should explore the remains of the chapel of Kilbride, for *Cille Bhrìghde*, Church of St Brigit, on the farm of Kilbride. This ancient building was about thirty feet in length and twelve in breadth.

The farm takes its name from this old church, which was built as a local memorial of the saintly virgin, Brigit or Bridget, the Mary of the Gael, who takes rank with Patrick and Columba, as a missionary of immense spiritual power and great popularity.

The author of the *Literature of the Highlanders* tells us that "her name became celebrated very early wherever the Gaelic folks did congregate. We find her associated with King Nectan of Albin, and with a church founded in her honour at Abernethy. So her fame was not confined to the Gaelic Regions of Erin" . . .

We, in our school-days in Islay, every year in February, on *La-Fhéill-Brìghde*, Day of the Festival of Brigit, donned our Sunday suit, went to school, bringing with us a few silver coins as a freewill offering to the teacher, who with his scholars kept this day as a festival-day, and thus paid unconscious honours to Saint Brigda. The boy and girl whose offerings were the highest were called the King and Queen of the school for that year.

Near the ruins of this church there are two standing crosses. One of them, the great Cross of Kildalton, is a monolith of grey granite nine feet high and stands inside the churchyard, well fixed in a roughly dressed block of the same kind of stone as basement . . . a beautiful specimen of Celtic work. Its elaborate ornamentation and its Biblical symbolism are intensely interesting. According to Dr Joseph Anderson, this cross "is one of two examples of the type with the encircling glory now remaining erect in Scotland, the other being St. Martin's Cross at Iona."

J. G. MacNeill, *Islay*, 1899

For one man the Kildalton Cross, and the other carved stones of Islay, became an obsession. Robert Chellas Graham, the Laird of Skipness in Kintyre, seemed to have plenty of everything – time, money and enthusiasm. His book on Islay's carved stones is systematic and encyclopaedic, but something of his passion for his work can be found in the introduction to that great work.

The oar strokes of war vessels were borne in from loch and bay, to mingle with the never easing sound of the ship-builder's hammer and the ring of the anvil, where sharper instruments than ploughshares were forged. Dunyveg and Finlaggan had their stirring garrisons. Churches that we see roofless and neglected were then watched and tended by zealous hands. Strange pageants of armed chiefs and long-robed ecclesiastics passed along roads which are silent and deserted now.

One can fancy oneself on the summer afternoon of one of those old days, standing below the great Cross of Kildalton. A faint breath of incense floats from the open door of the church, the stillness is only broken by one who, chisel in hand, bends over a long grey stone, and a device of tendrils, leaves and buds, winding round a central sword of cross, grows to his touch.

Beside the carver stands a group of men, who watch the progress of the work. Sea captains are there who know every rock and current of the chartless coast, soldiers whose knowledge of the trackless Highland glens is no less sure, priests too, whose career has also been one of travel and experience. One, now attached to an Islay church, may have studied in foreign lands, or passing from monastery to monastery, through sunny plains and over snowy ranges, may also have seen Rome.

Some such group we might call up before us, the ruined church we might restore, but we shall never know what the carving on the grey stone was like, when the sculptor gave his last touch and his last look at the completed work. Alas! That the tracery is disappearing so fast from these dying memorials of the dead.

Robert C. Graham, *The Carved Stones of Islay*, 1895

Is fuar gaoth nan coímheach.
Cold is the wind that brings strangers.

Reverend Donald Macintosh, *A Collection of Gaelic Proverbs and Familiar Phrases*, 1785, added to and republished by Alexander Nicolson, 1882

That proverb may be ancient, and is claimed to be a reference to Viking raids.

The Norsemen had first raided Iona in 795 AD and less than a century later had captured the stronghold of Dumbarton Rock on the River Clyde estuary. Islay lay directly in the path of their longships.

Towards the end of the eighth century, the Irish annals record the appearance of a new faction in Hebridean power politics – the heathen Scandinavian seafarers now known as 'Vikings'. While there are no written accounts of any Viking activity in Islay, it is clear from the attested raids in nearby Rathlin Island and Iona that Scandinavian warlords were operating in the area as early as AD795. Whether these particular raids were target specific, or part of a more ambitious campaign, it is impossible to say. But considering the dramatic escalation in Norse violence recorded in mainland Ireland in the early ninth century, it is hard to imagine that Islay, with its pivotal maritime location, would have remained unaffected for long.

David Caldwell, *Islay: The Land of the Lordship*, 2008

There are no contemporary accounts of Viking activity in Islay. Folk tales linking the name of the island to a supernatural Danish princess called Jula, and alluding to a battle between the 'Danes' and 'Fenians' at Gartmain on Lochindaal, may hint at vague community memories of Viking activity, but must be treated with caution. It can nevertheless be assumed that the majority of Viking warbands in and around the Irish Sea must have sailed down Scotland's west coast and directly past Islay to get there. Moreover, it would be surprising if at least a few of them had not stopped off along the way, given the island's acknowledged assets. This assumption finds a certain degree of support in the archaeological evidence.

While archaeologists have yet to confirm any Viking Age settlement sites in Islay, it is worth noting that the vast majority of artefacts removed from the island's soils and sand dunes that can be dated with any certainty to this period are Scandinavian. More significantly, they are also of a type normally associated with the pagan military elite of the tenth century, with the additional presence of female assemblages hinting at the entrenched presence of a pagan Scandinavian culture group at the heart of the erstwhile Christian *Gàidhealtachd* 150 years or more after the beginning of the Viking age.

Alan MacNiven, *The Vikings in Islay*, 2015

The lack of contemporary accounts of the Vikings on Islay didn't curb the imagination of William Livingston (Uilleam MacDhùnlèibhe), the nineteenth-century Islay bard.

The longest of Livingston's poems is a dramatic piece entitled *The Danes in Islay*. It is the only proper dramatic poem in the language. The subject is one that the poet could take up with much enthusiasm, as he pictured to himself the Norse army in a fleet of sixty-three sail entering the spacious Lochindaul, and dropping anchor there with no friendly intent. The bard's historical and antiquarian knowledge stood him here in great stead. The great Macdonald, Prince of the Isles, is the central figure, and next to him the aged but faithful Mackay of Rhinns, both who are immediately informed by their watchful scouts of the advent of those hereditary foes, the Norse invaders, on the green shores of Islay, which was once in their own possession. The fiery cross is sent all over the island to call together the brave subjects of the Macdonald to defend their homes and hearths. A battle takes place; and in the final struggle there are many heroes who do great and incredible deeds . . .

Nigel MacNeil, *The Literature of the Highlanders*, 1892

Here are some verses of a war chant from the poem, in which Livingston imagines the Norse psyching themselves up for battle – in the manner of a New Zealand rugby Haka – as they anchor in Lochindaal.

> So sinne 's cha 'n fhalbh mar a thàinig,
>   Tuagh, tuagh;
> Gheilbh sibh bhur nòineach am màireach,
>   Le tuagh, tuagh;

Buidealaich dhearg troimh gach fàrdaich,
    Tuagh, tuagh;
'S bhur mnathan 's bhur creach gu tràigh leinn,
    Tuagh, tuagh.

Bithidh sibh a' grìosadh 's a' teicheadh,
    Sgian, sgian;
Bheir sinne bhuaibh lùgh nan easgaid,
    Le sgian, sgian;
Na thig dhibh cha till iad am feasda,
    Sgian, sgian;
Cha' n fhaic iad a' mhaduinn 's am feasgar,
    Sgian, sgian;

Cha téid fear a dh' innseadh sgeòil dibh,
    Tuagh, tuagh;
Cluinnibh na fithich a' ròcail,
    Tuagh, tuagh;
Ni sinne dhaibh, cuirm do'r spòltan,
    Tuagh, tuagh.

Tollaidh sinn na gheibh sinn beò dhibh,
    Le sgian, sgian;
Cha' n fhalaich uamha no fròg sibh,
    Sgian, sgian;
So dhuibh caismeachd nan sgòrnan,
    Sgian, sgian;

Gheibh sibh so 's an còrr dheth màireach,
    Le tuagh, tuagh;
Cinn 'ur maithean air gad àraich,
    Le tuagh, tuagh;
Sgairt' o fhèithean am bràghad,
    Le tuagh, tuagh;
'S ga 'n dathadh air teallaichean nan ceàrdach,
    Tuagh, tuagh;
Ceann Mhic Aoidh againn 'ga iomain,
    Tuagh, tuagh;
'S gun fear beò 's an Roinn d'a chinneadh,
    Tuagh, tuagh.

Dòmhnull Aimhreidh am beul fo fhraoch,
    Is cach 'nan sineadh,
Gheibh esan damha-ghriosach ròstaidh,
    Far am bi e,
Gaoirgean eibhlean dearg
    Is tachdadh toite,
'S a rongairean Ileach gun bhuaidh,
    Ruagte, ropte.

Here we come, but we thus will not leave you –
    The axe, axe;
To-morrow will startle and grieve you
    With the axe, the axe.
A red blazing torch in each dwelling –
    The axe, the axe;
Your goods plundered, your captured wives yelling –
    The axe, the axe.

Fleeing, and cursing and wailing –
    The knife, knife;
The pith of your knees shall be failing
    For the knife, knife,
They who meet us shall leave that place never –
    The knife, knife;
Morn nor eve shall they see then for ever –
    The knife, knife;
None shall live to tell of the Reaver
    With the axe, axe;
But the raven above shall be croaking –
    The axe, axe;
And then feast on their limbs till he's choking –
    The axe, axe.

You now live who in blood then shall welter –
    The knife, knife;
Cave or hole cannot hide you or shelter
    From the knife, knife.
Through your throats one hoarse chorus ascending –
    The knife, knife;

In that cry screams and groans shall keep blending –
  The knife, knife.

All these ills shall your great men entangle –
  The axe, axe;
Ere their heads on our green withes shall dangle –
  The axe, axe;

The nerves of their necks we will rend them –
  With the axe, axe;

To the anvil* to roast them we'll send them –
  The axe, axe.
The head of Mackay we shall shinty –
  The axe, the axe,
Down the Rhinns, where his kin shall grow scanty,
  With the axe, axe.

William Livingston, *Na Lochlannaich An Ile (The Danes in Islay)*,
1882

High on our right, as if expecting reinforcements from Nosebridge Fort
and Knock Rònamail, rises the furrowed face of *Sliabh-a'-chath*, Hill of
the Battle, reminiscent of a battle, probably fought between Celt and
Norseman some nine centuries ago. This is the scene of Livingston's
celebrated martial poem, *Na Lochlannaich an Ile*, The Danes in Islay.
William Livingston, the Islay poet, was born on the farm of *Gartmain*,
which lies away to the left. His forte was to sing of arms and of men,
of battlefields and the exploits of heroes. MacKay of the Rhinns, one
of the bard's chief characters in this poem, shows clever strategy in
the disposition of his forces and real military tactics in the handling of
them. Livingston has made the Burn of Gartmain the Islayman's Bannockburn. This semi-historical drama is unique in the Gaelic language.

L. MacNeill Weir, *Guide to Islay*, 1911

There is one written account of a Viking raid on Islay. In 1098 the Norwegian king, Magnus Olafsson, sailed south from Orkney with a fleet, ravaging
the Hebrides as he went.

*Literally, to the fires of smithys.

From thence King Magnus sailed to Islay, where he plundered and burnt; and when he had taken that country he proceeded south around Cantire, marauding on both sides in Scotland and Ireland, and advanced with his foray to Man, where he plundered. So says Bjorn Krephende: –

> On Sandey's plain our shield they spy:
> From Isla smoke rose heaven-high,
> Whirling up from the flashing blaze
> The king's men o'er the island raise.

Magnus Barefoot's Saga, 1220, from the Icelandic of Snorri Sturleson, trans. Samuel Laing, 1844

While the Norsemen came to Islay to plunder, it seems they stayed to farm.

There are more Danish or Norwegian names of places in this island than any other; almost all the present farms derive their titles from them, such as Persibus, Torridale, Torribolse, and the like.

Thomas Pennant, *A Tour in Scotland and Voyage to the Hebrides*, 1772

A very noticeable feature of Scandinavian names in Islay is the frequent recurrence of the termination *bolstad*, represented by *pols*, *bolls*, or *bus*, and meaning homestead, townland or farm. This termination in Islay place names includes one-third of all the Norse names in the island; but in Lewis only about one-twelfth.

J. G. MacNeill, *Islay*, 1899

The Edinburgh University scholar of Scandinavian studies, Alan MacNiven, points out that there are 18 farm districts on Islay with names derived from Bólstaðr, the Old Norse for 'farm' – among them, Bolsay, Scarrabus, Eallabus, Cragabus, and Lurabus.

At a generous estimate, place-names containing Old Norse elements account for only a fifth of the total. Crucially, however, these names do not appear to be confined to any particular part of the island. Instead, they are spread fairly evenly across all of its landforms. Given the thousand years of change in population size, distribution and nomenclature since the height of the Viking Age, it is probable that the proportion of Norse place-names was once much higher, raising serious questions as to how the implantation and survival of so many Norse place-names could have been possible without a fundamental disruption to the societal status quo. Indeed, it might be asked whether the Viking Age in Islay saw cultural changes as dramatic as those which are now believed to have taken place in the Northern Isles of the Outer Hebrides.

Alan MacNiven, *The Vikings in Islay*, 2015

By the eleventh century the power of the Norse was waning. It was time for the resurgence of the Gaels. The man whose descendants would found the Gaelic Lordship of the Isles and Clan Donald was Godred Crovan. Crovan is also part-history, part myth.

On the roadside between Ballyvicar and Kintra is a large white standing stone, which is perhaps the most interesting historical memorial in Islay.

This large white stone, standing out solitary and conspicuous against the purple heather of the lonely moorland, unlike many similar monuments in Islay, has both a name and a history. It is called *Caraban* – White Stone – and marks the burial place of one of the doughtiest warriors of the time – Godred Crovan – the King Arthur of the Western Isles. Who was Godred Crovan? What is his history? His story is a tale of other and more war-like times.

L. MacNeill Weir, *Guide to Islay*, 1911

Weir, unaware that his own era was about to become hideously warlike, casts the minds of his readers back to 1066 when King Harold ruled England. Before he met his reputed end at the hands of a Norman archer at Hastings, Harold had defeated the invading army of the Norwegian King, Harold Hardrada, at Stamford Bridge in Yorkshire.

The Norwegian King, a man of giant stature and dauntless courage, fought at the head of his men with all that Berserker pugnacity for which the Viking breed was famous. His chief of staff was Godred – Godred the white handed. The battle was bloody and prolonged, but ultimately and absolutely, decisive. The Norsemen fought bravely but in vain. Harold Hardrada, the most famous of the Viking chiefs, lay among the flower of his warriors. Disaster befell the vanquished, but the triumph of the victor was short lived. While the English king was feasting at York a thane of Sussex suddenly appeared with the terrible tidings that Duke William of Normandy had landed at Pevensey and was laying waste the south coast.

Meanwhile Godred, escaping from the battlefield, made his way from Stamford Bridge to Islay. The fame of his prowess in the field preceded him, and he soon gathered sufficient men to dispute the title of King of Man and the Isles with Fingal. His exploits include the expulsion of Fingal, the invasion of Ireland, and the subjugation of Dublin and a great part of Leinster. Then it was that he turned his attention against Malcolm III of Scotland, commonly called Canmore.

If we turn from the study of the dusty records of the past to the local and living tradition of to-day we find the name of Prince Godred Crovan enshrined as the St George of the Western Isles.

Not content with Godred Crovan's achievement of becoming King of Man, Dublin and the Isles, tradition has made him 'the St George of the Western Isles'. And to be St George – you need a dragon.

As tradition avers, Islay had ceased to be a safe inhabitation for man at this time, on account of a fierce dragon, called by the natives Beithire which ravaged it. Crovan, who anchored his navy off Traighlaga, placed a number of barrels with long iron spikes projecting from their sides, between his ships and the shore, and proceeded, taking four horses with him, to the monster's den, which was at a place now called Imire-comhnard, about six miles into the interior of the island. He left three of the horses at three different stations, but rode on the fourth until he came within sight of the dragon. By shooting an arrow at it he roused it, and it immediately pursued him with alarming speed. When Crovan came to the third station he left the exhausted horse to be devoured by the monster, whose progress was thus retarded, whilst its wily destroyer, by mounting a fresh horse, was gaining ground. As the dragon neared him again he left it the second horse, and so with the third and fourth until he reached his well manned boat which carried him in safety to his fleet. The dragon, after devouring the fourth horse, pursued him; but was lacerated to death by the spiked barrels! In this way (according to the legendary lore of the natives) Crovan took possession of Islay; and gained a title to it of a far less questionable character than perhaps any subsequent possessor has had it by. He died in Islay in 1097, and Lagonan succeeded him, and was inaugurated as King of the Isles, in Islay and the Isle of Man, with full consent of Sigard, King of Norway: for although the Kings of Scotland were Lords paramount, they were either unwilling or unable to interfere with Islay at this time.

William MacDonald, *Sketches of Islay*, 1850

Godred Crovan's achievement was multi-faceted. Not only did he found the Scandinavian sea-going dynasty of Man and the Isles, and firmly established 'an extensive island kingdom which encompassed the western Scottish islands', but when his granddaughter, Ragnhild, married Somerled of Argyll, Godred became ancestor of a vigorous new race of Hebridean sea-kings, who would eventually wrest authority in the Isles from his own Norse descendants.

R. Andrew McDonald, *The Kingdom of the Isles*, 1998

Godred Crovan's heir, Olaf the Red, ruled for forty years before being murdered in 1153, when he was replaced by his son, Godred II. Godred II was unpopular, and provoked rebellion. In 1156, after a sea–battle that is believed to have been fought in the Sound of Islay, Godred had Islay, Mull and Jura wrested from him by the rising, part-Norse/part-Gaelic warlord who had married his sister – Somerled.

In the year 1156 on the night of the Lord's Epiphany (5th/6th January), a naval battle was fought between Godred and Somerled with great slaughter of men on either side. And when day broke they made peace and they apportioned between them the kingdom of the Isles; and the kingdom has been divided from that day to the present time. And this was the cause of the ruin of the kingdom of the Isles, beginning from the time when the sons of Somerled took possession of it.

Chronicle of the Kings of Man and the Isles, edited and translated by G. Broderick, 1973

That thirteenth-century Manx manuscript laments the 'ruin' of the kingdom of which the Isle of Man was the centre. But Somerled ruled Islay and the rest of his new won islands as a king, and founded a dynasty from which the Lordship of the Isles would rise.

At his death he was styled King of the Isles (*Innse Gall*) and Kintyre, and his power was manifest in his ability to gather together an imposing fleet of ships, said to be 160 strong with contingents from Dublin as well as the Isles and Kintyre. Such a fleet of ships would have carried a fighting force of at least 6,000 men, and possibly considerably more than that. The establishment of Somerled and his descendants in Kintyre and the Isles represented a considerable shift in power in the west away from the Isle of Man.

David Caldwell, *Islay: The Land of the Lordship*, 2008

Somerled died – assassinated or killed in battle – near Renfrew in 1164 as he attempted an invasion of mainland Scotland. Over centuries he has been revered as a Celtic hero, under whose leadership Gaelic Scotland re-emerged from under the power of the Norsemen. This song, which is recorded as having been made for 'Mackay of the Rhinns of Islay' by his sweetheart, is to an apple tree. It appears in Alexander Carmichael's vast collection of folklore among the waulking songs, but sounds like a magical incantation to promote the tree's fruitfulness, and invokes the memory of Somerled to this end.

> Chroabh nan ubhal, gu robd Dia leat,
> Gu robh gealach, gu robh grian leat,
> Gu robh gaoth an ear 's an iar leat,
> Gu robh Dùile mór nan sian leat,
> Gu robh gach nì thàna riamh leat,
> Gu robh Somhaorle Mór 's a chliar leat.
>
> Oh apple tree, may God be with thee,
> May moon and sun be with thee,
> May east and west winds be with thee,
> May the great Creator of the elements be with thee,
> May everything that ever existed be with thee,
> May great Somerled and his band be with thee.

Alexander Carmichael, *Carmina Gadelica*, 1900

Alexander Carmichael's collection of 'Hymns and Incantations' was mostly gathered between 1860 and 1909, and began when he was working as an exciseman, throughout the Gaelic-speaking areas of the Highlands and Islands. Carmichael has been criticised for adding literary polish to material he heard from the mouths of crofters and fishermen but, nevertheless, *Carmina Gadelica* remains an indispensable source of Gaelic folklore. The fact that Somerled was still celebrated in the songs of Gaels after seven centuries says a lot for the strength of oral tradition as well as for the reputation of the great warlord himself.

> A kingdom needs a king. The history of the western seaboard between 1100 and 1300 was dominated by vigorous sea-kings descended from the mighty Somerled of Argyll (d. 1164) and the equally formidable Godred Crovan (d. 1095). For a hundred years between the demise of Somerled and the death of the last Manx ruler in 1265, one of the major themes in the western seaboard was the struggle for hegemony between those two kindreds, which, though often violent, assumed a definite equlibrium. These sea-kings are compelling, spirited figures. They lived hard and died harder. Their praises were sung by Gaelic bards, and their formidable fleets of galleys inspired awe and terror in enemies and allies alike. They appear as thoroughly up-to-date rulers on the one hand, embracing contemporary trends in architecture and building magnificent stone castles and chapels like those at Dunstaffnage; yet on the other hand they were ready, willing and able to undertake old-fashioned plundering expeditions in the Hebrides or the Irish Sea long after the Viking Age had passed. Ranald the son of Somerled, Ragnvald the son of Godfrey, Ewan the son of Duncan, Angus Mór the son of Donald – these were men whose deeds were celebrated the length and breadth of the western seaways and beyond. Somerled's career was recorded in Scottish, Irish, Norse and Manx sources; both the St Albans chronicler, Matthew Paris, and Sturla Thordarson, the Icelandic author of Hakon's saga, praised Ewan of Argyll; Gaelic bards sung the deeds of Ragnvald of Man and Angus Mór of Islay. Yet, paradoxically, although they were mighty figures in their own day, these sea-kings seldom figure in modern history books. They might be called the lost kings of the medieval British Isles.

R. Andrew McDonald, *The Kingdom of the Isles*, 1998

Clan Donald and the
Lords of the Isles

The history of Islay may be succinctly described as the history of the
Southern Hebrides. Many are the tales told of the battle of Traigh
Gruinart, a battle fought between the Macleans of Mull and the Macdonalds of Islay – one of the most bloody fights in the history of the
Isles, and one that has given rise to a host of interesting legends that
are still told on a winter's evening around the farm-house fire. There
is the story of the Castle of Dunyvaig, a stronghold of the Lords of
the Isles, the tale of its bombardment by Sir Oliver Lambert and of
the escape of Coll Coitach and his men. There are the interests of
Loch Finlaggan and its little chapel – once under the patronage of
the Lord of the Isles – where Princess Margaret, daughter of the first
Stuart king of Scotland, Robert II, lies buried . . . The history and
legendary lore of Islay alone make rare reading.

Iain F. Anderson, *Across Hebridean Seas*, 1937

Much of Islay's history of this era is embellished with gracenotes of lore
and legend. Some historians may wince, but the general reader is invited to
enjoy the myths as much as the known facts.

The origins of the Macdonalds in Islay is said to be as follows: – During the Norwegian sway in the Western Isles, one of the Kings was
in the habit of coming to Islay every year with his household to hunt
the deer. Among the King's retinue was Gillebride, who for some
cause got out of favour. Being prohibited from returning to Norway,
he sent for his wife and family, and with them, took up his abode
in the cave. When his son Donald was about twenty-one, he used
to go and see what the Norwegian sportsmen were doing, and on
one occasion as he joined them, a seven-year-old stag started. There
was none among them so swift and powerful as young Donald. The
King's daughter fixed her eye and heart upon the stalwart youth, and
next day revealed her feelings to him. At the King's departure the

Princess could not be found, her lover having procured for her a safe retreat and hiding place. Three years thereafter, the King returned to the island – his barque being observed and watched by the Princess. When he landed, she went from the cave, which had hitherto been her habitation, and presented her first-born to His Majesty, who however took notice, that its clothing was unbefitting its royal descent, and enquired what would be sufficient to meet this want. The mother replied, if his Majesty would be pleased to grant the Island of Islay, the deficiency would be effectually met. On this the King gave up the island to the child, and thus the Macdonalds became Lords of Islay and the other Western Islands.

> Robert Oliphant, *The Tourist's Guide to Islay, The Queen of the Hebrides*, 1881

In the north east of Islay lies the freshwater Loch Finlaggan – power centre of the MacDonald Lords of the Isles. The ruins there date from the thirteenth century, although they may stand on the site of an older, Iron Age, fortification.

> In Islay, beside Loch Finlagan, one (or more) of the old Lords of the Isles held his court; and standing on a big stone seven feet square, received the homage of all his vassals, a ceremony graced by the sanction of the Church; "for," says the old chronicle, "the Bishop of Argyle and seven priests did anoint and crown him king of the isles, placing his father's sword in his hand, whereupon he swore to protect the Islesmen, and do justice to all his subjects".

> C. F. Gordon Cumming, *In the Hebrides*, 1901

Generations of travellers to Islay have made their pilgrimages to the seat of the Lords of the Isles. Donald Monro, a sixteenth-century cleric, wrote the first known account of the Hebrides. Monro was the Pre-Reformation Archdeacon of the Isles and is referred to as Dean Monro. His account of his tour of the Hebrides is a valuable historical document, not least for its early description of Finlaggan. The twelfth-century 'King of the Occident Isles' he describes is Ranald, son of Somerled.

> Ellan Finlagan in the middis of Ila ane fair Ile in fresh water Loch. Into this Ile of Finlaggan the Lords of the Iles, quhen thai callit thame selfis Kings of the Iles, had wanto to remain of in this Ile forsaid to

thair counsell for thai had the Ile well biggit in palace-wark according to thair auld fassoun . . .

Dean Monro, *Description of the Western Isles of Scotland*, written around 1563

Monro's vigorous Scots is hard work for modern readers, but this seventeenth-century translation by John Monipennie is easier.

There is also a fresh water loch, wherein stands the island named Falingania, some time the chiefe seat of all the isles men. There the governor of the isles, usurping the name of king, was wont to dwell. Neere unto this island, and somewhat lesse than it, is the Round Island, taking the name from the Counsell, for therein was the justice seat, and fourteen of the most worthy of the countrie did minister justice unto all the rest continually, and intreated of the waighty affaires of the realme in council, whose great equtie and discretion kept peace both at home and abroad; and with peace was the companion of peace, abundance of all things.

John Monipennie (ed.), *Certayne Matters concerning the Realme of Scotland*, 1603

Monro describes the 14-man council that deliberated at Eilean na Comhairle (Council Island):

In this Ile their conveinit 14 of the Iles best Barons, that is to say four greatest of the Nobles callit Lords; to wit Mcgillane of Doward, Mgrillane of Lochbuy, Mccloyde of Sary, and Mccloyde of Leozus. Thir four Barons forsaid might be callit Lords, and were haldin as Lords at sic time, Four Thanes of les living and estate; to wit, Mcginninin, Mcnaie, Mcneill of Gighay and Mcneill of Barry. Uther four great men of living of their toyall blude of Clan-donald lineally descebdit; to wit Clan-donald of Kintye, Mcane of Ardnamirquahame, Clan-Ronald, and Clan-Alister Carryche in Lochaber; with the Bishop and Abbot of Icolmkil. Thir 14 persons sat down into the Counsell-Ile, and decreitit and gave suits furth upon all debaitable manners according to the Laws made by Renald McSonharkle callit in his time King of the Occident Iles, and albeit their Lord where at his hunting or at ony uther games,

zit thai sate every ane at their Councell ministring justice. In
thair time thair was great peace and welth in the Iles throw
the ministraitin of justive.

Martin Martin describes the ritual by which he believed the Lords of the
Isles were inaugurated.

> There was a big Stone of seven Foot square, in which there was a
> deep Impression made to receive the Feet of the *Mack-Donald*; for he
> was crown'd King of the Isles standing in this Stone, and swore that
> he would continue his Vassals in the possession of their Lands, and
> do exact Justice to all his Subjects: and then his Father's Sword was
> put into his hand. The Bishop of *Argyll* and seven Priests anointed
> him King in preference of all the Heads of the Tribes in the Isles and
> Continent, and were his Vassals; at which time the Orator rehears'd
> a Catalogue of his Ancestors, etc.
>
> Martin Martin, *A Description of the Western Islands of Scotland*,
> 2nd edition 1716

The impression carved in stone, in which the new Lord placed his feet for
the ceremony, recalls the footprint carved on Dunadd Hill in Kilmartin
Glen on the Argyll mainland. These seem to have been of profound ritual
significance to the Scotti of Dalriada. The act of placing his feet in the carved
impressions may have symbolised the new king's dominion over his land.

> The ruins of this place and chapel still exist, and also the stone on
> which he stood when he was crowned King of the Isles. This custom
> seems to have been common to the northern nations. The Danes had
> their *kongstolen*.
>
> The ceremony (after a new lord had collected his kindred and
> vassals), was truly patriarchal. After putting on his armour his helmet
> and his sword, he took an oath to rule as his ancestors had done; that
> is, to govern as a father would his children: his people in return swore
> that they would pay the same obedience to him as children would
> their parent. The dominions of this potentate about the year 1586
> consisted only of Islay, Jura, Knapdale and Cantyre. So reduced were
> they, from what they had been, before the deprivation of the great
> Earl of Ross in the reign of James III.
>
> Near this is another little isle, where he assembled his council: Ilan-
> na-Corlle, or, 'the island of council'; where thirteen judges constantly

sat to decide differences among his subjects; and received for their trouble the eleventh part of the value of the affair tried before them.

In the island were buried the wives and children of the lords of the isles; but their own persons were deposited in the more sacred ground of Iona.

On the shores of the lake are some marks of the quarters of his *carnaugh* and *gilliglasses*, the military of the isles: the first signifying a strong man; the last, a grim-looking fellow. The first were light armed, and fought with darts and daggers; the last with sharp hatchets. These are the troops that Shakespeare eludes to, when he speaks of a Donald, who:

> From the Western Isles
> of Kernes and Gallow glasses was supplied.

Thomas Pennant, *A Tour in Scotland and Voyage to the Hebrides*, 1772

There was a square stone, seven or eight feet long, and the tract of a man's foot cut thereon, upon which he stood, denoting that he should walk in the footsteps and uprightness of his predecessors, and that he was installed by right in his possession. He was clothed in a white habit, to shew his innocence and integrity of heart, that he would be a light to his people, and maintain the true religion. The white apparel did afterwards belong to the poet by right. Then he was to receive a white rod in his hand, intimating that he had power to rule, not with tyranny and partiality, but with discretion and sincerity. Then he received his forefathers' sword, or some other sword, signifying that his duty was to protect and defend from the incursions of their enemies in peace or war, as the obligations and customs of his predecessors were. The ceremony being over, mass was said after the blessing of the bishop and seven priests, the people pouring their prayer for the success and prosperity of their new created Lord. When they were dismissed the Lord of the Isles feasted them for a week thereafter; gave liberally to the monks, poets, bards and musicians. You may judge that they spent liberally without any exception of persons.

Hugh MacDonald, *History of the MacDonalds*, c. 1660

Historians know little of the life of Aonghas Mór of Islay – son of Domhnall mac Raghnaill, and therefore the first 'son of Donald' and the first of the MacDonald line. But a rare insight into his world can be glimpsed in a thirteenth-century poem written to him by an Irish poet, requesting payment for a work commissioned from him by Aonghas Mór's recently deceased father. The poet pleads that a 'dread of the sea' prevents him from coming to collect the debt personally.

Asking a powerful medieval lord for money was, no doubt, a tricky business, so the poet butters up Aonghas by piling on the flattery. He refers to him in verse as 'king of Lewis' and 'king of the isles' and recalls his warlike feats.

We don't know the extent of Aonghas Mór's power, but readers of the poem are left in no doubt that he was a significant Hebridean warlord, with hosts of warriors and long ships at his command.

Here, in English, are the opening stanzas of the poem.

> Pay for your father's poem, Aonghas,
>   Since the house of the chief is now yours;
> Since you are the root of the tree and the flower,
>   Everyone will say you ought to pay.

> To you he left his castle,
>   Yours every breast-plate, yours every gem,
> His land, his followers, and his pointed weapons
>   Are yours, and his brown ivory pieces for chess.

> Yours are your father's slender dog-chains,
>   Every treasure chest is part of your lot,
> His house and tribute without division,
>   Yours Domhnall's cattle-herds and his studs.

> In his will he has left you
>   Every house from Mull to Kintyre,
> Aonghas, he has left you his galleys.
>   O pillar of green-branched Druim Caoin.

> Yours his assembly and swift horses,
>   Yours his hospitallers who cannot be taken away,
> As you are the son at the head of our battles,
>   It is yours to pay what your father has pledged.

> Acknowledge that you ought to pay for my poetry,
>   Oh hound of the Bann, O uncovered hair;

ISLAY VOICES

If you do not acknowledge it, tell another story,
  But I will lay your burden, of accusation on you.

I envy the high-poets the treasure,
  They gain from you, O lion of Loch Cé,
Who knows if it is justified envy –
  I am stifled by dread of the sea.

Coire Dhá Ruadh lies between us,
  O king of Tuam, I'm afraid;
On our course lies Corryvreckan
  I am beset by a seizing of fear.

Not less the difficulty that Corryvreckan
  Lies before me, O king of Ceól,
As its exuberance in sultry weather
  Will warp firm masts of sails.

I say, out of dread of the ocean,
  O darling of women, O man of Coll,
Over the sea to Aonghas of Islay
  It is a shame there is not one point of land.

While I put one foot before me
  O king of Lewis, into the ship,
The one behind I point westwards,
  When I go east, O pleasant one.

I would make a poor oarsman,
  Blue eye, on a perilous sea
Even on a calm river I tremble,
  When in charge at the helm.

I cannot calm myself as I ought to
  When crossing the waves;
I do not know if I'd be better sitting,
  But I'm afraid to lie down,

It is my grip that holds the ship together
  As I drag her towards me, O Prince of Fál;

So the waves won't break the ship asunder
    I grasp the gunwhale in my hand.

People have to ask, in my native district,
    What a ship is like, O king of the Isles;
From there little of the sea is visible
    Even from the highest steep hill there is.

Even if land reached as far as the sun rise,
    Most dangerous, I'd swear by your hand,
Is the sea, Aonghas, from here to Scotland,
    Grey-sprayed, down pouring, white.

Ceannaigh duain t'athar, a Aonghas (*Pay for Your Father's Poem, Aonghas*), in McLeod and Bateman, *Duanaire na Sracaire* (*Songbook of the Pillagers*), 2007

The second stanza of the poem contains a tantalising reference to 'brown ivory pieces for chess' that Aonghas inherited from his father, Donald. Could these have been the famous Lewis chess pieces?

The common theory is that the Lewis pieces were buried in the Hebrides by a Scandinavian merchant on his way to somewhere more civilised, like Dublin. Presumably eighteenth-century antiquarians couldn't bring themselves to believe that such beautiful objects could have been afforded and appreciated by, and played with, by Hebrideans – even ones descended from Somerled.

A MacSorley cannot be dismissed as a possible owner. Some of them were great warriors, holders of extensive lands, and were recognised as kings. One in particular is worth considering here, and that is Angus Mor, a great grandson of Somerled, whose main centre of power was the island of Islay. A praise poem written in his honour in the mid-thirteenth century describes how he inherited his ivory chessmen from his father Donald. It also describes him as king of Lewis – flattery yes, but Angus was clearly a big man in the world of the Isles, Scotland and Ireland. As son of Donald he was the first MacDonald, and also one of the commanders of the invasion fleet which King Hakon used to threaten Scotland in 1263.

Excavations directed by Dr David Caldwell at Finlaggan on the Isle of Islay, probably Angus Mor's main home, produced no chessmen but many tables-men – three of bone and about fifty of stone – probably all of later date than Angus. It is not without interest, however to note that Angus' praise poem also records how his father Donald left him his dog leashes and hounds. The bronze mounts from two dog collars were found in midden material dating to the thirteenth century. They include two fine quality swivel attachments with dragonesque heads.

Great men like these did not lead a sedentary life, but moved from house to house, went campaigning and visiting their lands, tenants, churches and clergy. It is possible that one such as these would have hidden or secured their chessmen in an underground chamber, no doubt adjacent to a favoured residence, until their return from a voyage.

David H. Caldwell, Mark A. Hall and Caroline Wilkinson, *The Lewis Chessmen Revealed*, 2010

In short, could the 'Lewis' chess pieces really have been the 'Islay' chess pieces?

While Finlaggan was the centre of law and administration, the MacDonalds also had a fortress at Dunyvaig on the south coast of Islay.

Dun Naomhaig was the principal stronghold of the Macdonalds of Islay and Lords of the Isles . . .

The name of Dun Naomhaig has given cause for debate, but it is said to be very ancient. In fact in 498AD it was the House of Aonghad Beag, the son of Erc. So, perhaps it is the *dun of Aonghas beag* a corruption of *dun Aonghaus Bhig*.

Peggy Earl, *Tales of Islay*, 1980

Dun Naomhaig, or Dunyvaig, is today an atmospheric ruin, most often seen by visitors to Lagavulin Distillery. Port Ellen too has a site associated with the MacDonald lordship.

There is a tradition, that while the Isle of Man was part of the kingdom of the Isles, that the rents were for a time paid in this country; those in silver were paid on a rock, still called Creig-a-Nione, or, 'the rock of the silver rent': the other Creg-a-Nairgid, or, 'the rock of rents in kind'. These lie opposite each other, at the mouth of a harbour on the south side of the island.

Thomas Pennant, *A Tour in Scotland and Voyage to the Hebrides*, 1772

Though they had their Parliament in Finlaggan it was to Kildalton Parish at Traigh Eirisgeir (the White Hart shore as it is called today) that the Manx tribute was paid. The tribute, in goods or kind, was paid at *Creag an Fion* just opposite the Ramsay Hall. Locally the name was *Creag an Fhion*, but it is believed that this was a corruption of *Creag na Nithean*, the 'rock of "goods"'. Creag an Airgiod, on the shore below Tichcargaman, is the place where the tribute in money was paid.

Peggy Earl, *Tales of Islay*, 1980

Aonghas Mór – 'the first MacDonald' – died around 1295 and was succeeded by his son Alasdair, but Alasdair supported the wrong side in the struggle for the Scottish crown between John Balliol and Robert Bruce. Meanwhile his brother, Angus Óg, threw in his lot with Bruce. After King Robert's army was routed at Methven, near Perth, in June of 1306, the King went on the run. Eventually, he fetched up in Kintyre where he was hospitably received by Angus Óg at his stronghold, Dunaverty Castle.

The alliance between Robert Bruce and Angus Óg is revealed by John Barbour in his epic poem, *The Bruce*. Barbour was Archdeacon of Aberdeen only fifty or sixty years after the momentous events of Bruce's life. So, while Barbour wasn't writing history in the way we understand it today, he would have been very well informed about the events of Bruce's life and the wars of independence.

Fortunately for the modern reader, the poem was translated and edited by Archibald A.H. Douglas and published in 1964. Douglas captured the directness and vitality of Barbour's writing:

Barbour tells us:

> Angus off Ile that tyme wes syr
> And lord and ledar of Kyntyr . . .
> The king rycht weill resavyt he
> And undertuk his man to be . . .

Douglas' translation makes it a little easier:

> Angus of Islay then was sire
> And lord and leader of Kintyre.
> The king right gladly welcomed he,
> And promised him his fealty,
> And offered freely out of hand

> Such service as he might demand.
> And for a stronghold to him gave
> Dunaverty, his castle safe,
> To dwell therein as he might need.
> Right thankfully the king agreed,
> And gladly took his fealty.

John Barbour, *The Bruce*, translated and edited by A.A.H. Douglas, 1964

It was Angus who arranged Bruce's flight to Rathlin Island off Northern Ireland. On clear days Rathlin can be clearly seen from Dunaverty and from parts of Angus's lands on Islay.

As Bruce's fortunes improved, so did Angus Óg's. Bruce rewarded the Islay warlord's loyalty with the grant of lands – some that had belonged to Angus's older brother, Alasdair Óg, a supporter of Bruce's enemies, the Balliols, and some forfeited by the MacDougalls, traditional enemies of the emerging Clan Donald.

On 24 June, 1314, Angus was at Bruce's side at Bannockburn. According to Barbour, Bruce had divided his army into four divisions, one commanded by the Earl of Moray, another by his brother Edward, and the third by James Douglas. Angus Óg and his islanders served in the final division under the command of Bruce himself.

> The ferd bataile the noble king
> Tuk till his awne governing . . .

Or, as Douglas translates it:

> The fourth division did the king
> Retain for his own ordering.
> The men of Carrick, from his land,
> Were all within his own command,
> As well as those from Bute, Kintyre,
> Argyll and the Isles (whereof was Sire
> Angus of Islay and of Bute),
> And many other men on foot.

In reward for his loyalty, Angus Óg was granted Angus Lordship of Mull, Jura, Coll and Tiree as well as swathes of Lochaber, Duror and Glencoe which were forfeited by Comyns and MacDougalls.

When he died at Finlaggan in 1330 he was a rich and powerful chieftain, worthy of burial amongst the Scots and Scandinavian kings on Iona. There is an interesting tradition which might explain why Angus Óg chose to be buried on Iona, and not on Islay.

> In the days of superstition, people were particularly anxious to have their dust interred in consecrated ground. But it is said, that an ancient traditional prophecy, "that this island should swim, when one tide would cover Ireland and green headed Ila" determined so many crowned heads to prefer this to every other.
>
> Robert Heron, *Scotland Delineated, or a Geographical Description of Every Shire in Scotland*, 1799

Angus Óg's son, John, and grandson, Donald, added to the family land and power through strategic marriages.

An account of John of Islay's marriages reveals the power and majesty of his court – and of John's ability to accumulate wealth and connections.

> Amic, the daughter of Ruaraidh, married in 1337 John of Islay, Lord of the Isles. The two being related, they were granted a dispensation by Pope Benedict XII. The Lady Amie had three sons.
>
> About the year 1358, John of Islay discarded Amie and married Margaret, daughter of Robert Steward, and grandaughter of Robert Bruce. When the Lord of the Isles came south to celebrate his marriage with the Lady Margaret, one hundred and eight ships full of kinsmen and clansmen, chiefs and chieftains, came in his train. Such a sight had never been seen in Scotland before, and people came from long distances to see this large fleet. The power and influence indicated by this enormous retinue created much comment and envy among the nobles of the south and even at the court.
>
> The Lord of the Isles retained possessions of the extensive territories of the Lady Amie, disposing of them afterwards to his several sons.
>
> The discarded lady took to a religious life, building and restoring oratories, churches, nunneries, monastries, and castles, throughout her ancestral lands . . .
>
> John, Lord of the Isles, was a man of much munificence, like all these princely Macdonalds. He gave largely to the Church, earning for himself from the priests of the period the name of "The Good John of Islay." He was buried in Iona in the year 1386, in splendour

and magnificence never surpassed, if ever equalled, in the case of the many kings of the five nationalities buried there.

About two years after his father's death, Ranald, the eldest surviving son of the Lady Amic, handed over the Lordship of the Isles to Donald, the eldest son of Lady Margaret, who soon afterwards fought the Battle of Harlaw.

Alexander Carmichael, *Carmina Gadelica*, 1900

Donald, now Lord of the Isles, knew the value of a good sword – and a strategic marriage.

This Donald was a great warrior. It was he who defeated the royal forces at Harlaw in 1411, and was therefore called Donald of Harlaw. In right of his wife, Mary Leslie, Donald claimed the earldom of Ross, a claim which was afterwards admitted by James I. This Donald, the grandson of King Robert II, was treated as an independent Prince by Edward IV of England.

J. G. MacNeill, *Islay*, 1899

By around 1420 the Lordship of the Isles was at its height – ruling the west of Scotland from the Mull of Kintyre to north-west Sutherland. But despite the expansion of the MacDonald empire, Finlaggan was still its administrative centre.

Remarkably, there still exists an example of the kind of legislation enacted there. The Islay Charter from 1408 is a unique historical document. Written in Gaelic, on goatskin, and signed '*MacDhomnuill*' by Donald Lord of the Isles himself, it is a very early example of Gaelic being used in public affairs.

The charter seems to have been written by Fergus Macbeth, whose family were hereditary doctors to the Lords of the Isles. 'Macbeth' is derived from the Gaelic for 'son of life', although they adopted the name Beaton sometime in the sixteenth century.

We have a specimen of the written Gaelic of this period in the famous Macdonald charter, the earliest Gaelic one extant. In 1408 Donald, Lord of the Isles, granted land in Islay to Brian Vicar Mackay of Rhinns, in that Island . . .

It is an interesting document, and is given here in a literal translation. It was written by one of the Beatons . . . who signs himself

"Fergus M'Beth." He was probably at the time physician to the Lord of the Isles. As Dr M'Lauchlan, who deciphered it, says – "The style of the charter is that of the usual feudal charters written in Latin, but the remarkable thing is to find a document of the kind written in Gaelic, at a time when such a thing was almost unknown in the Saxon dialects of either England or Scotland."

It is interesting to find that the Gaelic of the charter, written 470 years ago, is the same as that spoken in Islay at the present day. One word *brach*, "ever," is spelt phonetically just as it is pronounced now in the dialect of the island . . .

I, Mac Donald, am granting and giving eleven marks and half of land from myself and from my heirs to Brian Vicar Mackay and to his heirs, after him for ever and ever for his services to myself and to my father before me; and this on covenant and condition that he himself and they shall give to me, and to my heirs after me yearly, four cows fit for killing, for my house. And, in case that these cows shall not be found, the above Brian and his heirs shall give to me and my heirs after me, two marks and forty for the same cows aforesaid. And for the same causes I am binding myself and binding my heirs after me, to the end of the world, these lands, together with their fruit of sea and land, to defend and maintain to the above Brian Vicar Mackay, and his heirs for ever after him in like manner. And these are the lands I have given to him and to his heirs forever – namely, Baile Vicar, Machaire, Leraga-riabhoige, Ciontragha, Grastol, Tocamol, Ugasgog, the two Gleannastol, Cracobus, Cornunus, and Baile Neaghtoin. And, in order that there may be meaning, force, and effect in this grant, which I give from me, I again bind myself and my heirs for ever under covenant this to uphold and fulfil to the aforesaid Brian and his heirs after him to the end of the world by putting my hand and my seal down here, in presence of these witnessed here below, and the sixth day of the month of the Beltane, and this year of the birth of Christ, one thousand four hundred and eight.

McDonald.

Nigel McNeil adds:

It is a suggestive commentary on the uncertainty of sublunary things that these lands which Donald was to "uphold" "to the end of the world" to Brian and his heirs have passed through the hands of more than one family since – they being now the property of John Ramsay of Kildalton. Neither a Mackay nor a Macdonald owns any land in Islay now.

Nigel MacNeil, *The Literature of the Highlanders*, 1892

Since MacNeil's time, John Ramsay's estate has vanished and its lands are in the hands of several owners. However, the 'baile' (village or homestead) of Brian Vicar Mackay still lives on in the Islay farm name, Ballivicar.

Our route . . . lies across the low lying isthmus. The farm on our left is Cornabus, on our right is Ballyvicar, the Vicar's Farm, of Donald of Harlaw's Gaelic Charter.

L. MacNeill Weir, *Guide to Islay*, 1911

Fergus MacBeth, who wrote the charter, was one of a family of hereditary healers who were high status subjects of the Lords of the Isles.

. . . the clergy and the clan chiefs were well educated and travelled in Europe and their physicians were well read and talented.

Indeed, the surviving Gaelic medical manuscripts outnumber the handful of Latin medical manuscripts rescued from the Lowland monasteries after the Reformation. The Highland physicians had a high place in the hierarchy of the clan, taking second place to the bard at the banqueting table. The most distinguished of these hereditary families was that of the Beatons – the Latin form of the Gaelic MacBheathadh, MacBeath, or Bethune – who served the Macleods and the Lords of the Isles. Some legends say that the first Beaton came from Ulster with Angus Og's bride about 1303 but others assert that the name is a corruption of the pictish 'Bede', in which case the family was the one shown in the Book of Deer to have gifted land to Columba for his monastery. Whatever the explanation, the Beaton's medical knowledge came originally from Ireland. The family continued to be distinguished until the seventeenth century and held extensive lands in the west coast. For 200 years the office of principal physician of the Isles existed and in 1609 James VI confirmed to Fergus McBeath the land he held given to him by the Lordship of the Isles.

. . . Gaelic legends enjoy to tell how the metropolitan physicians substituted a sample of bull's urine for that from the King, but having spotted the trick, Beaton confounded these doctors and went on to cure the King.

David Hamilton, *The Healers*, 2003

From the early fourteenth to the early eighteenth century various branches of the Beaton clan practised medicine on a hereditary basis in the Hebrides and throughout mainland Scotland.

> Nor is it surprising to find a Beaton in Robert Bruce's service in view of the latter's close association with the west of Scotland and with the Clan Donald and their leader Angus Óg in particular.
>
> The centre of MacDonald power at this time was Islay and traditionally the Beatons settled in the parish of Kilchoman. Their presence there at least by the second half of the fourteenth century is confirmed by the erection in the churchyard of a fine cross in the West Highand style commemorating Beatons, apparently of the mainland division.
>
> John Bannerman, *The Beatons, A Medical Kindred in the Classical Gaelic Tradition*, 1998

But for all the skill of the Beatons and their like, unfamiliar and incurable illness could ravage entire communities.

> It is now believed that it was in 1430, shortly after the captivity of Lord Alexander, that the Great Plague or Pestilence prevailed so fearfully throughout Scotland, so much so that one third of the population of the whole kingdom was destroyed by it. In Islay the pestilence on this occasion was dreadful, for it is alleged the island was nearly depopulated. It was here the plague first broke out. A vessel from the Levant sea was stranded at Lochindaal, and the *fomites* or seeds of the disease were conveyed to the Island in the folds of a bale of scarlet cloth. Some unfortunate person first made the cloth into articles of clothing, and in the progress of doing so the disease was contracted, perhaps first by the tailor, then by the wearer, and so on until Islay was almost left desolate, only three families, consisting of 13 individuals, being left alive. The meagre annals of contemporary Historians do not enable us to detect any thing like the distinguishing symptoms of this awful scourge. It is also lamentable to observe that in the years 1349, 1354, 1378, 1560, 1604, and 1661 severe

pestilences infested all Scotland, and Islay suffered much at each of these periods.

William MacDonald, *Sketches of Islay*, 1850

The Highland healers were not working in isolation. Gaelic medicine was being influenced by the latest European developments, especially ideas from the medical school at Salerno in Italy.

... the advanced ideals of Salerno, which disregarded restrictions of colour, creed and class, permeate Gaelic medical writings. Its most renowned text, the *Regimen, Sanitatum Saliternae*, with its accent on the maintenance of health and prevention of sickness by a moderate way of life and attention to diet and exercise, is reflected in the *Regimen Sanitatis* (Rule of Health) compiled by John Beaton of Islay.

Mary Beith, *Healing Threads*, 2004

The text is comprehensive and follows orthodox lines, dealing with anatomy, botany, disease, therapy and the fees to be charged. The text is remarkable for an emphasis on prevention of disease – 'keep a firm grip on health' says the text, 'eat not too much' and 'spare the wine'. On rising in the morning exercises are recommended and walking is regarded as beneficial. Extracts of simple herbs are prescribed – violet (for headache and catarrh), nettle, mustard, hyssop, saffron, shepherds purse for bleeding wounds, fennel and parsley to increase the urine flow, celery for diseases of the mouth and stomach, mercury for lice and tannin for wounds.

David Hamilton, *The Healers*, 2003

However unwieldy in translation, the Gaelic *Regimen Sanitatis* throws interesting light on the health-conscious Highlander of the Middle Ages, for the concern with preventing disease and the pursuit of a sensible way of life parallel modern society's preoccupations. The three main principles of health with which the book begins guide the thinking throughout: the understanding and conservation of what makes for a healthy mind and body, the importance of noting the early signs of a breakdown in health and the means of preventing it, and the healing of the sick. One of the most significant aspects of the Gaelic doctors' beliefs was that health is maintained largely through applying common sense and, if somewhat sweepingly, that illness is chiefly caused by lack of it.

After rising in the morning the Gael was advised to stretch his arms and chest, have a good clean spit and rub dust and sweat from the skin. Hair was to be combed, hands and face washed *and* the teeth cleaned. After a prayer, some good exercise and walking in 'high clean places' was to be undertaken before breakfast.

Stringent advice on diet included guidance on cooking that took the then scientifically unidentified risks of salmonella poisoning into account:

> It should be known also that great injury is caused by the raw things such as oysters, and the things half raw as are the birds that are badly roasted . . .

In recommending eggs and egg custard for invalids, the manuscript notes:

> . . . if they are got in an unclean vessel they are very easily fouled, and they are the more healthy if broken into water.

Advice to cook peas, beans and other pulses with a pinch of cumin in order to prevent embarrassing bouts of wind is a tip worth remembering.

Mary Beith, *Healing Threads*, 2004

'Traditional' medicine is often thought as being mostly about herbal remedies, but Dr John Bannerman has shown that the Beatons were skilled surgeons, capable of carrying out lithotomies – removing stones from the bladder, kidney or urinary tract.

> . . . a poem in praise of Islay kindreds composed by Gille-Coluim c. 1550 describes the Beatons of Ballenabe in the following finely wrought couplet:
>
> > *'claim mhic beathadh a gnath ghrinn,*
> > *luchd snoidhe chnamh agus chuislenn.*
>
> > the kindred of Mac-beathadh, accurate in
> > their practice, carvers of bones and arteries.

and in describing the practice of surgery and venesection has no word of herbal treatment. Again in 1613 Gill-Anndrais Beaton . . . was credited with performing an operation which involved 'cutting a stone'.

This is not to suggest that the medical profession in Gaelic Scotland and Ireland had no native medical lore on which to draw. They were professionally organised and practising medicine long before the Islamic variety had reached the shores of Europe, as the law tracts of the seventh and eighth centuries amply testify. Since no native medical treatises have survived from this period, it should probably be assumed that this knowledge was passed on orally. Much of it would have found an echo in the medicine of the medieval manuscripts. The difference is not likely to have been in kind but in degree, to the extent that native herbs and substances unknown to Islamic medicine will have been used in ingredients in medical remedies and clearly continued in use, if we are to believe Hector Boece, alongside those of the foreign variety that could be procured.

However, towards the end of our period at least, there were medical practices or methods that were apparently recognisably Highland. One was lithotomy or cutting for stone, which operation we saw Gill-Anndrais Beaton performing in 1613.

John Bannerman, *The Beatons, A Medical Kindred in the Classical Gaelic Tradition*, 1998

The fame of the Beatons, or McBeaths, stretched far and wide, but Islay remained precious to them.

The Beatons were celebrated in the Medical department; one of whom was called to prescribe for King James VI, previous to his departure for England to take possession of the Crown after the death of Queen Elizabeth. The Royal patient recovered, and the physician being asked what reward he wished for, said, – "The farm of Coull." He was reproved for making such a modest request, and had Balinaby added to it. Thus were these two places originally separated from the Islay estate, as a reward for real merit, – a rare example of a rational appropriation of land.

William MacDonald, *Sketches of Islay*, 1850

As well as nurturing healers, the Lords of the Isles also prepared for the afterlife, and were generous patrons of the church.

A little further lie the low shores of the large island of Islay, rich in traces of old ecclesiastical buildings, no less than fourteen chapels having been founded by the Lords of the Isles. In the churchyard of Kil-arrow there is a remarkable gravestone, with the figure of a warrior with a conical head-dress, and tunic reaching to the knees. At his side is a dirk, and in his hand a sword. Near this stone is another bearing a large sword, and a garland of leaves – a Hebridean equivalent for a laurel crown.

C. F. Gordon Cumming, *In the Hebrides*, 1901

Related to the Scottish King and negotiating with the English crown, the Lords of the Isles were now playing the game of thrones, and not with an ivory chess set. But treating with England stoked the anger of James III and then James IV. In 1493 James IV officially abolished the Lordship, redistributed MacDonald lands and conducted military campaigns to clip the wings of Clan Donald. In 1503, John of Islay, the fourth and final MacDonald Lord of the Isles, died.

The forfeiture and the death of John had the effect of completely disorganising the clan; while all these clans which had been dependent upon the Lords of the Isles, although not connected by descent, having attained to considerable power under their protection, seized this opportunity, with one accord, of declaring themselves independent of the Macdonalds, and set about procuring from the king feudal titles to their respective lands.

There was no longer, therefore, any prospect of the Macdonalds again obtaining the almost royal state which they had so long enjoyed, and from this period may accordingly be dated the fall of that once powerful clan; although, before the Macdonalds finally resigned the contest, they appear to have made several attempts to place various of their branches at the head of the whole tribe; but these attempts proved equally unsuccessful, partly from the prompt measures adopted by the government, but principally from the effects of their own internal dissensions, as well as from the great opposition they received from the clans formerly dependent on the Macdonalds, but whose interest it had now become to prevent the union of the tribe under one head as formerly.

William Forbes Skene, *The Highlanders of Scotland*, 1837

With the forfeiture of the Lordship of the Isles in 1493, the MacDonalds ceased to be the dominant power in the west. But they were still a powerful clan, especially on Islay. In 1545 the MacDonalds of Dunyveg had much of their Islay land restored to them. It was a desirable property, and worth fighting for.

> . . . fertil fruitfull and full of natural girsing pasture with mony great deiris, mony woods, with fair games of hunting besides every town, with mekel leid over in Moychaolis, with ane water callit Laxan whereupon mony salmond are slane . . .
>
> Dean Monro, *Description of the Western Isles of Scotland*, written around 1563

By the time of Dean Monro's visit there were two powerful clans vying for Islay – the MacDonalds and the MacLeans of Duart.

> In this Ile thair is strynthie castells: the first callit Dunavaig biggit on ane craig at the sea side on the south–eist part of the cuntry pertaining to the Clan-donald of Kintyre. The second callit the castell of Lochgvrme, quhilk is biggit in ane Ile in the said fresch water loch far fra land pertaining to Clan-donald of Kintyure of auld, now usurpit be Mcgillane of Doward.

The scene was set for conflict between the MacDonalds of Dunyvaig and the 'usurping' MacLeans.

> The next dispute worthy of notice which occurred in the Isles was between the Macleans on the one part, and the Macdonalds of Islay and Kintyre on the other. This affair demands our attention, not so much on the account of its origin, which was merely a quarrel as to the right of occupancy of certain Crown lands in Islay, as because it was the commencement of a long and bloody feud between these tribes in which both suffered severely, and which led to the utter ruin of that powerful branch of Clan Donald. Of the early details of the feud, which was aggravated by previous disputes regarding the island of Gigha, little is found in the usual sources of information. The Isles of Mull, Tiree, and Coll were invaded by the Clan Donald of Islay, assisted by its kindred tribe, the Clan Donald of Sleat; and it may be supposed that the Macleans and their allies were not backward in similar hostilities. It is uncertain which tribe was the original aggressor; but from the tenor of certain proceedings before the Privy Council, it appears probable that the Macleans were to blame – a fact which,

indeed, is distinctly asserted by a historian, himself a Privy Councillor in the reign of James VI. According to this writer, the Rinns of
Islay (the lands in dispute) were actually occupied by Macleans, who
claimed to hold these lands as Crown tenants; but the decision of the
Privy Council established that James Macdonald of Islay was really the
Crown tenant, and that the Macleans, if they continued to remain
on the lands, must hold them of Macdonald, under the same conditions of personal and other services as the rest of Macdonald's vassals
in Islay held their lands. Such a decision must have been, no doubt,
very galling to a powerful and high-spirited tribe like the Macleans;
and we can scarcely be surprised at the deep-rooted hostility which so
long prevailed between them and the Clan Donald when we consider
the point of honour which was involved in their dispute. Such was
the inveteracy with which the rival chiefs pursued their quarrel, even
after the matter had been brought before the Privy Council, that in
1565 they were compelled to find sureties each to the amount of ten
thousand pounds, for their abstinence from mutual hostilities

Donald Gregory, *History of the Western Highlands and Islands of
Scotland: 1493–1625,* 1881

But rather than securing peace between the clans, royal meddling may have
exacerbated the feuds.

Under the House of Stuart, the Highlanders enjoyed a degree of
freedom suited to the ideas of a high-spirited people, proud of having,
for a series of ages, maintained their independence. The occasional
interference of the royal authority, and the policy frequently pursued,
of employing one chief to punish another, and of rewarding the
successful rival with a share of the lands forfeited by the vanquished,
has a greater tendency to perpetuate than to allay the endless feuds
between different clans and districts. It had another effect; it turned
the exasperation of the subdued clans against those who had attacked
them, and directing it from the person of a distant sovereign, whose
power was sometimes so weak that he had no other means of estab-
lishing his authority than that of setting the clans in opposition to
each other. In this state of hostility, their rage and irritations being
expended against their neighbours and rivals, the part the Sovereign
had taken attracted little notice; and thus loyalty and attachment to
his person continued unshaken. Of this we have striking instances in
the case of the Macdonalds of Cantyre and Islay, and the Macleans of

Dowart, whose lands were forfeited and granted to the Earl of Argyll in consequence of some acts of violence committed in the course of their mutual feuds; and yet no two peoples in the Highlands retained a stronger or more lasting attachment and loyalty than those two clans.

Major-General David Stewart, *Sketches of the Character, Manners and Present State of the Highlanders of Scotland*, 3rd edition, 1825

In 1583, the 17-year-old son of Mary Queen of Scots, King James VI, took control of his realm. Very soon the young King came to realise that the feuding warlords of the Highlands and Islands needed to be tamed.

After the young King had taken the government into his own hands, he was soon called upon to interfere in the feud between the Macdonalds and the Macleans, which owing to an unfortunate accident, now raged with greater fury than ever. The immediate cause of these renewed disorders, which speedily involved several other clans, was as follows. Donald Gorme Mor of Sleat, being on a voyage from Sky, with a retinue befitting his rank, to visit his kinsman, Angus Macdonald of Dunyveg, in the island of Isla, was forced by stress of weather to take shelter in that part of Jura belonging to Maclean of Dowart. At the same time, two gentlemen of Donald Gorme's clan, with whom he had lately quarreled, were by the same storm driven into a neighbouring harbour. On learning that their chief lay so near them, these vassals secretly carried off by night a number of cattle from Maclean's lands, and took to the sea, in expectation that Donald Gorme and his party would be blamed by the Macleans for the robbery and suffer accordingly. Their malicious design, unfortunately, took effect. For in the course of the following night the men of Sky were attacked by a superior body of the Macleans, and, as they apprehended no danger, fell an easy prey to the assailants. Sixty of the Macdonalds were slain, and their chief only escaped the same fate from the circumstance of his accidentally sleeping on board his galley on the night of the attack.

Donald Gregory, *History of the Western Highlands and Islands of Scotland: 1493–1625*, 1881

Donald Gorme MacDonald fled to Skye. Turning the other check was not an option open to sixteenth-century clan leaders. His campaign of revenge was brutal. But Angus MacDonald of Dunyvaig, who was married to a

Maclean of Dowart (Duart), believed that he could make peace between the clans, and took a retinue to Duart on Mull to negotiate.

> On the day after their arrival, Macdonald and his train – with the exception of Ranald McColl, Angus' cousin, who was left at liberty – were perfidiously seized and thrown into prison by their host. Here Macdonald was detained in close captivity, until, to preserve his life, he agreed to renounce, in favour of Maclean, the lands of the Rinns of Isla, so long disputed between the two families. For the performance of this agreement he was obliged to give his son, James, then a boy, and his brother Ranald, as hostages; whereupon he was set at liberty with his attendants. He then returned to his own Castle of Dunyveg, more than ever exasperated against his brother-in-law, and determined to obtain full revenge for the injuries inflicted both on himself and on his kinsman, Donald Gorme.
>
> Sometime afterwards, Maclean came to Isla to receive performance of the promises made by Macdonald regarding the Rinns of Isla, bringing with him his nephew, James Macdonald, one of the hostages, the other being left behind in the Castle of Dowart.

MacLean took over the now 'ruinous' castle on Loch Gorm, but was persuaded to move into Angus MacDonald's own house.

> Maclean accordingly came to Mullintrea, with eighty-six of his clan and servants, in the month of July 1586, and was sumptuously entertained on his arrival. In the meantime, the Macdonalds being secretly collected together to the number of three or four hundred men, surrounded the houses in which Maclean and his followers were lodged, and made them all prisoners, with the exception of two, to whom they refused quarter. One of these was a Maclean of rank and influence in the tribe, renowned for his valour and manhood; the other was Macdonald Terreagh, one of those vassals of Donald Gorme who were the original cause of the slaughter in Jura, and who, since that time, had attached himself to the Macleans. The house in which these two men were was burned to the ground, with its inmates, by the Macdonalds.
>
> When the report of the seizure of Maclean and his followers came to Mull, Allan, a near relation of the chief, caused a false rumour to be spread abroad that Ranald MacJames, the hostage left behind at Dowart, had been put to death. His object in this was to induce Angus

Macdonald to kill Maclean and his clansmen; in which event, Allan would have succeeded to the management of the estate, as guardian to Macdonald's children, who were then very young. And although this device did not succeed, yet it had this effect, that Coll MacJames, under the impression that his brother Ranald had really been executed, let loose his vengeance against the rest of the unfortunate prisoners. Two of them were executed every day, until at last Maclean himself alone survived of all those who had been seized by the Macdonalds at Mullintrea; and Macdonald's life was only saved by an accident that happened to Angus Macdonald as he was mounting his horse to witness the execution of his rival. These atrocities at length reached the ears of the King who employed the chiefs of the Campbells who governed the Earldom of Argyll during the minority of the seventh Earl, to mediate between the contending clans. By their influence, Macdonald agreed – on receiving a promise of pardon for his crimes, and on eight hostages of rank being placed in his hands by Maclean, for the performance of certain conditions, which the latter was forced to subscribe – to consent to the liberation of his opponent. After this, Macdonald went to Ireland to attend to his affairs in that country, when Dowart, regardless of the safety of his hostages and of his own promises, roused his clan to arms, and invaded Isla, a great part of which he wasted with fire and sword. On Macdonald's return to the Isles, he disdained to punish the hostages; but collected a large force of his vassals and friends, with which he invaded the Isles of Mull and Tiree, and put to death all the inhabitants that fell into his hands, as well as the domestic animals of every description. "Finally," says Sir Robert Gordon,★ "he came to the very Benmore in Mull, and there killed and chased the Clan Lean at his pleasure, and so revenged himself fully of the injury done to him and his tribe." While Macdonald was thus employed, Maclean ravaged and plundered a great part of Kintyre; and "thus for a while they did continually vex one another with slaughters and outrages, to the destruction almost of their countries and people."

Donald Gregory, *History of the Western Highlands and Islands of Scotland: 1493–1625,* 1881

. . . the adjoining field is called "Geathail-na-fola," or the field of blood, the place where upwards of fourscore Macleans were butchered, shortly before the battle of Traigh-Ghrunard, and probably the

★Sir Robert Gordon (1580-1656) Historian of the House of Sutherland.

place set apart for the execution of offenders, where, according to the well-known saying, benighted Highland serfs were want to "go up the ladder to please the laird."

Robert Oliphant, *The Tourist's Guide to Islay, The Queen of the Hebrides*, 1881

Sir Lachlan, for whom King James interceded, and for whose good behaviour the Earl of Argyll gave hostages, was no sooner released than he ravaged Islay, Angus Mor being at the time on a visit to the Antrim family in the North of Ireland. MacDonald retaliated, and they were both called before the King in Edinburgh in 1591, when they paid a fine to the Crown, and promised to become good subjects.

William MacDonald, *Sketches of Islay*, 1850

The Battle of Traigh Ghruineart

The turf war between the MacLeans of Duart and the MacDonalds of Islay reached a climax in a battle so bloody, infamous and prominent in the history and folklore of Islay, that it deserves a chapter to itself.

> Reached the head of Loch Druinard, a place celebrated for the battle of Traii-dhruinard, in 1598, between the Lord of the Isles, and Sir Lauchlan Maclean, of Mull; the last, with fifteen hundred men, invaded Ilay, with a view of usurping it from his nephew: the first had only eleven hundred, and was at first obliged to retreat till he was joined by a hundred and twenty fresh forces: this decided the engagement. Sir Lauchlan was slain, with four score of his principal kinsmen, and two hundred of his soldiers, who lay surrounding the body of their chieftain. A stone still on the spot, was erected in memory of his fall.
>
> Sir Lauchlan consulted a witch, the Oracle of Mull, before he set out on his expedition; and received three pieces of advice: first, not to land on a Thursday: a storm forced him into disobedience. The second, not to drink of a certain spring: which he did through ignorance. The third, not to fight beside Loch Druinnaird: but this the fates may be supposed to have determined.
>
> Thomas Pennant, *A Tour in Scotland and Voyage to the Hebrides,* 1772

Sir Lachlan Mor Maclean of Duart claimed ownership of Islay. On 5 August 1598, at Traigh Ghruineart on the western shore of Loch Ghruineart, he landed with nearly 1,000 men to take it by force. Although not the power they once were, the MacDonalds refused to relinquish their traditional fiefdom. But their chief, Sir James MacDonald of Dunnyveg, who was Sir Lachlan Mor's nephew, was prepared to do a deal – offering his maternal uncle large areas of Islay. The MacDonalds were well trained, but outnumbered, and had sent for reinforcements from their allies in Kintyre.

Their mutual friends now endeavoured to effect a reconciliation by arbitration; and it is said that Sir James of Islay offered to resign the half of the Island in perpetuity to his uncle. As nothing but full possession of the whole would satisfy Sir Lachlan, the dispute was left to the decision of a bloody battle, which raged for several hours on Traigh Ghruinard, with alternating prospects of success; when, as the Macdonalds were seemingly being beaten, they derived encouragement from the arrival of their friends the Cantyre men, more especially as, at the same momentous juncture, Sir Lachlan fell by a well directed arrow of an insignificant looking creature called "Du-sith," who, in the early part of the day offered his services to Maclean, and on being spurned by the courtly knight, went immediately to Macdonald who received him with grateful feelings.

Many of the Macleans, now without a leader, were slain as they fled to Kilnave Church, where, on account of the reputed sanctity of the place, they expected to find refuge.

William MacDonald, *Sketches of Islay*, 1850

After the battle the McDonalds perpetrated a most dastardly deed. When the McLeans were defeated, those who survived fled, making for the place where their ships were anchored, but the sailors had made off with them when they realised that the McLeans were losing the fight.

Peggy Earl, *Tales of Islay*, 1980

The MacLeans took refuge in Kilnave Church where they should have been safe, but the MacDonalds locked them in and set fire to the church.

They met with no mercy however, for the edifice was set on fire around them; and thus perished the whole muster of Macleans, excepting the body of reserve who took to their galleys and escaped to Duart, and one brave fellow named Mac Mhuirich who effected his escape through the roof of the church. He was pursued by the Macdonalds, but he eluded their grasp by swimming to a small Island, called Ellein-na Badaig, where he concealed himself until the fury of his foes was abated. This individual settled in Islay. His descendants are still in the neighbourhood of Gruinard, and are called Clamnhuirich-na-Badaig. The corpse of Sir Lachlan was picked out from among the slain and conveyed, on a car, to Kilchoman Church-yard, by a female of the Macleans. It is said that her son, a youth about eighteen, accompanied her to drive the horse, who, on observing the head of Sir Lachlan waggling with the jolting of the car, smiled. This levity incensed her already wounded feelings to such a degree that she attempted to stab her own son, – an extraordinary proof of her attachment to her chief. As report goes, Sir Lachlan was warned not to land in Islay on a Thursday. And not to drink out of Tober Neil Neonaich (literally Whimsical Neil's Well) near Gruinard. These injunctions, as well as the very *oracular* information that a Maclean would fall at Gruinard, he disregarded, and went boldly to the field which proved so fatal to himself and his men. Sir James Macdonald and 60 of his men were severely wounded, besides 30 who were slain.

William MacDonald, *Sketches of Islay*, 1850

Another account of the burial of Sir Lachlan has a bloodier ending than William MacDonald's. In it, the woman driving the body of her chief in a cart to his last resting place at Kilchoman is known as the Highland Nurse. Her son laughs at the sight of Sir Lachlan's head bouncing up and down on the cart.

He laughed but once. Such disrespect for the mighty slain, her beloved chief, flamed the fury of the faithful Highland Nurse. Leaning forward, she grasped the chieftain's dirk and plunged it in the heart of her own child.

L. MacNeill Weir, *Guide to Islay*, 1911

There are several versions of this story. One is that the nurse with whom McLean was fostered lived in the Rhinns of Islay. She heard that Lachlan Mor McLean, her foster son, had been killed at the Battle of Traigh Ghruinard and she felt she had to find him and bury him. She had a son called Duncan, and she made him get the horse and put on its harness. With a sledge they then set off for the battleground and found McLean's body. With difficulty they managed to get McLean onto the sledge. Duncan sat with the body to keep if from falling off, while his mother led the horse.

The road was rough and uneven and as the sledge was shaken McLean's head wagged which made Duncan laugh. This angered the foster-mother so much that she stabbed her son to death.

As their route was by way of Carnduncan, she buried him there and the huge cairn which was raised over him is still to be seen today. This is how Carnduncan got its name.

Peggy Earl, *Tales of Islay*, 1980

The battle has fired the imaginations of generations of Ileachs, not least the poet Thomas Pattison. He was born in 1828, the son of a tenant of Skerrols Farm, and educated at the Parish School of Bowmore, before studying at Edinburgh and Glasgow Universities. Pattison became a minister, but enjoyed a reputation as a poet, and as a translator of poetry from Gaelic. He died in 1865, and his book *The Gaelic Bards* appeared posthumously.

> Never shall his clan behind him
> Gather in the joy of fight;
> Never draw their cold blue weapons –
> Hard and deadly – glancing bright.
>
> Poorly now the chief's attended,
> Rudely now the hero's led;
> Yet he wakes not from his slumber
> Of yon red and mossy bed.
>
> For the sad stamp's on his features
> Which Dubh Shee's hard arrow bore;
> On the moor Clan Gillian redden'd
> With their brave and boiling gore.
>
> Only two are with the driver
> Of a rolling, rocking car,
> Stretch'd whereon the dead man's carried
> From the fiery field of war.
>
> Two that walk in silent sorrow –
> Ladies of his kindred are –
> Mourning, to the field of slaughter
> Come to seek him from afar.
>
> As they drive him slowly onward,
> O'er the bad and broken way,
> His head, with all its matted tresses,
> Nodded where he lifeless lay.
>
> Then the driver laugh'd who saw him,
> Large and massy, lie along,

Senseless, soulless – him so lately
    Foremost in the martial throng.

Laugh'd! and quicker drove him onward,
    Yet again to see the head
Nodding, without will or reason,
With its light of manhood fled.

Nodding at the boor who jeered him
    With that mean, malicious scorn,
Nursed in secret by the envy
    In the vulgar spirit born.

Then the ladies hastened forward –
    Not a word the younger said,
While her tears rained down in anguish
    On the wan face of the dead.

But the elder damsel answered: –
"Laugh'st thou at my fallen Chief?
May thine own vile carcass, caitiff,
    Fill thy mother's heart with grief!"

Out she drew the chieftain's dagger,
    As she hurled this angry cry
At the boor who gloomed before her,
    With his dull and threatening eye.

And she struck him down, and left him
    Stretched beneath the sunbeams there,
Like a wild fowl by the falcon
    Swept from out the fields of air.

Then, alone, their dead they carried,
    While one nursed the manly brow –
Nursed, on her bosom gently,
    Like a holy heavenly vow.

Thomas Pattison, *Sir Lachlan Mor*, 1890

L. MacNeill Weir tells us more about the *Du Sith* (in English, the *Black Fairy*). He is certainly an archer, and possibly a fairy. Flint arrowheads – Elf bolts – were once thought to be the weapons of fairies, rather than those of our Neolithic ancestors.

> Before the engagement Sir Lauchlan was drinking at the fateful spring, the Well of Queer Neil, when there came to him a little dark man who was offering his services in the fight. Now MacLean was a man of gigantic strength and the body of a Hercules. He looked down contemptuously on the little man and told him he didn't mind what side he fought on. The inordinate conceit, characteristic of the diminutive, was hurt by Sir Lauchlan's contempt, and the dwarf then made the same offer to Sir James MacDonald.
>
> "Will I accept your help?" said Sir James, "why I'd be glad of a hundred like you."
>
> "Well," said the little fellow, "you see to the others, I'll settle MacLean." MacLean, clad in steel from head to foot fought, as always, at the head of his men. The fight was fierce and long. All day long, while the tide of battle ebbed and flowed, the little fellow kept following MacLean, biding his time. At last he planted himself in a milk-white thorn and from it saw Sir Lauchlan raise his visor. Instantly an arrow stuck him in the forehead at the division of the hair and came out the back of his head. It was said to be one of these arrows known as Elf-bolts.
>
> Now when Sir James learned that his uncle was dead he was sorry, and inquired who had killed hm.
>
> "It was I," said the little man, "who killed your enemy, and unless I had killed him he would have killed you."
>
> "What is your name?" said Sir James.
>
> "I am called *Du Sith* [Black Fairy], and you were better to have me with you than against you."
>
> L. MacNeill Weir, *Guide to Islay*, 1911

A folklorist recorded a story of the 'second sight' relating to the grave of Sir Lachlan. In it, a *taïsher* or *taibhsear* – a person with the second sight – arrived at his home near the burial ground at Crossapol on the island of Coll.

> He arrived at home to find his only child, a boy about twelve years of age, dead in the burying-ground, where he had gone to play and fallen asleep. Its entrails (*màthair a mhionaich*) were protruding. The

seer, in his distraction, belaboured the surrounding graves with his stick, accusing their tenants, in his outcries, of indifference to him and his, and saying he had many of his kindred among them, though they had allowed this evil to befall his child. That night a voice came to him in his sleep, saying, he should not be angry with them (shades of the dead), seeing they were away that day in Islay keeping "strange blood" from the grave of Lachlan Mor (*cumail na fui choimhich a uaugh Lachuinn Mhòir*), and were not present to have rescued the child. This Lachlan Mor was a man of great stature and bodily strength, chief of the Macleans of Dowart, and therefore related to the Macleans of Coll, who had been killed at the bloody clan battle of Gruinard Beach, in Islay, and was buried at Kilchoman Churchyard. On hearing of the seer's vision the Laird of Coll dispatched a boat to Islay, and it was found that on the day the child was murdered an attempt had been made to lift the chief's gravestone for the burial of a sailor, whose body had been cast ashore on a neighbouring beach. The attempt had failed, and the stone was left partly on is edge (*air a leth-bhile*). The shades had laid their weight up it, so it could not be moved further.

This story the writer has heard more than once adduced as positive proof of the reality of the second sight (*tabhsearachd*), that is, of the capacity of some men to see and hear spirits, or whatever else the spectres are.

John Gregorson Campbell, *Witchcraft and Second Sight in the Highlands and Islands of Scotland*, 1902

Elsewhere in *Witchcraft and Second Sight*, Campbell warns of the danger of disturbing the dead.

It was part of the lesson impressed on the young Highlander, to treat that which belonged to the dead with reverence. The unnecessary or contemptuous disturbing of graves, bones, or other relics of humanity was reprobated, and sometimes warmly resented. This praiseworthy feeling towards the dead was strengthened by the pride of race and ancestry, which formed so prominent a feature of the Highland character, and by sundry tales of wide circulation . . .

The battle of Traigh Ghruineart was a rich subject for the nineteenth-century Islay bard, William Livingston, who composed an epic poem about it. Here is the lament for Lachlan Maclean from Livingston's poem.

Fhir mhòir an do leagadh thu,
Gu h-iosal,
Gun anail 's tu diblidh,
Fo' n fhòid, fo' n fhòid,
A' d' shìneadh,
Sgal pìob, sgal pìob,
Nach eisd thu, nach éisd thu,
Ni's mò, nis mò,
'Nuair a thogar fir Alba,
Gu feara ghniomh, gu fera ghniomh,
'S gun thusa le d' Rìgh, le d' Rìgh,
'S gun thusa le d' Rìgh,
'S gun thu beò, 's gun thu beò,
Bithidh na Leathanaich threun,
'S ceann catha, nan Ileach,
Fo bhròn, fo bhròn,
O nach tig thu, mar b' àbhaist,
Gu àros, Rìgh Seumas, Rìgh Seumas,
'S gun do thogadh leis fein thu,
'S tu òg, 's to òg,
Cha'n fhacas a' d' Iatha, air talamh
Na h-Eòrpa, na h-Eòrpa,
Air talamh, na h-Eòrpa,
Fear eile do shamhuil, do shamhuil
Fhir àillidh, fhir àillidh,
Cha d 'fhàgadh a' d' dhéigh dhuinn,
A' d' dhéigh dhuinn, a' d' dhéigh dhuinn,
O na rinneadh do d' chreubh,
Caisil-chrò, Caisil-chrò
O na rinneadh do d' chreubh,
Caisil-chrò,
Fhuaradh do chlaidheamh a d' ghlaic,
Le greim bàsmhor, greim bàsmhor,
'S cha'n'eil fear ann
'S an àl so, 's an àl so,
Na 's urrainn a làmdadh,
Fo'n t-sròl, fo'n sròl,
Togar do chumha Ie Muile,
'S Ie Ìle, 's Ìle,
Le urram a dh'innsear,

ISLAY VOICES

Do chòir, do chòir,
Le urram a dh'innsear,
Do choir.

William Livingston, *Blàr Traigh Ghruineart, Cumha Mhic
Ill'eathain*, 1882

Great man, are you fallen
Laid low,
Without breath, and you wretched,
Beneath the turf, beneath the turf,
Lying stretched,
Skirl of the pipes, skirl of the pipes,
Will you not listen, will you not listen,
Any more, any more,
When the men of Scotland are raised
To the manly action, to the manly action,
And you not with your King, your King,
And you not with your King,
And you not living, and you not living,
The valiant Macleans,
And the leaders of the battle, the Ileach,
Will be sorrowful, sorrowful,
Since you will not come, as you did,
To the palace of King James, King James,
And you were raised by himself
And you young, and you young,
There was not seen in your day
In Europe, in Europe
In Europe,
Another of your ilk, of your ilk,
O elegant man, O elegant man,
There was not left behind for us,
Not behind for us, not behind for us,
Since there was made for your body,
A bier, a bier,
Since there was made for your body,
A bier,
Your sword was found in your grasp
With a deadly grip, a deadly grip,
And there is no man,

In this generation, this generation,
That can handle it,
Under the ensign, under the ensign,
Your lament will be raised by Mull
And by Islay, by Islay
And with honour will tell
Of your claim, of your claim,
And with honour will tell
Of your claim.

William Livingston, *The Battle of Traigh Ghruineart, Lament for MacLean*, 1882

MacDonald No More

Sorley Boy MacDonald – Somhairle Buidhe Mac Domhnaill (*Somhairle of the yellow hair, son of Donnell*) was the warlike and energetic son of Alexander MacDonnell, Lord of Islay and Kintyre. Under Sorley Boy, Clan Donald firmly established itself in Antrim, the north-easterly county of Northern Ireland. Antrim can be seen from Islay on clear days.

This Antrim sept of Clan Donald was a constant thorn in the royal flesh of Scotland. In 1608, James – now King of England as well as of the Scots – sent an Anglo-Scottish military expedition to subdue the troublesome Celts in the west. On Islay, Angus MacDonald of Dunyvaig surrendered his castle, and the following year the Highland chiefs were forced to sign the Statutes of Iona – an Act designed to clip their military, political and cultural wings. From now on, Gaelic Scotland would increasingly be expected to dance to Lowland and London tunes.

> . . . the king, irritated by the disturbances raised by private wars, waged between these and other clans, resumed the grant made by his predecessor, and transferred it to Sir John Campbell, of Calder, who held it on paying an annual feu duty of five hundred pounds sterling, which is paid to this day. The island was granted to Sir John, as a reward for us undertaking the conquest; but the family considered it a dear acquisition, by the loss of many gallant followers, and by the expense incurred in support of it.
>
> Thomas Pennant, *A Tour in Scotland and Voyage to the Hebrides*, 1772

James, the son of Angus MacDonald of Islay, was languishing in Edinburgh Castle under sentence of death. At last, his old father signed away the Mac-Donald claim to Islay.

> It was in 1612 that the King and his Council compelled Angus MacDonald of Islay, father of gallant Sir James MacDonald, the last McDonald of Islay, to write at Edinburgh a Renunciation of Islay.

Renunciation of the Lands of Islay, Angus MacDonald,
1st January 1612

Be it kend till all men me Angus Mcdonald, forsamekle as I have instantlie receavit fra the richt honorabill Sir Johne Campbell of Calder the soume of sex thousand markis, thairfoir witt ye me to have renuncit, discharget, and overgevin, fra me and my airis, to and in fauoris of the said Sir Johne Campbell all richt, tytil, propertie, and possessioun quhilkis I ather haid, hes, or ony wayes may have had in and to the landis of Ilay possessit be me and my subtenentis . . .

J.G. MacNeill, *Islay*, 1899

As the tide of MacDonald power ebbed, the influence of Clan Campbell flowed through the west.

Hereupon the inheritance of the Macdonalds of Islay and Cantyre was gifted to the Earl of Argyle and the Campbells. Violent struggles ensued between these parties, especially in 1614, 1615 and 1616, when the Macdonalds were finally overpowered, and Sir James obliged to take refuge in Spain; but he was afterwards received into favour. The power of the Macdonalds in Islay having thus passed into the hands of the Campbells, has never since been recovered, and their sway in Argyleshire has wholly disappeared.

George Anderson and Peter Anderson, *Guide to the Highlands and Western Islands of Scotland*, 1863

The political vacuum left by the end of MacDonald power was filled by the Campbells of Calder, or Cawdor, a north east of Scotland clan, related to the Campbells of Argyll. But MacDonalds – hostile to the Campbells, and with their own allegiances – remained on Islay in large numbers.

Events in the civil wars of the mid-seventeenth century were to lead to an escalation of hatred between the two clans and opportunities to demonstrate their anger in action, not just on the field of battle but in atrocities, and the cold-blooded murder of prisoners.

David Caldwell, *Islay: The Land of the Lordship*, 2008

Dr Caldwell tells of one alleged atrocity.

. . . a wicked woman of the family of Dunstaffnage (Janet, wife of George Campbell), who was then in command of Islay, made a practice of seizing followers of the MacDonalds in the night, binding them hand and foot, and transporting them to deserted rocks and islands where they were left to die. Donald Campbell of Ellister, who kept a birlinn for trading to Ireland and the North Isles, was able to rescue them and land them on Rathlin or the coast of Ireland . . .

. . . The story of the wicked Janet taking matters into her own hands has probably been exaggerated in the telling, but the main point is that supporters of the MacDonalds were being forcibly evicted, and that can hardly be doubted.

In the wars between Crown and Covenant, Islay MacDonalds supported the Crown. But they had an agenda – hatred of the Campbells, who supported the Covenanters.

In the year 1642, no fewer than 500 young men of the Clan-donald left Islay under Sir Alexander Macdonald, known as Alastair Mac Cholla, to join Montrose. This was a severe blow to that Clan in Islay, for not one of these 500 ever returned alive.

When Montrose's men were beaten in Cantyre in 1647, and subsequently massacred to the number of 300 by Argyll and Leslie at Dunaverty Castle, Sir Alexander Macdonald retired to Islay with 300 men, and thence to Ireland, leaving his father Colla Ciotach in charge of the Islaymen under arms at Dunnaomhaig. Argyll and Leslie prevailed here also. They took the fort, transported the soldiers to France under the charge of Campbell of Calder, hanged the veteran Colla Ciotach (to whom the inimitable Pibroch of "Cella nan Gael" was played extempore, to warn him from the Fort). Sir Alexander, his son, was afterwards betrayed by a countryman for the Government reward, and was cruelly murdered at Dungannon in Ireland.

William MacDonald, *Sketches of Islay*, 1850

It would be impossible, except in the compass of many volumes, to give even a small part of the tragic history of this famous stronghold, bound up as it immediately is in the story of Islay and the Isles. In the final chapter of the long Iliad of its misfortunes, the unscrupulous malevolence of the Bishop of the Isles and the shameful treachery of the Duke of Argyll were matched only by the sordid avarice of Campbell of Calder, who took the castle finally.

The most picturesque figure in the story is Coll Mac Gillespick. He is famous in Highland tradition as Coll Ciotach, Coll the Left Handed, the hero of many a tale.

On 1st February, 1615, Dunyvaig was bombarded by a large force under Sir Oliver Lambert. Next day after an attempt at compromise, the fort was surrendered. That night Coll Ciotach and his men made their escape by boat. The boat, however, proved leaky and they were obliged to land. Six of them were captured and executed, but the elusive Coll escaped. Eight of the principal chiefs of the west were give commissions of fire and sword against him, but he led them, hide and seek, round the Western Isles. A man-of-war sent after him had no better success.

Tradition has it that on one occasion when, like a hare returning to his home, Coll was approaching Dunyvaig and, as it happened, coming straight into the jaws of a trap, his brother, a famous piper, warned him of the ambuscade. He stood up on a mound on the seaward side of Dunyvaig and played the well-known air, "A Cholla, mu rùin." An enemy slashed the piper across the hand, severing the little finger. Now it is a fact in pipe playing that five fingers of one hand are necessary and only four of the other, but it was the essential little finger that was severed. But the brother of Coll, so the story goes, stoically changed hands and played on undaunted. Coll understood the warning and escaped once more. He was, however, ultimately captured, tried by a jury of Campbells, and was hung from the mast of his own galley placed over the cleft of a rick at the castle of Dunstaffnage. He made the last request, when on the scaffold, to be buried beside the Duke of Argyll that they might have a snuff together.

L. MacNeill Weir, *Guide to Islay*, 1911

Today, the besieged and battered Dunyveg still stands as an impressive ruin. But another MacDonald stronghold, on Loch Gorm, has almost vanished entirely.

In an island in this loch stood once a massive square castle, with a round tower at each corner. In the sixteenth century it was a stronghold dread enough to cause despair to anyone who, from the margin of the loch, counted its towers and marked its bulwarks. In 1614 Sir James MacDonald strengthened the fortifications of the island of Loch Gorm by covering them with a belt of earthworks of great thickness at which one hundred and twenty Islaymen laboured. But towards the end of 1615, the Earl of Argyll, Sir John Campbell of Calder, Sir

James MacDonald's brother-in-law, and Sir Oliver Lambert, Commander of the King's forces, empowered by the Privy Council to take possession of Islay, and having with them His Majesty's ships, the *Phoenix*, the *Moon*, and the *Bran*, a scow to carry the ordnance and a barque with provisions, landed with cannon and troops in Islay, and attacked and captured the castles of Dun Naomhaig (Dunyvaig) and Loch Gorm. In this unequal struggle brave and accomplished Sir James MacDonald was deprived of the ancient inheritance of his fathers.

L. MacNeill Weir, *Guide to Islay*, 1911

In this lake, there is a small island, fortified very strong. Its bastions are all entire. To this fort, it is said, M'Donald of Islay betook himself in his difficulties. Now the owls of the desert nestle in it.

Statistical Account, 1791–1799
Parish of Kilchoman, The Rev. Mr. John M'Liesh, Minister

After the forfeiture of the Lordship the vassals and cadets of the family rose five times to try to restore it, and the memories of its glories were a source of rightful pride to the clans descended from Donald. So as late as the eighteenth century, a bitterly Whig visitor to the Highlands wrote: 'The poorest and most despicable Creature of the name McDonald looks upon himself as a Gentleman of far Superior Quality than a man in England of £1,000 a year.'

The fall of the Lordship was followed by a century of anarchy in the Highlands, during which the houses of Argyll and of MacKenzie of Kintail rose into power. Argyll and his Campbell clansmen in particular, secured much of the land formerly held by the MacDonalds. But neither Argyll nor MacKenzie replaced the Lord of the Isles as great patrons of the arts of the Gael. By the seventeenth century the learned classes of Gaeldom were disappearing and Highlanders were getting their education at Lowland universities. The degradation of the old Gaelic civilisation to a folk culture was beginning. For instance, the old Gaelic physicians who had been learned in the best contemporary medical science were being superseded by Lowland doctors and only the use of charms and simples by country people lingered on.

I. F. Grant, *Highland Folk Ways*, 1961

The forfeiture of the MacDonald lordship was a political mistake for Scotland and a calamity for the Gaels living in the lordship because the MacDonald supremacy was not replaced by an equivalent or even greater royal supremacy sufficient to command the respect and obedience of the former MacDonald vassals whose spontaneous loyalty to their MacDonald lords over generations could only have been replaced in time by another loyalty won by royal dignity, magnanimity, patience and sagacity and those requisite qualities were hardly likely to be forthcoming in the circumstances of the times.

In spite of his personal visits to the lordship in 1493 and subsequent years the King was really an absentee ruler unlike the MacDonald lords who had moved freely throughout their territories and had kept in constant touch with the clansmen who gladly acknowledged them as unquestioned hereditary rulers. James was also at a further disadvantage in being really an alien to the Gaels both in blood because of his ancestry and also in language in spite of the flattering assertion that his linguistic attainments included a knowledge of Gaelic whereas the MacDonald lords were nearer in blood to their fellow-Gaels and certainly needed no interpreters when speaking to their clansmen and vassals!

Colin M. MacDonald, *The History of Argyll*, 1950

No longer does MacDonald rule on Islay, nor do those galleys, which with sails unfurled, are depicted on the old tombstones, steer proudly across the seas to Ireland, to Mull or to Skye. But the memory of this imperious family remains, and will remain for all the time in the isles of the west.

Seton Gordon, *Highways and Byways in the West Highlands*, 1936

Folk Belief

Much of the early 'history' of Islay – the distant memory of *Na Samhaiceanthe* or 'silent' hunter gatherers; the mysterious Fir Bolg; the invasion of the Gaelic-speaking Cenel Oengus; the miracles of Saint Columba; a drowned Norse Princess – at least partly belongs in the realms of tradition, folklore and superstition. It was this body of tradition that inspired the life work of one of the world's great folklorists

John Francis Campbell, the Victorian scholar and polymath, was a descendant of Campbell of Shawfield who had bought Islay in 1723. But, despite being a son of 'the big hoose', Iain Òg Ìle, Young John of Islay, revelled in the lives and culture of his father's Gaelic-speaking tenants and the common people of Islay and beyond. He became an authority on Celtic folklore and, among other works, published a massive, four-volume collection of Highland tales.

This story, which he heard from the Reverend Thomas Pattison on Islay, tells of MacEachern, an Islay blacksmith, and of his dealings with the fairies.

Years ago there lived in Crossbrig, a smith of the name MacEachern. This man had an only child, a boy of about thirteen or fourteen years of age, cheerful, strong, and healthy. All of a sudden he fell ill; took to his bed and moped whole days away. No one could tell what was the matter with him, and the boy himself could not, or would not, tell how he felt. He was wasting away fast; getting thin, old, and yellow; and his father and all his friends were afraid that he would die.

At last one day, after the boy had been lying in this condition for a long time, getting neither better nor worse, always confined to bed, but with an extraordinary appetite, – one day, while sadly revolving these things, and standing idly at his forge, with no heart to work, the smith was agreeably surprised to see an old man, well known to him for his sagacity and knowledge of out-of-the-way things, walk into his workshop. Forthwith he told him the occurrence that had clouded his life.

The old man looked grave as he listened; and after sitting a long time pondering over all he had heard, gave his opinion thus – "it is not your son you have got. The boy has been carried away by the 'Daoine Sith,' and they have left a *Sibhreach* in his place."

"Alas! And what then am I to do?" said the smith. "How am I ever to see my own son again?"

"I will tell you how," answered the old man. "But first, to make sure that it is not your own son you have go, take as many empty eggshells as you can get, go with them into the room, spread them out carefully before his sight, then proceed to draw water with them, carrying them two and two in your hands as if they were a great weight, and arrange when full, with every sort of earnestness round the fire." The smith accordingly gathered as many broken eggshells as he could get, went into the room, and proceeded to carry out all his instructions.

He had not been long at work before there arose from the bed a shout of laughter, and the voice of the seeming sick boy exclaimed, "I am now 800 years of age, and I have never seen the like of that before."

The smith returned and told the old man. "Well, now," said the sage to him, "did I not tell you that it was not your son you had: your son is in Beorra-cheill in a digh there (that is, a round green hill frequented by the fairies). Get rid as soon as possible of this intruder, and I think I may promise you your son."

"You must light a very large and bright fire before the bed on which this stranger is lying. He will ask you 'What is the use of such a fire as that?' Answer him at once, 'You will see that presently!' and then seize him, and throw him into the middle of it. If it is your own son you have got, he will call out to save him; but if not, this thing will fly through the roof."

The smith again followed the old man's advice; kindled a large fire, answered the question put to him as he had been directed to do, and seizing the child flung him in without hesitation. The "Sibhreach" gave an awful yell, and sprung through the roof, where a hole was left to let the smoke out.

On a certain night the old man told him the green round hill, where the fairies kept the boy, would be open. And on that night the smith, having provided himself with a bible, a dirk and a crowing cock, was to proceed to the hill. He would hear singing and danc-ing and much merriment going on, but he was to advance boldly; the bible he carried would be a certain safeguard to him against any danger from the fairies. On entering the hill he was to stick the dirk in the threshold, to prevent the hill from closing upon him; "and then," continued the old man. "on entering you will see a spacious apartment before you, beautifully clean, and there, standing far within, working at a forge, you will also see your own son. When you are questioned, say you come to seek him, and will not go without him."

Not long after this, the time came round, and the smith sallied forth, prepared as instructed. Sure enough as he approached the hill, there was a light where light was seldom seen before. Soon after a sound of piping, dancing, and joyous merriment reached the anxious father on the night wind.

Overcoming every impulse to fear, the smith approached the threshold steadily, stuck the dirk into the threshold as directed, and entered. Protected by the bible he carried on his breast, the fairies could not touch him; but they asked him, with a good deal of displeasure, what he wanted there. He answered, "I want my son, whom I see down there, and I will not go without him."

Upon hearing this, the whole company before him, gave a loud laugh, which wakened up the cock he carried dozing in his arms, who at once leapt up on his shoulders, clapped his wings lustily, and crowed loud and long.

The fairies, incensed, seized the smith and his son, and throwing them out of the hill, flung the dirk after them, "and in an instant a' was dark."

For year and a day the boy never did a turn of work, and hardly ever spoke a word; but at last one day, sitting by his father and watching him finish a sword he was making for some chief, and which he was very particular about, exclaimed, "That is not the way to do it;" and taking the tools from his father's hands he set to work himself in his place, and soon fashioned a sword, the like of which was never seen in the country before.

From that day the young man wrought constantly with his father, and became the inventor of a peculiarly fine and well-tempered weapon, the making of which kept the two smiths, father and son, in constant employment, spread their fame far and wide, and gave them the means in abundance, as they never before had, the disposition to live content with all the world and very happily with one another.

John Francis Campbell comments:

The walls of this house where this celebrated smith, the artificer of the "Claidheamh Ceann-Ileach," lived and wrought, are standing to this day, not far from the parish church of Kilchoman, Islay, in a place called Caonis gall.

Many of the incidents in this story are common in other collections; but I do not know any published story of this kind in which the hero is a smith. This smith was a famous character, and probably a real personage, to whom the story has attached itself.

The gentleman who has been kind enough to send me this tale, does not say from whom he got it, but I have heard of the Islay smith, who could make wonderful swords, all my life, and of the "Swords of the Head of Islay".

John Francis Campbell had a fascinating theory about the origin of fairy belief.

Men do believe in fairies, though they will not readily confess the fact. And though I do not believe myself that fairies *are*, in spite of the strong evidence offered, I believe there was once a race of small people in these islands, who are remembered as fairies . . . the fairy was probably a Pict.

John Francis Campbell, *Popular Tales of the West Highlands*, 1860–62

There was a man living in Connispie at one time, and his wife having given birth to a child, and there being no whisky in the house, he left his wife in bed, and went away to Blackrock for whisky. On his home journey with the whisky, just when he was passing the mouth of Gortan glen, he happened to lift the wing of the plaid he had about him, and threw it over his shoulder, wishing just to sort it on him, as it had been falling down by his side, when who should drop down beside him but his wife. She had been taken away by the fairies, and had just been passing down the glen, through the air, at the moment when he happened to throw his plaid over his shoulder, and the smell of the plaid brought her down. She returned home along with her husband, and when they reached it, they found, what to all appearance was another woman in the bed. They asked the women who had been left in charge when the man had gone for the whisky, but they all declared they had seen nothing, and were of opinion that it was the woman that was in the bed all the time, and they had not disturbed her, thinking she had fallen asleep. The man went to the bed, and took whatever it was, and put it on the fire, and what did it turn out to be but a block of wood, which the fairies had put there in place of the man's wife, when they took her away with them.

School of Scottish Studies Archives, University of Edinburgh, from John Gillespie, Port Charlotte, Islay, published in *Tocher* *14*, 1974

Fortunately, there is a magical substance that can be used to overcome the spitefulness of fairies. Iron is to fairies what garlic is to vampires.

Who were these powers of evil who cannot resist iron? Those fairies who shoot stone arrows, and are the foes of the human race? Is all this but a dim, hazy recollection of war between a people who had iron weapons and a race who had not, the race whose remains are found all over Europe?

John Francis Campbell, *Popular Tales of the West Highlands*, 1860–62

Whoever, or whatever, fairies were, there were charms, rituals and substances to use against them.

I heard about a man who was one time at a marriage at Port Askaig, and when the company broke up, this man along with others were on their way home, early in the morning. He halted a minute after the others, to make his water, just under a hill that is there in which fairies dwelt. Just when he was going to make his water a company of fairies gathered about him. What he did was – he took an end of his plaid, and having made his water in a fold of it, he threw the water among the fairies. As soon as this was done, the fairies made off, crying after them that it was good for him that he had the learning to know what would put them away, for had it not been for what he had done, he would have been taken away with them.

The reciter, who professes to attach credibility to the story, adds that there is nothing in the world better than urine for protecting one, old or young, from fairies.

School of Scottish Studies Archives, University of Edinburgh, Mrs D. Brown, Port Charlotte, Islay, published in *Tocher 22*, 1976

But it seems that if you treated fairies with respect and generosity, they would repay you well. This tale was originally recorded in Gaelic.

One night the fairies visited a man there . . . at Finary . . . and the fairies came upon him one night – to his door – and the fairy, one of the fairies said to him:

"My meegle, moogle, maagle sent me
To ask you for the dubhràmhach"

. . . the riddle for riddling the meal – it was his mother who had sent him for it. And she (the housewife) gave them the riddle and they went away taking the riddle with them. But they left plenty for it – they paid well for it.

And they used to come for the dubhràmhach, as the fairies called it, whenever they needed it. And everything prospered for this man and woman. They would give the fairies everything they possessed. The fairy would only ask for things he knew they had. They used to work with barley at that time, the fairies: they used to know how to grow barley.

School of Scottish Studies Archives, University of Edinburgh, Recorded from Donald Ferguson, Port Wemyss, Islay by D.A. MacDonald and Alan Bruford, published in *Tocher* 28, 1978

Martin Martin, a native of Skye, would have been familiar with some of the lore and rituals he encountered on Islay, although he disapproved of such paganism.

Some of the poorer sort of People in these Islands retain the Custom of performing these Rounds Sunways, about the Persons of their Benefactors three times, when they bless them, and with good success to all their Enterprizes. Some are very careful, when they set out to Sea, that the Boat be first row'd about Sun-ways; and if this be neglected, they are afraid that their Voyage may prove unfortunate. I had this Ceremony paid me (when in the Island of *Ila*) by a poor Woman, after I had given her an Alms: I desired her to let alone that Compliment, for I did not care for it; but she insisted to make these three ordinary Turns, and then pray'd that God and *Mac-Charmig*, the Patron Saint of that Island, might bless and prosper me in all my Designs and Affairs.

Martin Martin, *A Description of the Western Islands of Scotland*, 2nd edition, 1716

ISLAY VOICES

Although Islay has lore of Saint Columba, ancient ecclesiastical buildings and a long tradition of Christianity, it clung to elements of paganism right up till modern times. Ulsterman Billy Frazer became an assistant lighthouse keeper at Rhuvaal just after World War Two. Billy, who had skippered an RAF rescue launch during the war and was a competent seaman, found some of Islay's seafaring practices baffling – until he learned the lore of the 'sunways', or clockwise, ritual.

> When the boatmen first brought us up, it's just a wee jetty and when he came alongside, and there was rocks ahead and he kept walking back and forward and back and forward to get this boat clear into the mid-stream again. And I said to the principal keeper, 'That man hasn't a clue what he's doing', and he says 'For goodness sake, he's been a boatman all his life'. 'Well,' I said 'All he has to do is come a-stern and turn the boat and he's away'. He says 'You haven't been in this part of the world long have you?' 'Well,' I says, 'I haven't'. He says 'They'll never turn a boat against the sun'. That was just the things that happened in these places. You learnt, but I tell you it sunk in, there was no more nonsense. So after that I kept my mouth shut you know and I didn't try to be too clever, because the islanders knew what they were doing. I liked Islay, it was a big island of course.'

> Interview for TV documentary 'The Lighthouse Stevensons',
> Billy Frazer, 2011

Ancient sun worship preconditioned Celts to carry out rituals *deiseil*, or in a sunwise direction. The opposite course – *Tuaithuil*, or widdershins – was held to be unlucky. The pagan habit was even held to in rituals involving clearly Christian monuments.

> In Islay there is a subtle link between the orthodox medieval medicine and the vestiges of a folk belief that, as likely or not, long preceded as well as outlived the clan physicians. The finely carved Kilchoman cross, of a style that has been dated to the second half of the fourteenth century and standing over eight feet tall, has at its base man-made hollows or cups, one of which has a stone which has to be turned sunwise while making a wish, rather in the manner of working a mortar and pestle. The incomplete Latin inscription on the stone translates: 'This is the cross by Thomas, son of Patrick, doctor, for the souls of his father, mother, wife and of all the faithful departed, and of said . . .'

> Mary Beith, *Healing Threads*, 1995

But a stone need not be finely carved and with a Latin inscription to have healing powers.

> The toothache stone is a large meta–gabbro boulder, not unlike a human molar in shape, in a small valley below the pump house at the back of Port Charlotte. Into cracks in the stone have been hammered numerous nails, both iron and copper, either as a form of sympathetic magic, or so that an attempt could be made to pull them out with the affected teeth.
>
> Website, Royal Commission on the Ancient and Historical Monuments of Scotland, 2015

> Toothache, as anyone who suffers from it will agree, is 'the hell of all diseases', and the only cure is to have the offending molar extracted, but the people of Port Charlotte had a better idea. When they felt the first pangs they made for the Toothache Stone in the glen. Armed with nails and a hammer they hammered the nails into the stone and at the end of their exertions their toothache had gone!
>
> Peggy Earl, *Tales of Islay*, 1980

Prominent stones have the habit on Islay of attracting traditions, as they do moss.

> . . . at Lower Cragabus, there is a monolith and a few burial cists formed of large stones. At the foot of this Pillar-stone there is a heap of small stones. Its local name is *Càrn Chonnachain*, Connachan's Field. Mr. Hector Maclean says: Connachan was the strongest of the Fenians. The others were envious of him, and learned from his mother that nothing would weaken him but women and strong drink. They brought a lot of handsome women from Ireland, and had dances every night. He was plied with strong drink, and in a month's time he became so weak that he was easily mastered and killed, and they buried him in the cairn.
>
> J. G. MacNeill, *Islay*, 1899

Supernatural or miraculous powers were often attributed to Islay's springs and wells.

> A mile on the South-West of the Isle is the celebrated Well, call'd *Tonbir in Knahar*, which in the ancient Language is as much as to say,

the Well that sallied from one place to another: For it is a receiv'd Tradition among the vulgar Inhabitants of this Isle, and the opposite Isle of *Collonsay*, that this Well was first in *Collonsay*, until an imprudent Woman happen'd to wash her Hands in it, and that immediately after, the Well being thus abus'd, came in an instant to *Ila*, where it is like to continue, and has ever since been esteemed a *Catholicon* for diseases by the Natives and adjacent Islanders; and the great resort to it is commonly ever Quarter day.

The quarter days that this Catholicon – or universal remedy – was most effective on were important civic events that happened around religious festivals close to the two solstices and two equinoxes. On these days rents were due, farm servants were hired and school terms started.

It is common with sick People to make a Vow to come to the Well, and after drinking, they make a Tour Sunways round it, and then leave an Offering of some small Token, such as a Pin, Needle, Farthing, or the like, on the Stone Cover which is above the Well. But if the Patient is not like to recover, they send a Proxy to the Well, who acts as above-mention'd, and carries home some of this water to be drank by the sick person.

There is a little Chappel beside the Well, to which such as had found the Benefit of the Water, came back and return'd thanks to God for their Recovery.

Martin Martin, *A Description of the Western Islands of Scotland*, 2nd edition 1716

All over Scotland there are caves where pipers are said to have disappeared, and where their ghostly music can still be distantly heard. Islay is no exception.

A way up in the north of the island is the largest cave in Islay, The Great Cave of Bolsa, and indeed one of the biggest in Scotland.

About this mysterious cavern tradition has many a tale to tell. Its immense size, its many recesses, the strange sounds which re-echo from its depths, all combine to verify the tragic stories. To explore the cave, it was said, a stream of blood had to be crossed, and once that water had been crossed there was no hope of return for the foolhardy adventurer. This stream was called *Totan dearg*, and it was more awful than the Lethe of the Greeks. A tiny rivulet trickling over the ochreous earth is the basis for this legend.

Once upon a time a piper ventured to fathom the mysteries of this uncanny place. His only weapon was his bagpipes, and accompanied by his dog he set out. He never returned. He played his own coronach, "Cha till me tuille." – "I shall never return." Some time afterwards his dog came out at a well near Druisker, about seven miles from the cave and, horrible to relate, he was hairless – singed in a subterranean fire. And even yet among the wild solitudes which surround Bolsa Cave, the plaintive lament of the hapless piper comes down the wind, but woe, woe to him that hears it. Those skilled in the language of the pipes say that he is lamenting the fact that he has not three hands – two to play and one to fight the fiends that encompass him.

L. MacNeill Weir, *Guide to Islay*, 1911

John Gregorson Campbell was a passionate collector of folklore, active in the late 1800s. Despite being the Free Church Minister on Coll and Tiree, he enthusiastically teased out pagan tales and superstitions from his parishioners and other Gaels. A fluent Gaelic speaker, he painstakingly translated and transcribed them. Here he writes about 'Highland hobgoblins and suchlike objects of terror'.

CLACHLAIDH NA FEUSAIG, ISLAY

At the bottom of a dell, or hollow, through which the public road lies, in the island of Islay, there was a gate across the road, bearing the above name, which means "The Beard Gateway." At this place things unearthly were encountered after dark. One night a man saw an indistinct object coming towards him. He could give no account of it, but that its mouth was wide open, as if to devour him, and that from the width of its gape he could see its lungs (*sgamhan*) down its throat. He was accompanied, fortunately, by a large Newfoundland dog, which rushed between his legs at the "thing," and a terrific fight ensued. He ran away home, leaving them at it. In the morning the dog came without any hair on its body, and shortly after its return expired.

About the middle of February, a party was coming home from the market held on the Level Bridge (*Imire Comhnard*) at Ballygrant (Ugly Town). Before parting they entered a roadside inn. One of them, Ewan M'Corkindale, had, after leaving, to pass through the Beard gateway and the haunted dell. His companions made fun of him, and asked him if he was not afraid of the *Bodach*, the carle, or old man, who haunted the dell. Out of fool-hardiness Ewan proposed "the health of the *bodach*, the old man, and let the *cailleach*, the old wife, go to the dogs." When he reached the haunted spot two apparitions, an old man and an old woman, met him. The old woman endeavoured to attack him, but the old man kept her off, and ever after, at every opportunity, the same scene was rehearsed, the old wife attacked him and the old man defended him. The latter also told him to go to a smithy in Ireland, others say to two brothers in Cantyre, and get a dirk made, and as long as he kept this on his person, the old woman would not venture to attack him. The dirk bent three times in the making, and from its possession Ewan acquired the title of "Ewan of the dirk" (*Eoghan na biodaig*). As he was working one evening by moonlight in the harvest field, he left the dirk on a stook of corn, along with his vest. The carlin wife got between him and the dirk, and gave him such a squeeze that he put out three mouthfuls of blood. The *bodach* came, but too late, to his rescue. It however, told him, that if he survived till cock-crowing, five years would be added to his life. Ewan woke up now and then to ask if the cock crew yet, but when it did it was too late. Very likely the poor man died of some rupture or heart disease. The dirk was preserved by his son.

Iron – Ewan's dirk – was widely believed to ward off fairies, and the tradition of the 'lucky horseshoe' still persists. Rowan trees were seen as effective against witches, and many old ruined cottages in the highlands and islands still have rowan trees standing sentinel beside them. Such counter-charms were made to protect both people and livestock. John Gregorson Campbell writes:

The mountain ash (*Caorrunn*) was the most powerful charm of any.

> "A Rowan tree and a red thread
> Gars a' the witches dance to dead."

Its efficacy was known in England as well is in the Highlands. The peg of the cow-shackle (*Cnag chaorruinnsa bhuaraich*) should be made of it, as well as the handle and cross (*crois na loinid*) of the churn staff. In Islay, not twenty years ago, a man had a rowan-tree collar for securing his cow at night, and every time the animal visited the bull he passed this collar thrice through the chimney crook. On Beltane-day annually he dressed all the house with rowan.

Campbell shares the useful lore of how to detect a witch.

Early in the morning, on the first Monday of each of the four quarters of the year, the smoke from a witch's house *goes against the wind*. This may be seen by any one who takes the trouble of rising early and going to an eminence, whence the witch's house can be seen.

Campbell also tells of charms – to be recited only on Thursdays or Sundays – that were effective against the Evil Eye.

A woman in Islay worked wonderful cures with the following. It is a wretched specimen of superstition, but it is given to show how ancient creeds accommodate themselves to modern modes of thought. The ancient charm, instead of being entirely abandoned, became a sort of prayer:

> "If eye has blighted,
> Three have blessed,
> Stronger are the Three that blessed,
> Than the eye that blighted;
> The Father, Son and Holy Ghost;
> If aught elfin or worldly has harmed it,
> On earth above,
> Or in hell beneath,
> Do Thou, God of Grace, turn it aside."
> Thus was to be said thrice.

John Gregorson Campbell, *Witchcraft and Second Sight in the Highlands and Islands of Scotland*, 1902

There was a woman living in Port Ellen and if the fishermen met her on the way to their boats, they would turn back. She was red-headed and that was one reason, but she was also supposed to have the 'Evil Eye' and the gift of *Cronachadh*. The house in which she lived was bought by a family in the village, and she had to leave it, which annoyed her very much. When the people who had bought the house were flitting, one of them met her and thought this an ill omen.

Unbelievably bad luck followed that family. The member who had met the red-haired woman developed a throat infection and in a comparatively short time was dead. Then the mother died, and then another sister and two brothers. Coincidence – or what?

Peggy Earl, *Tales of Islay*, 1980

The evil eye was sometimes used by those disappointed in love against their more successful rival. Fortunately, there were counter charms.

> Donald takes three threads of different hues, and ties three knots on each, three times imprecating the most cruel disappointments on the nuptial bed: but the bridegroom to avert the harm, stands at the altar with an untied shoe, and puts a sixpence beneath his foot.
>
> Thomas Pennant, *A Tour in Scotland and Voyage to the Hebrides,* 1772

Islay has also its witches and wizards, and their Charms and Amulets were, till of late, very much dreaded by the generality of the people. These imposters reaped rich and abundant harvests among their dupes; but by means of the wholesome instructions communicated to the people by the ministers of the Gospel, superstition is fast giving way. A male and female who stood at the head of the profession have died lately, and it is supposed their places shall not be filled.

> William MacDonald, *Sketches of Islay,* 1850

One of Islay's most popular legends concerns a sinister horseman who is said to haunt Laggan Bay, or Traigh Mhor, the Big Strand. Before the building of the long straight road that passes Islay's airport, the 'road' from Bowmore to the Oa was along the strand. It's a forboding place on a stormy night, but a perfect setting for a horror story, as Robert Oliphant recounts.

> . . . there is a curious legend told, which we must here take some notice of, although we are by no means believers in those old super-stitious notions of spectres by the sea shore or ghosts of the drowned and unburied; but in the present case, many of the old people are staunch supporters of its truth. Not unfrequently have we with breathless interest listened to the recital of the story of this spectral apparition – the rider of the snorting steed with spurting fire from eyes and nostrils as it flitted past.
>
> The legend is, that on this long and dreary stretch of strand, there nightly rode the famous *marcaich' an eich dhuibh*, with all the majesty of an eastern caliph. The bay . . . is fully 9 miles in length, with not a single house, except about the centre, the old public "Knock Angle," but which is now in ruins. Here the sea in stormy weather rushes in with tremendous force, the waves reaching to an altitude

of fully 20 feet, and whose awful power is spent on the sandy beach and adjoining warren . . .

Crossing by the old route in stormy weather was no joke, and during the night time many a brave fellow lost his life in the attempt. Here as the eerie traveller wended his way along the strand, the ocean spectre, the rider on the black horse, would invariably make his appearance, and what was very singular, he never attempted to outrun his companions, no matter what their pace might be, he always kept at a little distance from them.

Amongst the people there was no end of conjecture who this mysterious stranger was – some allowed it to have been the spirit of a travelling packman who had met with foul play and the deed never discovered – others again venture to suggest, it was the ghost of some drowned and unburied voyager to a foreign land – the latter supposition being thought the more probable took firm hold upon the people; and from the fact; as the story goes, – a neighbouring farmer having occasion to be very early one Sabbath morning on the beach in search of some stray cattle, to his great surprise and no small terror, discovered a number of dead bodies washed ashore, with several packing cases and other articles of merchandise – the latter he mustered courage to ransack and unlawfully appropriate the contents to himself, leaving the former neglected and uncared for – the bodies, however were accorded decent burial in the little lonely church-yard of Kilnaughton where they now repose in peace. The wretched and unfeeling farmer, it was believed, became exceedingly rich, and to all appearance prospered for a time, but ultimately he got into difficulties and died in obscurity.

Oliphant goes on to relate Islay's own Tam o' Shanter legend.

Amongst the last who happened to come into contact with our mysterious visitant, was one Godfrey McNeill – this Godfrey was a captain in the British Army, courageous and very daring. Having some business at Bridgend on one occasion which detained him longer than he expected, it was pretty late before he started for home, having fallen in with some old cronies, in whose hilarious company he passed a few hours very pleasantly . . .

> "He thought na on the lang Scots' miles,
> The mosses, waters, slaps and styles."

About witching time, our hero reached the strand, when bitter was
the blast and angry was the sea, which caused poor Godfrey to quake
for very fear. Suddenly his attention was attracted by the piteous
whining of his dumb companion, whose "droopin' heid and clappit
tail," betokened danger nigh for:

> "Brutes, they say, aye sooner ken,
> When some uncanny thing is near."

Bewildered for a moment, our hero raised himself, when, instantly,
he espied the sable steed and dusky rider following closely at his heels;
but being in no good humour for further parley, Godfrey quickly
turned upon his saddle, and with a boastful challenge, thus addressed
the apparition:

> Tho' you the very Devil be.
> I care not even a single straw;
> My pony white shall win the race,
> And we shall first be at Kintraw.

Applying his spurs to the flanks of his little steed, he fled over the
Laggan river, remembering the universally known fact, that no dia-
bolical power can pursue beyond the middle of a running stream. No
sooner did the echo of this effusion die away, than the mysterious
spectre dashed in among the breakers amidst sparks of fire and was
seen no more.

> "Ye'll say 'tis juist an auld wife's tale,
> And there's no one believes it noo;
> Yet they were truthfu', honest folk
> Wha tauld the tale I tell to you."

Robert Oliphant, *The Tourist's Guide to Islay, The Queen of the
Hebrides*, 1881

To illustrate the above tale Oliphant draws on a quote from Burns, two from
the Lanarkshire poet Janet Hamilton, and what may be an Islay verse, as it
mentions Kintraw, the farm at the southern end of Laggan Bay.

Godfrey MacNeill – known as Captain Gorrie – was a real character,
and a brave one.

Captain Godfrey McNeill of Ardnacross, was a brave soldier, a keen
sportsman, a superb athlete and a fearless rider. Captain Gorrie, as he
was known, was involved in rash exploits and fast races; it is said he was

once chased across the island by the Devil! In 1785, the cargo vessel *Jeanie* was wrecked in Laggan Bay, and Captain Godfrey organised the recovery of both crew and cargo. As a mark of their gratitude, the owners of the *Jeanie* presented Captain Godfrey with a silver bowl. The bowl has remained in the MacNeill family for 11 generations, until being kindly donated by Jeannie MacNeill, the last owner, to the Museum, where it is now on display.

Website, The Museum of Islay Life, 2015

One Islay folklore collector clearly identifies the other character in the tale – the ghastly rider – as the devil.

The horse affected Gorry with his nervousness and he became really afraid. He looked furtively behind and almost collapsed when he saw a big, black horse and rider whom he knew to be the Devil. Gorry spurred on his horse but he could not throw the Devil and his black steed off his track. Faster and faster Gorry pursued his course till at last, thankfully, he and his gallant grey horse arrived at the stable door.

Captain Gorry was safe but the weary horse stumbled, fell, rolled over, and died. The Captain was very upset. He wrapped his own soldier's cloak round the horse and buried him with full military honors.

Peggy Earl, *Tales of Islay*, 1980

Among the animals widely associated with superstitions are serpents. Adders are native to Islay, and have their place in local folklore.

Vipers swarm in the heath: the natives retain the vulgar error of their stinging with their forked tongues; that a sword on which the poison has fallen will hiss in water like a red hot iron; and that a poultice of human ordure is an infallible cure for the bite.

In this island several ancient diversions and superstitions are still preserved: the last indeed are almost extinct, or at most lurk only amongst the very meanest of the people.

Thomas Pennant, *A Tour in Scotland and Voyage to the Hebrides*, 1772

Assistant lighthouse keeper, Billy Frazer, found superstition about adders still alive shortly after World War Two.

We had a peat bank outside the lighthouse. Och, it was something new to me and we used to cut it and that was where I first met the adder. And when you cut the peat you laid it out for so long and then when it dried you turned it over and then when it was dry you built it into wee stacks, and that was how the north islanders lived. I knew about adders and I knew they were very dangerous, and I lifted this peat and here was this adder, and I had this tusker, as they called the spade, in my hand and I killed the adder. And then I took it in and put it on the top of the boiler in the wash-house. So that night the occasional keeper came from a place called Bunnahabhain and a farmer, a very big farmer he was, he tellt me. 'There's about a 1000 acres.' But he didn't tell me there was only 13 of them arable, you know. And I said to him, 'Hugh, I killed an adder today.' He said, 'Where is it?' I said, 'It's on top of the boiler in the wash-house.' He says, 'It's not dead.' I says, 'Well if ever I've seen a dead snake, it's dead!' So he came in and looked at it and the thing was stiff and 'No,' he says 'it doesn't die until the sun sets.'

Interview for TV documentary 'The Lighthouse Stevensons', Billy Frazer, 2011

More than two centuries before Billy Frazer learned of traditional serpent lore on Islay, Martin Martin had been convinced that superstition was dying out on Islay.

There are several Instances of Heathenism and Pagan Superstition among the Inhabitants of the Islands, related here: but I would not have the Reader to think those Practices are chargeable upon the generality of the present Inhabitants; since only a few of the oldest and most ignorant of the Vulgar are guilty of em. These Practices are only to be found where the Reformed Religion has not prevailed; for 'tis to the Progress of that alone, that the Banishment of evil Spirits, as well of evil Customs, is owing, when all other methods prov'd ineffectual.

Martin Martin, *A Description of the Western Islands of Scotland*, 2nd edition, 1716

More than two and a half centuries after Martin Martin's visit to Islay, folklorists found traditional lore and belief alive and well on the island.

An old man, a native of Islay says that when he was young it was a common Hallowe'en custom to steal Kail (gaoisean Càil) from which to have their future read; and he tells of one time he and several others tried it. Each pulled his stock, and away they went in company to an old woman who lived near to where he was brought up, and who had the credit of being a good hand at "reading Kail Stocks". They all knew each other's stock, but agreed to present them as a lot, to the woman, without letting her know which was which. And he declares that when she came to his gaois, she read his future as truly as it could be read. She said that "the one to whom this gaois belongs will be twice married, and will have two children by his first wife," which turned out to be quite true, and everything else she said was just as true as that. He adds that his own case makes it impossible for him but to believe that there was real virtue in the old custom referred to.

School of Scottish Studies Archives, University of Edinburgh, from Dugald Bell, Port Charlotte, Islay, published in *Tocher* 23, 1976

My mother's uncle, he was an old man when he died, and I only wish now that I had written down the stories that he told me, but he said that at that time the roads weren't very good, and if there was a main road, – where they lived was just a sort of track so that you could hardly even take a horse and trap – you had to go on horseback, and if anybody was ill it was quite difficult to come for the doctor, and so if a person was ill in the house and they wanted to know whether it was a serious illness or not, or whether it was worthwhile getting the doctor, they went outside and they turned up a stone. If there was a living creature under that stone, a worm or a beetle, something that was moving, then it was all right, they went for the doctor because there was a chance of that person being saved, but if there was nothing under the stone they just said, "Well, that's all right, they're going to die in any case," and they didn't bother!

School of Scottish Studies Archives, University of Edinburgh, Recorded from Mrs Earl, Port Ellen, Islay by Mary MacDonald, 1969, published in *Tocher* 11, 1973

Campbell's Kingdom

Much is made in popular Scottish history of feuding between Campbells and MacDonalds. Clan Campbell certainly won the prize of Islay, but for many of that name the island was a millstone round their necks. Sir John Campbell of Cawdor took possession of Islay in 1614 – and found the natives hostile, and the expense crippling.

> On his return from France, Sir John Campbell took possession of Islay, and found it no easy or lucrative affair. Indeed the Calder family were much in the same predicament which the Argyles were with it, losing men and money. During the time of the grandson of Sir John, matters in Islay were in a desperate state. In a quarrel with the tenants, some of the Clerks or Factors, while enforcing their claims, were murdered. To avenge this, the disaffected tenants, to the number of eighteen, were ordered to repair to Baile-Ne'll near where Port Ellen now stands. There they were invited to a spacious barn, where, as was supposed, a sumptuous feast was provided for them, and were admitted one by one. Each man as he entered had a noose thrown over his head and was dispatched! Thus the tragedy went on until only three remained outside; one of whom said that he would not enter until he knew what had become of his comrades. These three took to their heels, and although their enemies pursued them a considerable distance they all effected their escape.
>
> William MacDonald, *Sketches of Islay*, 1850

The Campbells of Calder – or Cawdor – were a branch of the clan from Morayshire. Shakespeare's witches greet Macbeth prophetically: *'All hail, Macbeth, hail to thee, thane of Cawdor!'* And Thane of Cawdor Macbeth soon became.

For over a century the Calders mismanaged Islay, using hired hands to administer it during the childhoods of the heirs to the estate and title.

In 1677 Sir Hugh Campbell began the first stage of what is now Islay House. Today it is an A-Listed building, but it is also remarkable in that it was designed as an unfortified house – something unthinkable to Sir Hugh's Campbell ancestors and MacDonald predecessors.

Sir Hugh died in 1716, and his debt-ridden grandson was forced to dispose of parts of the estate. Enter another branch of Clan Campbell – a Campbell from Skipness in Kintyre who had bought the Shawfield estate between Rutherglen and Glasgow. In 1725 Daniel Campbell bought Calder's Islay, and a chunk of Jura, outright.

> MR CAMPBELL of Shawfield is proprietor of the whole island, and possesses one of the best and most compact estates, enjoyed by any commoner in Britain. On the forfeiture of the M'Donalds, Islay, Jura, and the lands of Muckairn, were made over to Campbell of Cawder, who was then a favorite at Court, on condition of his paying £500 yearly of a feu-duty out of Islay, which is the reason of the duty being so high, and Calder sold all these lands again to Shawfield, for £12,000; which, if the rage for renting land continues, will, by and by, be the income from it.
>
> Statistical Account, 1791–1799
> Parish of Kilchoman, The Rev. Mr. John M'Liesh, Minister

Daniel Campbell of Shawfield, who was a Member of Parliament, had supported Prime Minister Walpole's imposition of a Malt Tax that increased the cost of a barrel of beer by sixpence. The tax was so unpopular that an angry mob wrecked Campbell's Glasgow home. Compensation for the damage done, paid by the city's ratepayers, gave Campbell the funds he needed to buy Islay.

The next writer, who was a Unionist politician, claims that resistance to the Malt Tax in Glasgow was fanned by Jacobites and opponents of the 1707 Treaty of Union. Whether the mob was being provoked or not, the city was a powder-keg waiting to explode.

> . . . Daniel Campbell of Shawfield, who had been an active supporter of Walpole's scheme, was in danger of being made the victim of the popular rage. Two companies of soldiers were drafted into the city on the 23rd of June. On their arrival they found the guard-house locked against them; and whether from disaffection or timidity, the provost besought the officer not to attempt to force it, but to disperse his soldiers to their quarters throughout the city. With amazing facility the officer consented to this course, and thus gave direct encouragement to the rioters, who proceeded to attack Shawfield's house. The officer sent to offer to the provost the help of his men to stay the destruction, but his offer was refused, and the house was sacked and wrecked. Next

day, on assembling his men, the commander of the force found them attacked by a riotous crowd, upon which he fired. This increased the fury of the mob, which broke into the town-house and seized what arms they found there; and then, acting as it would seem under some sort of guidance of which it is not difficult to origin, proceeded to attack the soldiers. At the entreaty of the magistrates their worthy officer withdrew his men to Dumbarton, pursued by the mob, and did not consider himself safe until he had found refuge in the castle there.

Sir Henry Craik, *A Century of Scottish History*, 1911

What sort of estate did Daniel Campbell buy with the compensation for the destruction of his Glasgow mansion? Martin Martin had visited Islay a decade or two before Daniel bought it.

All the Inhabitants are Protestants; some of them observe the Festivals of *Christmas* and *Good Friday*. They are well proportion'd, and indifferently healthful: the Air here is not nearly so good as that of *Jura*, from where it is but a short Mile distant; but *Ila* is lower and more marshy, which makes it liable to several Diseases that do not trouble those of *Jura*. They generally speak the *Irish* Tongue, all those of the best Rank speak *English* . . .

. . . This Isle is reckon'd the furthest West of all the Isles in *Britain*: there is a Village on the West Coast of it call'd *Cul, i.e.* the back part; and the Natives say it was so call'd, because the Ancients though it the back of the world, as being the remotest part of that side of it.

Martin Martin, *A Description of the Western Islands of Scotland*, 2nd edition, 1716

The number of inhabitants is computed to be between seven and eight thousand. About seven hundred are employed in the mines and in the fishery: the rest are gentlemen farmers, subtenants or servants. The women spin. Few as yet have migrated.

The servants are paid in kind; the sixth part of the crop. They have houses gratis: the master gives them the feed for the first year, and lends them horses to plough annually the land annexed.

The air is less healthy than that of Jura: the present epidemical diseases are dropsies and cancers: the natural effects of bad food.

Thomas Pennant, *A Tour in Scotland and Voyage to the Hebrides*, 1772

When Daniel Campbell of Shawfield acquired Islay, he inherited the Stent Committee.

Stent, (*Scot*) *n* assessment; valuation, tax – *vt* to assess, to tax, to levy.

The Chambers Dictionary

On Islay, land was traditionally measured in 'extents', which were defined not by the area of their holdings but by the sum their tenants paid to the landlord. To 'stent' something, was to tax it.

The Stent Committee was unique to Islay. It was a collection of local gentlemen – those of 'the best rank' – who gathered to decide what taxes needed to be raised to pay taxes to the Crown, and to carry out improvements on the island. It had been set up in 1718 and one of its main responsibilities was the repair of roads and bridges. This was something required by Parliament – although it was local cottars who, unpaid, had to provide the tools and the sweat.

This was the 'age of improvement' and the provision of schools, teachers and a surgeon feature heavily in the Stent Committee's accounts.

Att Killerow, November 5th 1719

The Baillie and Gentlemen of Islay having conveen'd, Do hereby Stent the Cesses payable for Decer next and March 1720 terms, and is as follows: –

Imprimis the King's part,	£25 0 0
It. The Surgions fees	40 0 0
It. Killdalton Schoolmrs Sellary	12 0 0
It. For the Collector's Sellary	66 0 0
It. for building an Schoolhouse for Killdalton parish	20 0 0

The Stent Book and Acts of the Balliary of Islay, 1718–1843

For nearly 120 years successive Campbell lairds worked with the Stent Committee, raising and spending taxes. Tumultuous matters on the mainland – like the 1745 Jacobite rebellion – passed the Stent Committee, and Islay, by.

In 1745, when Prince Charles came to Scotland in order to obtain possession of the Throne of his ancestors, the people of Islay took very little interest in the matter, so little indeed that none espoused the Prince's cause and only one hundred young men accompanied the recruiting party of the Government under the auspices of the

Duke of Argyll. After the Battle of Culloden the Islaymen returned home, well replenished with the enemy's booty. It was then the Moidart horses were introduced to Islay; and this superior breed is still in great demand there.

William MacDonald, *Sketches of Islay*, 1850

The dreams of the exiled Stuart dynasty were finally extinguished – along with the lives of about a thousand or more Highlanders – on the field of Culloden Moor. But Scotland was changing in other ways. The hard-scrabble subsistence economy of growing of a few crops and raising a couple of beasts was giving way to the new agricultural practices that were needed to feed growing towns and cities – and make profits for estate owners.

'The Great Daniel' died in 1753 at the age of 82. His eldest son had pre-deceased him, and he was succeeded by his grandson, who was also named Daniel Campbell.

Daniel Campbell the Younger inherited an estate in flux. Islay, which had once attracted waves of invaders and immigrants, was now haemorrhaging people – to the army, to industrial employers in the lowlands, and to the emigrant ships. In the twelve years leading up to 1775, about 1,300 people left Islay for North Carolina. Critics of emigration believed that development opportunities were being missed and that the future prosperity of islands like Islay was being damaged.

This is the more to be regretted as the Improvement of the Hebrides is undoubtedly a great national Object. Their Extent is important: upwards of two millions of Acres. Their Inhabitants numerous: being above seventy thousand persons, yet the number is small compared to the territory they inhabit. Thirty Acres for each Individual, is a proportion hardly known in any other European country: and shews; how little these Islands have hitherto felt the Beneficial Influence of Arts and Industry.

Their soil remains, as it was left at the Creation: The Inhabitants, when compared to their Fellow Subjects, with respect to Arts, are in almost the same Situation as in the Days of Oscian, yet they are Countries capable of being greatly advanced by Agriculture; capable of many of the most important Species of Manufacture: possessed of the most valuable Fisheries in Europe: and inhabited by a sensible, hardy, and laborious Race of People.

The Rev. John Walker, *Report on the Hebrides*, 1764

As well as being a Church of Scotland Minister, John Walker (1731–1803) was one of the most distinguished natural philosophers of his day, with knowledge of botany, zoology, chemistry, geology, meteorology and economics – a true son of the Scottish Enlightenment.

This expertise prompted the Kirk and the Board of Annexed Estates to commission Walker to make two expeditions to the Highlands and the Hebrides to report back on the state of the economy, the people and their faith. In seven months Walker travelled more than 3,000 miles. His report gives us a last glimpse of a way of life on Islay that was soon to vanish.

The wages of a Labourer are 6d. and even 8d. a Day. This article was never so high till of late, occasioned by the great number of Men sent to the War, and the Removal of so many of the labouring People to Ireland.

The chief Export of Ila is black Cattle, of which 2,800 were sent last year out of the Country, at £1 16sh. A Head, which amounts to £4,140. The Grain raised on the Island is sufficient to serve the Inhabitants, and in good Seasons, they spare a considerable Quantity.

It exports likewise some Kelp, and a considerable Quantity of Butter and Cheese.

About 80 Dozen of Rabbit Skins at 5sh. P. Dozen, are sent annually to Glasgow.

As there are no Foxes, Badgers, Weazles nor Fumarts* in Ila, it abounds in Poultry of all kinds, especially in Geese, of which there are between 4 and 5,000 in the Island, whose Quills and Feathers might be rendered an Article of some Profit, but at present neglected.

The Rev. John Walker, *Report on the Hebrides*, 1764

As well as exporting large numbers of cattle, Islay enjoyed a reputation for raising horses.

The island of Islay is famous for horse raising; the saying goes that an Islay man will carry a bridle and saddle for a mile in order to ride half a mile.

William J. Watson, *The History of the Celtic Place Names of Scotland*, 1926

We are said to keep too many horses, which is against the system of black cattle: Yet these horses bring a good deal of money into the

*Polecats or, sometimes, ferrets

country, the Irish being very fond of them, as they are neat lively creatures, and fit for the saddle. Our manner of husbandry requires also a good many horses, 4 being yoked in each plough; and peats, corn and fulzie carried home on horseback. As the country is champaign, and the roads good, an Islayman will scarce stir from home without his *pad*.

Statistical Account, 1791–1799
Parish of Kilchoman, The Rev. Mr. John M'Liesh, Minister

The Reverend M'Liesh used some interesting words in his account. Fulzie is a Scots word for dung; champaign, an archaic word for open level countryside; and a pad-horse is an easy paced horse suitable for riding on roads.

Writing in 1764, John Walker states that a new crop had been introduced to Islay 'about 25 years ago', and had already become a significant food.

Potatoes are now cultivated all over the Islands, but to a greater Extent in Ila, than any where else, where many Fields of them are to be seen of 10, 12 or even 15 Acres each; all planted in lazy Beds with the Spade.

It has been questioned whether the Cultivation of Potatoes is in fact advantageous to the Highlands, or ought to be encouraged, as they tend to discountenance Industry, by affording so great a Quantity of Sustenance with so little Labour. But there are some strong Reasons for thinking that they cannot be too extensively cultivated, especially in the Islands, provided, they be confined to waste Land.

In Ila there is a greater Quantity of Potatoes raised, than what is consumed by the Inhabitants, the Overplus being transported to the Ports of the Clyde and other Places. This Abundance is not only of great use in reclaiming the Soil, but has also a very friendly Influence upon the Progress of the Linen Manufacture in the Island and must certainly have the same Effect in every other Country. For where the Manufacturing People depend entirely for their Sustinence upon Grain, the train of Labour necessary for that Purpose, becomes almost their Constant occupation throughout the Year; but when chiefly supported by Potatoes, their Sustinence not only comes cheaper, but leaves them more time to employ in Manufacture.

The Rev. John Walker, *Report on the Hebrides*, 1764

Daniel the Younger had dedicated himself to agricultural improvement, and even ordained the way in which peat was to be cut.

Rules with Regard to the Cutting of Moss, 8th September, 1767

That such as will be indwellers at Bowmore and Ardlarach (except fewers,) after the Term of Whitsunday 1768, must cut their Turf in a regular Beng★ as will be shown them: – Those residing at Bowmore are to begin cutting at the beginning of the moss betwixt Knockna-firah and the Church. Those at Ardlaroch to begin . . . of the moss nearest their Houses and corn.

That the Moss must be Cutt regular to the Bottom, and the pair-ings laid regular after them.

That if any person or persons DO cutt Terf contrary to the Intention of the above Rules such person or persons SHALL be liable to the sum of Ten Shillings Stirling for the first offence twenty for the second and his, hers or theirs Turf thrown into the Holes in which they were cutt.

The Day Book of Daniel Campbell, edited by Freda Ramsay, 1991

This attention to order was more than a Georgian fad. Irregularly cut peat caused quagmires to form that were dangerous to cattle, and made the im-provement of soil difficult. But not all tenants obeyed the rules.

Came to Islay 10th July 1779 . . .

The people of Kilmeny have again Cutt their peats in the Green Meadow below the road – they must certainly be fined . . .

The people of Bowmore have also Cutt vile Holes and taken out Peats above the road and must be stopt.

The Day Book of Daniel Campbell, edited by Freda Ramsay, 1991

Islay people, like many Highlanders, had long grown and woven flax to make their own linen clothing. But in 1746 the British Linen Bank was incorporated in Edinburgh to stimulate the linen industry and make it a money-spinner for estate owners. John Walker tells that Campbell of Shaw-field's tenants were soon required by their leases to grow 'lintseed' (linseed) from which to produce flax yarn.

No Country can be better adapted, both for the raising and the manu-facturing of Flax, than Ila. The Goodness of the Soil and Climate, the great Abundance of enriching Manures, the cheapness of Labour, the general Vacancy of the People and the neighbourhood of Ireland,

★ peat bank.

all conspire to render it one of the most eligible Seats for the Linen Manufacture to be found in North Britain.

The Rev. John Walker, *Report on the Hebrides*, 1764

But Walker thought that Daniel Campbell the Younger was missing a trick.

The Inhabitants have been very little aided in their Prosecution of the Manufacture, and therefore it still subsists among them in a very rude State, though with proper attention and Encouragement, it might be brought to great perfection. The Difficulties to be encountered here, are not such as prevail in a Country, where the Manufacture has hitherto been unknown. The People have for many years been engaged in it, and though they pursue it in a very awkward way, yet they feel the Advantage of it, and are anxious to embrace any Improvement that may be offered.

Walker's visit to the Hebrides came at the end of the Seven Years War, which had broken out between Britain and France in 1756 over their rival imperial ambitions in North America, and had escalated into a global conflict fought on four continents that involved all the major powers. Britain's man-devouring Army and Royal Navy had recruited heavily in the Hebrides, but disease had also bled the islands.

Ila sent to the Army and Navy, during the late War 500 Men, which was nearly a fourteenth of its whole inhabitants. Yet this great Proportion it could spare perhaps every 10 years without Detriment, was it not for several Causes, which conspire to prevent its Population. Among the Children, the Measles are peculiarly Mortal. The small Pox are less hurtful than in the other Islands, because the disease generally visits Ila once a year; yet of those who are seized with it a much larger Proportion die, than in any district upon the main Land where this is the Case, and Inoculation has not yet been introduced. The Bloody Flux also is a prevailing and fatal Distemper.

The Rev. John Walker, *Report on the Hebrides*, 1764

'The Bloody Flux' is the old name for dysentery, a disease rife where homes are overcrowded and sanitation poor or non-existent. It was only one of the fatal scourges that wracked Islay. A mile or so north-west of Ardbeg lies a ruined village where, it is said, the inhabitants were wiped out by plague.

Nearby are the ruins of what is locally called The Plague Village. At least eight or nine cottages must have been there. The story goes that a ship with the plague on board called at Ardbeg, and the villagers went down and caught the disease, and the whole village was wiped out. This was in the early part of the nineteenth century, when cholera was rife in many parts.

'Islay', by the Isle of Islay Federation, Scottish Women's Rural Institutes, 1968

According to local tradition a young man from the village, who had travelled the world, came back to Ardbeg as a crew member of a ship. On a brief visit to his native village he fell ill and died of "The Plague". The villagers immediately put themselves into quarantine. People from the surrounding area brought food each day to a rock near the infected village. When the food was no longer taken away, they knew that the last of the villagers had died. In due course the houses were burned, leaving only the stone walls and a corn kiln to mark the spot where the village had stood.

Clifford N. Jupp, *The History of Islay*, 1994

But the scourge of disease was not alone in winnowing away Islay's population. Lack of work and opportunity was driving Islay folk to emigrate.

The Migration of the People of Ila, and indeed of all the southerly Islands to Ireland, is more detrimental however to their Population than all their Diseases. These Emigrants are generally the young Men and Women, who either are induced to leave their Country for want of Employment, or enticed by the Hopes of reaping more by their Labour in another Kingdom. And as these Islands raise a greater number of People than are requisite for their present System of Agriculture and Labour, this Emigration must continue till they can be allured to remain at Home, by being profitably employed.

In the 1st of August 1764 about 80 Young Men and Women embarked for Ila, in one Vessel from Ireland. They usually go about that Season of the Year, to the Harvest, but scarce any of them ever return. Nor do they even continue long there, but generally join the Emigrants, which now go annually in great Shoals from the North of Ireland to America.

The Rev. John Walker, *Report on the Hebrides*, 1764

But what of those left at home? Despite the potential for fisheries and agriculture identified by the Reverend Walker, and Daniel Campbell's improvements in communications and farming, the lives of Islay's poor cottars remained hard.

A set of people worn down with poverty: their habitations scenes of misery, made of loose stones; without chimneys, without doors, excepting the faggot opposed to the wind at one or the other of the apertures, permitting the smoke to escape through the other, in order to prevent the pains of suffocation. Their furniture perfectly corresponds: a pothook hangs from the middle of the roof, with a pot pendant over a grateless fire, filled with fare that may rather be called a permission to exist, than support a vigorous life: the inmates, as may be expected, lean, withered, dusky and smoke-dried. But my picture is not of this island only.

Notwithstanding the excellency of the land, above a thousand pounds worth of meal is annually imported, a famine threatened at this time; but was prevented by the seasonable arrival of a meal ship; and the inhabitants like the sons of Jacob of old, flocked down to buy food.

Thomas Pennant, *A Tour in Scotland and Voyage to the Hebrides*, 1772

Tho it still rained our patience was so far wore out that we set out this morn and scarcely had we proceeded a mile toward Kilarow when we met an object that attracted our attention, a highland house so miserably constructed that it tempted us to have drawings made of every particular in it. Twas build of stones so loosely laid together that wind and rain could rarely be stopped in their course by them. There were two doorways one of which served at all times for a window for the house was furnished with only one door or rather substitute for one a faggot of sticks not more closely tied up than faggots in general are which was occasionally placed in one or the other doorway as the family found it most convenient.

In the middle of the house was the fire over which hung a pot . . . not on the chimney but under that hole which was made in the roof as an expedient to let out a part of the smoke which it did but not till after the house was full so that none seemed to be looked upon as superfluous but the mere overflowings. Round this on miserable benches sat the family consisting of a weaver, his wife her mother a

stranger woman and six children. These had two beds to accommodate them the rest of the furniture consisted of a loom and a lamp.

Few as nice conveniences were to be allotted to the use of ten
people yet they all appeared cheerful and content rather more so
than common and the man in particular answered all our questions
with that becoming care that total absence of mauvals that the whole
Scotch nation are blessed with in a degree so superior to the English
to which chiefly I am inclined to attribute the great success that their
adventures meet with in our capital.

Joseph Banks's Diary, 3rd August 1772

Presumably, the absence of 'mauvals' Banks refers to are bad habits, baubles
and pretensions, from the French *mauvais* (adj) – bad, worthless.

Daniel Campbell the Younger died in 1777, and his estate passed to his
brother, Walter, who owned Islay until his death in 1816.

Mr Campbell has improved large tracts of land of moor ground within
view of his own house, which lies about three miles from the village;
and, from his method of cultivation they have produced large crops.
He spares neither pains nor expense; and in this respect several of his
tenants attempt to imitate him. It is computed that he lays out yearly
from 700£ to 1000£ per annum upon improvements, though his
stay here is but 2 or 3 months in the year.

Statistical Account, 1791–1799
United Parishes of Killarrow and Kilmeny, Rev. Mr. John
Murdoch

We have a clear idea of what Islay was like under Walter, because of the
detailed accounts contained in the first *Statistical Account of Scotland,* which
was published between 1791 and 1799. Local ministers the length and
breadth of Scotland were asked to give as full descriptions as possible of life
in their parishes.

Here is a selection of what the ministers of Islay's three parishes – Kilchoman, Kildalton and Oa, and Kilarrow and Kilmeny – wrote about the Islay
of Daniel Campbell's era.

Cultivation – Of late the farmers have got into the way of growing
early oats, which gives them an earlier harvest; for our crops have
been often much hurt by the winds and rains, that set in from the

W. early in the autumn. Seed time commences about the 22nd of March; and by the middle of October all the crop is generally got in. The broad scotch plough, with 4 horses, is most generally in use. There are several tacksmen in the parish, who employ cottagers to work their farms, and tend their dairy. This must be the case with gentlemen who have large farms, as it would be impossible to take servants into their houses to carry on all their business; and as there may be some of them, whose circumstances enable them to be above taking such drudgery upon themselves.

Climate and Diseases – Our climate is the same with that of other maritime places. If we have our Westerly winds and rains, we are free of the frosts and snows of the east, snow never continuing above a day or two with us. An instance of the wholesomeness of that climate, may be seen in the healthfulness of our people, who are seldom or never visited with any epidemical distemper, and generally live to a good age. The small pox, which used to make a vast devastation, is now easily got over by inoculation; one surgeon having, last season, performed that operation upon more than 800 children, very few of whom died. Some people advanced in years were also inoculated, with good effect. The poor were inoculated gratis, and the operator enjoys their blessing.

Black Cattle – The rearing of cattle is a principal object with the gentlemen of Islay, who have the merit of having brought the Islay cattle to vie with the best of their neighbours at market, and to be much run upon. The farming business may be pursued to advantage on Islay; but black cattle have been its greatest riches of late years. There are about 800 of these annually sold out of this parish, at the average price of £3.15s.; they are carried by drovers to Dumbarton and Falkirk, and even to England occasionally.

Employment – The Highland dress has not made much rapid progress among us, as with our neighbours to the N. We are more clad in the long coat, hat, and breeches, than the inhabitants of any of the Hebrides.

Fishing, Fuel, etc – Lochindale affords all kinds of sea fish, and Portnahaven, a fishing village, in the Rinns of Islay, is famous for its cod fishing: And for their encouragement, Mr Campbell of Shawfield has given them some boats, lands and timber for houses. Another great advantage, we have, is, that no country is better supplied with fire and water. Almost every farm has its peatmoss within itself, of an excellent kind, affording charcoal for the smith, as we have no coals. These peats, with the fish oil they burn in lamps, make the habitation of the meanest cottager warm and cheery.

Roads and Bridges – None of the Western Isles can boast of such good roads and bridges as Islay. The inhabitants are every year called out to work upon them; and any gentleman may drive for 30 minutes through the isle in his carriage. To complete the line, our communication with the main shore is kept up by a packet, which goes and returns regularly every week, with the mail, passengers and goods on board. This packet has £40 of salary from the country and £30 from government. The expense of government is more than defrayed by the post-office here, as seafaring people, along with those in the country, send a great many letters through that channel.

Schools – An industrious good schoolmaster is a most valuable member of society and much needed in this parish, to assist in guarding the youth from the errors of popery, as we are just in the very neighbourhood of Ireland.

Improvements – Changes and improvements in all countries, take their rise from the spirited exertions of particular individuals, who seem born for the purpose of rousing the multitude from a state of ignorance and torpor. Within these dozen years, the present proprietor has more than doubled his rents; yet the tenantry, as well as himself, are better off than ever. They have given him, as it were, an addition to his estate, by rescuing many acres, of moor and moss, from a state of nature, and bringing them to yield good crops of corn and grass. On the other hand, the proprietor has given the tenants such advantageous leases, that they have greatly bettered their circumstances, as well as increased their numbers, and are enabled to live much more comfortably than formally. And indeed they are so sensible of the advantages they enjoy, and in general are so contented with their situation, that very few have emigrated from the island: And the farms of such who have, have never continued long unpossessed. When tenants are emancipated from the avarice of monopolisers, they seem to breathe a purer air, and improvements go on rapidly; for nothing has tended more to excite the spirit of emigration, than the *Demon* of

Monopoly, which leads the avaricious to add land to land, and farm to farm. The writer of this article, cannot approve of the maxim, "That *the more rents* you lay on, the tenants will *work the better*." This, like the Egyptian bondage, is exacting bricks without straw, and tends to check, rather than incite, the spirit of industry. But if moderation and lenity, that have hitherto been observed in Islay, continued to be adhered to, we may venture to promise, that the people would rather stay at home, to improve the lands of their native island, than go abroad to cultivate the wilds of America, Amen!

Statistical Account, 1791–1799
Parish of Kilchoman, The Rev. Mr. John M'Liesh, Minister

Soil, Cultivation, Roads Etc. – They carry out their manure in small creels on horseback, and they bring home their peats in the same manner; whereby much time is spent doing very little work. This is partly owing to the want of good public roads; for the inhabitants only work at them 2 days of the year, and the statute labour is never commuted. They do little or nothing for the reparation of private roads. It is much to be wished, that the tenants knew the value of good roads, and that they would use carts to manure the ground, as they do in the next parish, where they have a good public road, which is upheld at a small expense to the tenants. The people of Killarow are encouraged to improve a little in agriculture, by the example of Mr Campbell of Shawfield, who is one of the best farmers in the west of Scotland: And perhaps his Islay estate is capable of as much improvement as any in the kingdom.

Population – The poor people who have families, spend much of their time in spring, in preparing some potato land, and in carrying manure from the shore on their backs, which they spread on such moss land as they procure; for the sea-ware is very abundant and proves good manure for moss ground. The farmer, again, is employed in cutting their own peats, and the peats of those on whom they depend for a house, or a cow's grass, and any other advantages they enjoy; which are all paid for in labour of this kind. They are also frequently employed, on similar terms, in harvest, as they get ground for sewing flax-feed, which they pay for by assisting the farmers in cutting down their barley and oats; nothing else being sown here except potatoes, which is the only support of the poor. They also catch some grey fish, and cod, which they dry, and keep for winter provisions; and sometimes get a few herring in the winter season; but the herrings are only driven here in storm weather, and seldom continue any time.

Poor – The number of those who apply to the kirk-session for charity, seldom exceeds 20, as we have no fund for their relief, except which is collected on Sabbath in the church, which is very trifling. However, the wants of the poor are partly supplied by the tenants at their own houses, where they give freely what is necessary for their maintenance and clothing. The natives are very hospitable to strangers; and are often imposed on by vagrant beggars, who are very capable of working for their own support. Giving charity to such persons is an encouragement to idleness and vice which every friend to mankind ought to discourage, and reward the opposite virtues of industry and sobriety.

> *Statistical Account*, 1791–1799
> Parish of Kildalton, The Rev. Mr. Archibald Robertson

. . . the whole population of Islay has increased greatly within these 40 years, owing principally to the tenants, who are in possession of large farms, dividing their possessions among their children, which encourages marriage. Some, however who are reduced in their circumstances, are obliged to emigrate.

> *Statistical Account*, 1791–1799
> United Parishes of Killarrow and Kilmeny, The Rev. Mr. John Murdoch

According to folklore, clergymen were taking a risk in compiling statistics. This tale was recorded in Gaelic.

Well, there was a field yonder, a bit away. Every year when it was under oats, they would have it cut in the morning – and in stooks – when they got up in the morning. But the farmer said that, indeed, he would watch them the next time there were oats in it. He watched it, and he was up for nights watching it, but the fairies came at last to cut it. And he waited a short while and he went down then to where they were. And the fairy said to him, "Are you counting us?" "Yes," he said, "Well," he [the fairy] said:

> "we are four sixes, four sevens,
> fourteen men plus eight,

nine hundred and fifteen,
those are all that are in the field."

The field was never cut again, because he counted the people. You should not count people.

School of Scottish Studies Archives, University of Edinburgh, recorded from Calum MacLachlan, a native of Kilchoman, Islay by Morag MacLeod and John MacLean, 16 February 1971.

We know a good deal about conditions in eighteenth-century Islay from the records of the Stent Committee, the local 'parliament' of Islay's great and good. Here is a selection of its records, beginning in 1744 when it provided the funds to establish the island's first Post Office at Kilarrow.

Killarow, 11th Jully 1744 years

This Meeting taking into Consideration That its necessary a post office be Erected in the Country for a year. They Agree That not only the Sum of One hundred and Thretty pund Scots mony already in the Collect hands since last Stent, being half of our proportion of the money stented on the shyre for a Watch But also That whatever the said post office shall cost the Country, over and above the said soume the same is to be stented with the next stenting, and appoint The Bailys of Jura and Ilay, Shindarline, Balinaby, Askamiln, and the Clk a Committee for Erecting and Regulating said post office . . .

Lesser tenants and cottars were 'drafted' to maintain the island's roads. The work was unpaid and seen as part of their payment for their homes and smallholdings.

Att Killarrow, the 20th July 1753

With respect to working on the Highways the meeting here now present doe appoint that onn Munday and Tuesday the 2nd and 3rd of July New Stile and Wednesday the 4th bee the days to work upon throughout Islay, that the people of the parish of Kilchoman work on the roads as formerly appointed in last meeting. Balynaby to Direct the working in Killarow parish and to order all the men of Glencatadill and to the water of Lagan from (the) water of Killaro on the road from Killaro to Duich water where they wrought last year. That Ronald Campbell in Balychlavan Act as survey'r off Killmeni parish and Give directions where and how to wk, appoint proper overseers – and the road from Kil'w to Portaskog to bee by Balygrd, and well seen to with the key of Portasgog.

The packet – or regular mail-ship – service to the mainland, was another concern of the business minded Stent Committee. Here they refer to the tax levied to run the services as a *cess*, a term for a tax used only in Scotland, Ireland and India. Ffailziw – *Failziw* or *Failyie*, is a default or a penalty for breaching a bargain.

At Killarow the 20th Day of December one thousand Seven
Hundred and Seventy one years.

. . . To be levied with the Cess towards defraying the Expenses of the Pacquet till the twentieth October next, Besides the sums formerly pay'd by Shawfield, Mr Ffreebairn and Collonsa, £32 : 8 : 6 Sterl'. But the meeting ordain Mr Hamilton their Collector to make Retension of the said sum unless the Pacquet be repaired, and the Pacquet Master perform as ffollows, viz: – That the Pacquet must make a Return once every week, wind and weather permitting. That the Pacquet master and owners must get sufficient Masts, Sails, Rigging, Cables, Anchors, &c. That there must be four Beds made in the Cabine and four new Matresses in them, and that there be locks on two of them and none but Cabine passengers admitted to them. That there be three sufficient Sailors and a Boy always in the Pacquet. That if any accident happens the pacquet The Master must ffreight another vessel at his or his owners Expence to answer the Service. That in case any Accident happen the pacquet at Loch Tarbert, and that another vessel cannot be found to carry the Bag to Isla, the Pacquet Master must send an Express by the fferrys with the Bag at his own Expence. That upon the Pacquet's arrival on Isla the Bags are to be sent immediately to Killarow by Express. That the Pacquet Master must send a List of the Goods on Board. That a Coppy of the above Articles is to be Delivered to the pacquet Master, and by him to be keept for the perusal of any Gentlemen passenger who may choose to call for it. That the Pacquet must be repaired as above on or before the twentieth Jan next. That a Committee of Gentlemen is then to view her, and that according to their Report the above sum is to be paid, And that the above hail Articles are to be performed under the penalty of Ten pounds Ster' in case of ffailziw to be retained out of the sum here Stented. That the Pacquet must always be keept clean in the Bottom, And that the Pacquet master must freight a sufficient vessel at his own Expence to answer the Service if the Pacquet is Repairing. That the pacquet is not to go out of her course to call at any place or for any person, and that the Pacquet master is not to take any by freights.

John Robertson.

The cess levied was £32. 8. 6d. But however well financed and well run the Islay packet was, it was still at the mercy of an unforeseen international event. The outbreak of the American Revolutionary War unleashed the Kirkcudbright-born 'Father of the American Navy' into Islay's waters.

> . . . in the autumn of 1778, the notorious Paul Jones made a descent here. In the Sound he captured the West Tarbert and Islay packet. Among the passengers was a Major Campbell, a native of the island, just returned from India where he had realized an independence, the bulk of which he had with him in gold and valuables, and the luck-less officer was reduced in a moment from affluence to comparative penury.
>
> George Anderson and Peter Anderson, *Guide to the Highlands and Western Islands of Scotland*, 1863

Although it was a tax-raising and spending body, the Stent Committee never doubted its right to lay down the law to the common folk of Islay. In March 1792 it condemned meetings and combinations – early trade union activity – by disgruntled weavers on the island.

> It being represented to this Meeting that there is unlawful combinations and Meetings held by the Weavers in the Island, particularly in the Parish of Kilchoman, for the purpose of shortening or cutting off the usual measure called the Islay Ell, which has for time Immemorial been the Standard measure given by the Weavers with every Species of their Manufacture, and for reducing the measure to the English yard, and for continuing the prices for the English yard as high as that for the Islay Ell – This Meeting highly disapproved of such Illegal meetings and combinations, and recommend it to the Gentlemen of the different districts in Islay to Prosecute before any of his Majesty's Justices of the Peace, and Weaver that they shall find Guilty of such Practices.

In December the same year, the Stent Committee turned its attention from troublesome weavers to troublesome dogs.

> The meeting considering that the number of useless Dogs in this Country are a great grievance, and that for many obvious reasons their number should be diminished, and it being also represented that a number of Half Greyhounds very destructive to Hares are kept by Many – This meeting recommends to the Gentlemen of the different quarters of Islay to Intimate to the people of their neighbourhood that all useless and superfluous Dogs are to be killed, and that the owner of any Dog found chasing Sheep or Lambs or running Hares shall be liable for the Damages, and the Meeting also recommend that no dog be seen at Church or other publick Meetings – and they appoint their Clerk to send Extracts of this Minute to the different Clergymen of the Island, who will be so good as direct the same to be Published in the different Churches that none may pretend Ignorance.

'Gentlemen, Heretors and Tacksmen' of the Stent Committee enjoyed a fair degree of conviviality at its annual meetings. In 1792, their expenditure included the following:

The Bill to Miss Simpsons,	£10. 6. 2.
General Meeting Bill, 1792	
To Dinner	2. 10. 0.
To ½ Doz Clerat @ 3/,	0. 18. 0.
To 20 bottles port @ 2/6,	2. 10. 0.
To 10 Do, White @ 3/,	1. 10. 0.
To 4 Doz, punch and 4 Bottles @ 8,	1. 6. 8.
To Drams 2/, ale and porter 20/,	1. 2. 0.
To Glasses,	0. 2. 6.
To Servants,	0. 7. 0.
	————
	£10. 6. 2.

The line 'To Glasses', refers to breakages. The 1778 bill makes this clear.

> Glasses broke, 10 @ 6d each is 5/.

In 1806, the Committee decided that the conviviality was getting out of hand.

> This Meeting having taken into Consideration the enormous amount of the Bill of Entertainment, Resolve that the following rules shall be attended to in future, viz.:- That for each Guest Sitting at Table, the Landlord shall allow and produce a half Bottle of wine and a Bottle of Punch – a Bottle of Brandy to the whole Company – with small Beer – that the Landlord shall charge for each Sitting to Dinner at the rate of 3/-, that the Servants shall be Limited to a half mutskin of Whisky to each in name of Drink, and that the Landlord shall make no charge for Horses.

This outbreak of Calvinistic sobriety was short-lived. The following year, the self-denying rule was reversed.

> This Meeting having revised the Consideration of last year's resolution respecting the Restriction as to the Liquor, &c.: The Meeting now think that this restriction is not necessary, and that the Meeting will proceed in that as formerly, without regarding the Minute of Last Year.

We know that the first Ileach named in history was the seventh-century pig owner, Feradach, who St Columba prophesied would be 'blotted out of the book of life' for the murder of a Pictish nobleman. Twelve centuries later, according to the Stent Book, Islay folk were still rather keen on pigs.

Bowmore, 11th April 1804

It has been now represented to the Meeting that the Town of Bowmore is very much annoy'd by a destructive Crowd of Pigs running up and down the Streets, and that many of the Inhabitants, regardless of Propriety, keep their Dunghills upon the Streets. This meeting consider themselves Authorised to order a better Police, appointing Archd Adair and Mr Hector Simpson as Superintendents, who are hereby recommended, to Publish to all the Inhabitants of Bowmore, that eight days after the date of that Publication, each owner of a Pig which shall be found loose upon the street shall pay a Fine of not Exceeding 2/6 Sterling for each offence, and those who erect their Dunghills upon the Street shall after the above notice pay 5/- Sterling for each offence; as well as those who do not remove their Dunghills upon receiving Intimation – which different fines, when uplifted, are to be applied and laid out for the improvement of the Streets of Bowmore.

In 1812, America declared war on Britain, which was already locked in conflict with Napoleonic France. The causes of the American conflict were chiefly unresolved issues left over from the American Revolutionary War, but in the autumn of 1813 Islay found itself in the front line. Locally, that year became known as 'the year of the burnt ships.'

On the fourth of October 1813, the inhabitants of Islay were thrown into an agony of despair, on account of the arrival of a piratical vessel from the United States of America called "The True Blooded Yankey," commanded, as is supposed, by a certain Captain named Duplait. This Privateer was a fine man–of–war being pierced for 26 guns, and carrying 260 men. She arrived in Lochindaal about dusk, and having been boarded by two experienced pilots she cast anchor near Skiba, now called Portcharlotte. The harbour happened at this period to have been crowded by merchant vessels of all sizes. The commander of the pirate observing this he determined to have them all simultaneously set on fire, and he carried his fell purpose into effect; having previously rifled such vessels of such articles as he coveted. Between 20 and 30 vessels were either burned or sunk by this rover in one night. It was a fearful spectacle to behold so many fine vessels with their precious loading, all in a flame at the same time; occasioning a loss of private property amounting to nearly £600,000. Early on the following morning she departed from Lochindaal and proceeded to Brest, laden with spoil. She was afterwards taken as a prize by the British and carried to the River Plate, where she was condemned. Thus ended the career of the redoubtable and "True Blooded Yankey."

William MacDonald, *Sketches of Islay*, 1850

The True Blooded Yankee had been a French ship that was bought and fitted out by a Rhode Island man resident in Paris, as a privateer to harry the British. All privateers with Rhode Island connections had the word 'Yankee' in their names. Edgar Maclay, an American journalist, historian and one-time lighthouse-keeper, takes up the story . . .

On September 30, 1813, the following notice, copied from a Paris newspaper, dated September 25th, was posted in Lloyd's Coffee

133

House, London: "The True Blooded Yankee, American privateer, has been completely refitted for sea, manned with a crew of two hundred men, and sailed from Brest the 21st inst. supposed for the purpose of cruising in the British Channel. Her orders are to sink, burn, and destroy, and not to capture with the intention of carrying into port." These orders were faithfully carried out, an immense amount of damage being inflicted on British commerce at the hands of this "Yankee" scourge.

Edgar Stanton Maclay, *A History of American Privateers*, 1899

'Nuair a thainig Bliadhna na Soithichean Loisgte, b'e sin 1813 . . . thainig an "Full-Blooded Yankee", soitheach-cogaidh. Rainig iadsan a stigh an loch, agus stad iad aig Aird Nis, shìos, ann an Nereabolls, agus chaidh am muillear agus an gille a mach do'n t–soitheach, agus dé ach 'nuair chaidh iadsan air bòrd air an t-soitheach cha leigeadh iad air falbh iad, na h-Ameirigeanaich, agus thug iad orra an toirt a nìos do'n acarsaid aig Bodha-Mór, agus sin far an do chuir iad na soithichean nan teine, 's bha iad airson dol do'n Tigh Bhàn, agus sgrios a thoirt air an Tigh Bhàn agus a h-uile rud a bh'ann a thoirt leò. Có-dhiù, cha d'rinn iad sin . . . agus sheòl iad a mach air ais, agus 'nuair a bha iad a' dol seachad air Nereabolls, leag iad am muillear mu sgaol. Bha bàta beag a' mhuilleir air bòrd air an long, 's nuair a bha iad mu choinnimh Nearabolls thubhairt aon de na seòladairean, 'n uair a bha a' muillear 's an gille 's a' bhata bheag ri cliathach an long, "As a so suas, cumaidh thusa tuillidh uisge air do mhuilinn, a mhuilleir." 'S ann anns a Ghàidhlig a bha so.

When the Year of the Burnt Ships came, that was 1813 . . . the "Full-Blooded Yankee", a war ship, appeared. They entered the loch [Loch Indaal] and they stopped at Aird Nis, down in Nereabolls, and the miller and the lad went out to the ship, and when they went on board the ship, they would not let them go, the Americans. And they forced them to take them up to the anchorage at Bowmore, and there they set the shipping on fire, and they were going to go to the Tigh Bàn [the White House – Islay House] and to sack the Tigh Bàn and to plunder everything that was in it. However, they did not do that . . . and they sailed back out, and when they were passing Nereabolls, they released the miller. The miller's small boat was aboard the vessel, and when they were off Nereabolls one of the sailors said, when the miller and the lad were in the small boat at the side of the vessel,

"From now on, keep you more water to your mill, miller." This was spoken in Gaelic.

> School of Scottish Studies Archives, University of Edinburgh, recorded from Gilbert Clark, Port Charlotte, Islay, by Ian A. Fraser, on 20 November 1970, published in *Tocher* 6, 1972

Who was the privateer crewman serving on *The True Blooded Yankee* able to speak to the miller in Gaelic?

The Stent Committee was less concerned with 'piratical vessels' than with the ferry service to the mainland. In 1812 Henry Bell's paddle steamer, *Comet*, began plying the Clyde, and twelve years later the Stent Committee embraced this new technology.

> This Meeting being impressed with the utility to the island by the appointment of a Steamboat to ply in place of the Packet, do unanimously Stent themselves in the sum of one Hundred and ten pounds sterling for this current Year – and from their inclination would be induced to increase the sum – did the General Production of the Island warrant an increase of Salary – and in conceding this allowance.
>
> They trust that the Steam-Boat will continue to do the duty the Packet was in the use of performing, so that the exports and imports may be regularly carried on as formerly.

But not all seaborne traffic was welcome. In 1817, after two years of bad harvests, Ireland was close to famine, and many of its rural poor were on the move.

> It is now stated that a vast importation of Irish Beggars have already arrived upon the island, and that others are likely to follow from the misconduct of our own Boatmen – the Community at large are warned to beware of harbouring foreign beggars, and if they are found guilty that the penalties prescribed by the Meeting of the Commissioners at Inverary will be levied from those trespassing, and of course Boatmen bringing over from Ireland passengers of this description will be punished according to Law, and the Clerk to this Meeting is now instructed to make out Advertisements to this effect to be sent particularly to the Ports of Lagivillin, Portnahaven, and Skibba and the Loudians.

For more than a century the Stent Committee worked in tandem with Islay's owners, and accomplished a great deal. In 1816, Walter Frederick Campbell

– grandson of Walter Campbell – had inherited the estate and the Stent Committee with it. But when poor harvests and economic depression brought Islay's Campbell regime to an end, the Stent Committee disappeared overnight.

> The last meeting of the Islay Stent Committee was on the 19th May 1843. There was no indication of its immediate demise. It can be surmised that when the sequestrators arrived to wind up Walter Frederick Campbell's affairs, the irregularity and illegality of the Committee's proceedings were quietly pointed out.
>
> Norman Newton, *Islay*, 1988

Today the Bowmore inn which saw many of the Stent Committee's convivial gatherings is still in the hospitality business, as upmarket tourist accommodation. But in the early days of the Stent Committee its meetings were held in Kilarrow, the village on Lochindaal close to Islay House, and near present day Bridgend.

> Heretofore the principal town in the island was the ancient town of Kilarow, in the neighbourhood of the burying place. It was a busy, thriving market town with its tollbooth, its inn, its shops, its smithy, its carpenters' workshops, its meal mill, its lint mill, its post office and its school.
>
> J.G. MacNeill, *Islay*, 1899

But Kilarrow was too close to Islay House for Daniel Campbell's tastes. In 1768 he founded Bowmore, about three miles further along the coast, and cleared the people of Kilarrow to it. Nothing now remains of Kilarrow, except its atmospheric graveyard, close to Islay House. Its name, however, continues in the name one of Islay's parishes, Kilarrow and Kilmeny. Meanwhile, the planned village of Bowmore has become Islay's 'capital'.

> To the south-west of Jura lies the island of Islay. Its greatest length is twenty-five miles; its breadth eighteen. It is deeply indented on the south by the great bay called *Loch-in-daal*, at the head of which formerly stood the village of *Killarrow*. The principal village now, is *Bowmore*, where there is a post-house, and where several neat buildings have lately been erected. This new town has a convenient harbour.
>
> Robert Heron, *Scotland Delineated, or a Geographical Description of Every Shire in Scotland*, 1799

The village of Bowmore was begun in the year 1768, and laid out on a regular plan. By order of the proprietor, the new church was built at the end of one of the municipal streets, in a very elegant manner, and upon a new plan. It is ornamented with a steeple, fronting the quay, built upon foundations with freestone. It cost about 1000£. There are already 110 houses built in the village, 50 of which are covered with blue slates, 20 with tiles, and the rest are thatched. The inhabitants are increasing. The number at present (1793), of old and young, is about 500.

Statistical Account, 1791–1799
United Parishes of Killarrow and Kilmeny, Rev. Mr. John Murdoch

Islay owed many of its edifices to the Shawfield family; and among the number the Parish Church at Bowmore, which was built at the expense of the above Daniel Campbell in 1768, who also projected the village of Bowmore. Port Charlotte and Port Ellen were projected by the late proprietor; the former called after Lady Charlotte Campbell, his mother; and the latter after his much lamented late wife, Lady Eleanor, the daughter of the Earl of Wemyss. He also built the Light House, which he continued to keep up at his own expense.

William MacDonald, *Sketches of Islay*, 1850

Travellers were full of praise for the Campbells' great house, gardens and woods that surrounded them.

We here passed two very agreeable days at Islay House. The prevailing aspect of the country, as viewed from the sea, is rather bare and barren, and those parts where the chief amenities prevail being somewhat low and flat, the plantations are seen as it were greatly fore-shortened, and so diminished in effect. But as we approached the dwelling-house we found a great extent of richly wooded walks, with far-spreading rosaries, and other intermingled garden grounds, and an extensive semicircular lawn, screened by a sheltering belt of shrubbery from the "injurious sea". It would take long to tell of all the wonders of art and nature which are here combined. Neither need we dwell on those elegancies of civilised life which, always grateful to the feelings, showed to additional advantage when we thought of the wild barbarians we had lately seen along the pillared shores of the Emerald Isle.

Besides its arboreal beauties, the vicinity of Islay House is remarkable for its tasteful and extensive aviaries, its various ponds for aquatic fowl, its plots of intermingled grass and gravel, where strut in all their pride of place an assortment of most beautiful bantams, to say nothing of more secluded enclosures devoted to the rearing of the different species of pheasants and other game. There are also a pair of very lively otters, which will take a fish from any one's hand, and will also gladly bite that same, when they find nothing between the finger and thumb. Islay's own dwelling place is large and irregular, not distinguished by any architectural beauty, but possessing a pleasant patriarchal character from its numerous offsets and dependencies, and presenting indeed almost a village aspect, when its various tops and chimneys are seen among the tufted trees.

We understand that almost all the outer adornments are owing to the exertions of the present hospitable proprietor. Few trees were planted by his predecessors, and even so late as fifteen years ago this quarter of the island did not greatly differ from the surrounding hills, which if not barren in the pastoral sense of the word, are at least treeless and unadorned. There are now, however, about 1300 acres of young plantations in the most thriving state. Indeed the growth of trees of all kinds here within these last few years has been quite remarkable. After exploring the wooded wilderness of pleasure grounds by which the dwelling is surrounded, and inspecting the ponds, aviaries, and other zoological enclosures, we made an excursion upwards along the river side, through a beautifully wooded avenue, or private road, of several miles in length, by which the house is approached from the north-eastwards. The soil which stretches along the stream is a deep mossy loam, now made dry by draining, and any natural monotony of character which its original tendency to flatness may have imposed upon it, is relieved by the varied verdure of the plantations, interspersed with cultivated glades and sunny meadows. The proprietor retains some thousand acres in his own hands, and gives employment to a very numerous body of attached retainers.

James Wilson, *A Voyage Round the Coast of Scotland*, 1842

In 1841, Walter Frederick Campbell hired William Playfair, one of Scotland's greatest architects, to improve Islay House.

This magnificent mansion is pleasantly situated near the centre of the Island, about a quarter of a mile from the commodious Inn of

Bridgend, and at the head of the spacious Bay of Lochindaul. It is surrounded by far spreading plantations; and the pleasure grounds, private drives and walks, around and connected with it, are extensive and varied, and laid out with much taste and judgement, suitable in all respects, both for convenience and recreation. The gardens, hothouses and fountains are superior to any private gardens in the west of Scotland; so charming that they remind the visitor rather of the enchanting grounds and fairy scenery mentioned in Eastern story, than of a reality.

William MacDonald, *Sketches of Islay*, 1850

The Campbells of Shawfield would leave an indelible mark on Islay – not least in the building of their own home.

It is believed that the family of Calder had a cottage on the same place where Islay House now stands. The first Daniel Campbell, Esq., of Islay, either built a plain new house of three storeys on the foundation of the old one, or otherwise made an addition to the walls of the former residence. This served as the Shawfield mansion until 1760, when the east staircase was built at the expense of the fifth Daniel Campbell of Islay, the great, great grandson of the third Daniel, under the superindendence of Mr George Shanks.

William MacDonald, *Sketches of Islay*, 1850

The lives of Islay's common people were very different from those who lived at Islay House – and not much different from that described by Thomas Pennant and Joseph Banks nearly eighty years earlier.

The dwellings generally are of a very rude and inferior order, suggesting the idea that the personal happiness and the improvement of the taste of the people were but little thought of by those who regulated these affairs.

William MacDonald, *Sketches of Islay*, 1850

But the planned village of Bowmore, further along Lochindaal from the old Kilarrow, impressed.

Bowmore is for situation the joy of the island. Viewing it at sunset from the opposite side of the loch, its houses look like gems in a crown. Like a guardian angel watching the living town, Bowmore, and protecting the silent village, the churchyard, stands at the head of the principal street the parish Church of Kilarow – a curious circular building, one of two churches in Scotland built on the corn-stack principal. This church is the older of the two , and owes its conical peculiarity to a French architect. Was the same architect the writer of the bombastic Latin inscription on a tablet affixed to the outer wall? It may be translated thus: "For the study of piety, and the culture of truth and honour, Daniel Campbell, lord of this island, built this church at his own charges, and dedicated it to the Supreme Deity in the year 1767".

J. G. MacNeill, *Islay*, 1899

The town lies on the east side of, and is about three miles from the head of Lochindaal, or what we might appropriately term the "Loch of Delay," from the fact, that previous to the days of Bell's application of steam power, and when paddles and screws were things unknown, large numbers of sailing vessels trading between Scotland and the West of Ireland, not unfrequently, to escape the fury of the outer tempest, and the angry mountain waves of the sea, had to seek refuge in Lochindaal, where they were often delayed by prevailing adverse gales of long continuance, especially during winter – hence the name "Lochindaal." Which in Gaelic signifies the "Loch of Delay."

Robert Oliphant, *The Tourist's Guide to Islay, The Queen of the Hebrides*, 1881

Is the word Bowmore a corruption of *Pol Mòr*, Great Pool? The late Hector MacLean says that "When the church and the first houses of Bowmore were built, Scotch artisans were brought to the island and it would be quite natural for Lowlanders speaking Scotch to corrupt Pollmòr into Bowmore." This seems to be correct, for, about 150 years ago, the north end of Main Street, where once the Old Pump stood, nearly opposite Douglas House, was a piece of bogland covered with reeds.

J. G. MacNeill, *Islay*, 1899

Bowmore quickly established itself as the legal and business centre of Islay.

A few days after the sittings of the Sheriff Court in August, the annual Horse and Lamb Market takes place. This is the principal fair held in Bowmore during the year, and two or three days are generally set apart of it, when there is a good deal of business transacted, as well as its being a season of much enjoyment and recreation. If the weather be fine, we recommend the stranger to see the fair, and the fun and frolic incidental to it, which cannot fail to afford him some amusement. From early morn, to well on in the forenoon, the continual stream of horses, carts, machines, pedestrians, cattle, &c., &c., keep pouring into the village from all the quarters of the Island, when by noon we may say, the Fair is at its height. Generally speaking, there is always a good show of horses – a fair attendance of dealers from the low country and elsewhere . . .

The Portnahaven fishermen are always in attendance with a good stock of the Stenlock fish caught at Barra, which find a ready market. A goodly number of servants are also present at this fair, looking for, and expecting fresh engagements, – many of the female portion, decked out in all the colors of the rainbow, keep constantly perambulating the streets during the day, and every now and again are to be seen earnestly surveying the tempting display of bonnets and other domestic commodities, so dazzling to the eye, in the various milliners' and drapers' windows, each apparently intent on some fine garish purchase in which to appear on proper holiday attire.

Robert Oliphant, *The Tourist's Guide to Islay, The Queen of the Hebrides*, 1881

The stenlock fish that the Portnahaven men were selling are defined in the *Scottish National Dictionary* as:

STENLOCK, *n.* Also *-lack, stan(e)lock, -lac, stainlock*. The coalfish, *Gadus virens*, esp. in its fully-grown or SAITHE stage.

This extract from 'Fair Day', by an Islay poet, gives a lively impression of the regular Bowmore fairs.

An August afternoon – blue sky – bright sun,
The village streets, that wont so quiet be,
All full of bustling life and busy talk.
And tread of men, and tramp of horses' feet;
With hundreds occupied in countless ways,
Single, together, moving or at rest.
Spreading a murmur like a cataract.

ISLAY VOICES

There, on one spot, are sunburnt faces seen.
With massy features and bluff hardy look,
And broad and brawny forms, all clad in blue.
The deep sea fishers these, whose luggers ride
The breezy sea that clips the Hebrides;
And these their wives, so garrulous and glad,
Who sell their hard smoked fishing by the score,
And black coarse oil, to meet the winter night.
With them their daughters come, all trig and smart,
And youngsters eager for the holiday,
Now wildly staring, for they never looked
On such a crowd of busy men before.

Leaving that scene of busy interchange,
You see the group about those horses met,
One is the ploughman in his best array;
That broad squat man, so round and corpulent,
With dry black hair, and full brown eye and bright,
The shabby coat, and clothes that once were good,
With his hands deep into his pouches held,
And look of ready cash about his face, –
That man who, jingling, jingling, stands and looks,
Is a horse-couper. And the tall thin man
With the broad shoulders who, with out-stretched neck,
O'erlooks his comrade's round and dusty hat,
And wears a coat that reaches to his heels –
He is the friend – the friend and referee.
But that's an amateur whose brows are knit.
Who, better dressed and sprucer on the whole
Than the two dealers, sees a bargain close,
And stepping up, with calculating care
Pokes on the ribs the horse that's to be sold, –
Looking as wise as Solomon the while –
Then with one weighty sentence turns away.
These are his friends and satellites behind,
Who hang upon his skirts, – look as he looks,
Turn as he turns, and wander as he goes;
Thinking him paragon of mortal men.

Thomas Pattison, *Fair Day, Gaelic Bards*, 1890

At stated intervals, a cattle fair is held in the island, which is attended by dealers from the mainland of Scotland. All the beasts purchased on these occasions are driven to Port Askaig, to be ferried to Jura, and thence to the mainland. One day during my stay here, upwards of a hundred cattle were driven to the ferry, and in consequence of the stormy weather were unable to cross. The drovers, a hard race, might, if they would, have kept them on the hills above the port, where, by the custom of the island, cattle in transit have the right of grazing; but, there being no whisky-shops on the heaths, they never stop there under any circumstances, but drive their charge to the sea-shore, where the unfortunate animals must remain without food until ferried to Jura. For two nights and a day they stood about on the barren shore, without, as I have said, a particle of fodder, green or dry; lowing piteously; occasionally poking one another with their horns, as if in mockery of sport; badgered by dogs, trained, seemingly, to fasten onto their tails by their teeth, and to suffer themselves to be swung round rather than let go their hold; and battered with huge clubs by the drovers, whenever they turned their heads in the direction of the inland road. That the occurrence was common appeared clearly enough, for from morning to night little girls in pairs visited the milch cows, round and round, and over and over, one stroking the famished beast to keep it quiet, the other draining a scanty drop of milk into a tin pan. The sight was pitiable in the extreme; but the worse was to come. Late in the second morning the weather moderated so far as to allow the ferry-boat to cross, and the poor animals were driven, about ten at a time, by shouts, blows, barks and bites, to tumble into the boat. I scarcely think that one could have made the passage uninjured, so reckless were the drivers, and so inadequate the means for transporting the cattle. But this process I could not endure to watch, so turned my back on Port Askaig, and strolled along the cliffs.

Sir Smith Child, *Three Weeks on Islay*, 1861

The village of Bridgend, close to Islay House and the site of the now vanished village of Kilarrow, is today the location of Islay's Auction Mart for cattle and sheep. In the past Kilarrow's May Market was an important event in Islay's agricultural, social and romantic calendar.

During the month of May the all-important May Market is held at Bridgend, which is also the principal feeing time for servants; and where:

"The lads and lasses are thrangin'
And a'body's noo in a steer."

Here also, many a hearty Highland greeting is witnessed, with diverse amorous demonstrations of Donal wi' his dearie.

Throughout the day on the Market stance, which, by the way, is a very large field or common at the head of the Loch . . . many a hard bargain is struck between buyer and seller, with the ne'er-to-be-forgotten luck's penny thrown back. While this buying and selling is going on, many a serving lad and lass have made their bargains too . . .

Robert Oliphant, *The Tourist's Guide to Islay, The Queen of the Hebrides*, 1881

In 1829, Walter Frederick Campbell came up with a plan to improve the lot of poor cottars, by offering them a chance of self-sufficiency on the then unimproved land known today as the Duich Lots.

As I humbly conceive that the plan I have pursued may prove of use in the Highland districts, I hereby subjoin a short account of the manner in which I have hitherto carried on the improvements of my estate in the Island of Islay, in hopes that, at all events, it may serve as the ground-work for something better, and thus lead to the cultivation of a portion of the vast tracts of land in my native Highlands, which are at present in a state of unproductive barrenness.

The tract of land on which I made the experiment, lies to the west of the Island of Islay, along the shores of the Bay of Laggan. It comprises three farms – Machry, Glenagadale, and Duich; but is generally called the Flat of Laggan.

It comprises a distance of about six miles in length, and from two to three miles in breadth. In the immediate proximity to the sea, a good deal of land has been brought into cultivation; but about a mile from the coast, the land was in a state of nature, and was counted of little or no value to the farms to which it was attached, being very wet moss, and producing nothing but the most stunted heather. A stripe of land was cut off the farms in 1829, and notice was given that portions of it would be granted, free of rent, for a term of years, to any persons of good character who came forward to demand it. In consequence of this notice, a great many people, who had been living as cottars on the different farms of the island, came forward to demand grants (each producing a certificate of character). The land was then divided into lots of twenty acres each, and was numbered on a plan. A selection was then made of the candidates; the name of each was written on a separate piece of paper, and put into a hat, and numbers, corresponding to those on the plan, were written in like manner on slips of paper, and put into another hat. A name and a number were then drawn, and the lot marked with that number on the plan, was the portion to be granted to the name drawn with it. In this way the land was portioned off; and has been held, up to this time, by the persons who drew, with one or two exceptions. The terms on which the grants were given, were, that they should hold the land free of rent for eight years, and provided that they had ploughed the whole of the twenty acres during the first eight years, they should be entitled to hold it for eight years more, at a shilling an acre.

I ought to mention, that, though no rent was demanded, each lotter is burdened with a servitude of six days' labour in each year; which labour is expended in forming roads and digging main drains.

The manure used has invariably been sea-ware and shell-sand, vast quantities of which are thrown up on the Bay of Laggan.

The houses were built by the crofters themselves – in some instances I gave them wood.

Transactions of the Highland and Agricultural Society of Scotland. Mr Campbell on the Improvement of Waste Land of a District in the Island of Islay, Walter Frederick Campbell, 1834

The result of the experiment on the 18th August 1834, were, that 47 cottars had brought into arable culture under oats, bear, and potatoes, varying in quantity from 1¼ acre to 20 acres, averaging for each cottar 5.7 acres, and extent of 208 acres; that four cottars had cultivated none; and that three had only enclosed their lots.

It is believed that this is the first, as it is certainly the most extensive experiment, in the improvement of waste land, which has hitherto been made in the West Highlands of Scotland.

The commentary concludes . . .

The work goes on steadily enough, and the "cotters or small lairds" are all contented and happy.

Transactions of the Highland and Agricultural Society of Scotland, commentary on Walter Frederick Campbell's account, 1834

Historian David Caldwell suggests that as well as satisfying the dreams of cottars of good character, 'the muir' may partly have been used as a dumping ground for disorderly tenants, and that the lots soon became known as 'Canada' – a distant land from which few returned.

But there is no disputing the fact that the Campbells of Shawfield had changed the face of Islay. As well as building the grand 'big hoose', they had revitalised agriculture, promoted fisheries, improved the infrastructure and created well-planned modern villages, not least Bowmore. But their reign lasted only 120 years. Walter Frederick Campbell – 'despondent beyond measure' – ran out of money. In 1848 his estate was sequestrated.

> Islay is again in a transition state. It has slipped out of the hands of the gentleman who recently held it, and is now in the hands of Commissioners and a Trustee, and advertised to be sold in a few days. We forbear to detail the doings of these parties because they are sufficiently well known, and because the time for passing sentence upon them, has not yet arrived. But not withstanding all this we cannot forbear reminding them, that the position which they now occupy, as *pro tem* Lords of Islay, is one of great responsibility, and that they, like all those who have preceded them, will one day be called to account for their stewardship. To fit them for this, let them muse over the grave of Sir Lachlan Maclean at Kilchoman, and take a quiet walk among the ruins of the Macdonalds' palace at Finlagan, and there learn, if they have not already learned it, "that, however exalted the station of any individual may be, or however extensive and conspicuous his sphere of action, its duration is extremely short; and that the revolution of a few years puts an end to all artificial distinctions, and place the high and the low, the rich and the poor, the victor and the vanquished, on the same level."

> William MacDonald, *Sketches of Islay*, 1850

Walter's bankruptcy meant that his son – one of the era's most remarkable scholars – didn't inherit Islay. But John Francis Campbell became a distinguished folklorist. He was a gifted linguist and had an easy empathy with his 'social inferiors' – including John Murdoch, the son of one of his father's tenants. Murdoch was to become a renowned journalist and campaigner for the rights of crofter and cottar. Although he was the scourge of the landed classes, Murdoch had a (not uncritical) admiration for the Campbell laird.

At the time I speak of, Walter Frederick Campbell, laird of Islay, was in the prime of his early manhood. He was really a handsome man, possessing good features, great vigour and a love of what are called manly sports. Around him were mature men of which such a man might be proud. And that he was animated by a good Highland feeling is shown by the training he arranged for his son, John Francis.

John Murdoch, unpublished autobiography, 1889–1898

As soon as I was out of the hands of nursemaids, I was handed over to the care of a piper. His name was the same as mine, John Campbell, and from him I learned a good many useful arts. I learned to be hardy and healthy and I learned Gaelic. I learned to swim and to take care of myself, and to talk to everyone who chose to talk to me. My kilted nurse and I were always walking about in foul weather or fair, and every man, woman or child in the place had something to say to us. Thus I made early acquaintance with a blind fiddler who could recite stories. I worked with the carpenters; I played shinty with all the boys about the farm; and so I got to know a good deal about the ways of Highlanders by growing up as a Highlander myself.

John Francis Campbell, *Popular Tales of the West Highlands*, 1860–62

I found John Francis a young, soft, gentle, growing boy in the charge of *Am Piobair Mor*. This was John Campbell, a Lorne man of quiet, steady character, well informed and a good piper. He wore the Highland dress and spoke good Gaelic; and, from what we read in *The West Highland Tales*, he must have had some Highland lore in his head. Such was the early tutor which the then laird of Islay placed over his son. One result was that the son spoke the language of the country from his youth and took part in all the hardy exercises of the people. And without making a long story of what followed, this part of John Francis Campbell's education formed his great inheritance when he came to man's estate.

John Murdoch, unpublished autobiography, 1889–1898

There is a fascinating theory that the dashing and sophisticated *Iain òg Ìle* (Young John of Islay) turned the head of a St Kilda girl called Marion Gillies. Anne Lorne Gillies' majestic *Songs of Gaelic Scotland* suggests that the smitten girl may have written a love song to John Francis Campbell. Here is a little of that song:

ISLAY VOICES

Mo ghaol òigear a' chùil duinn

Mo ghaol òigear a' chùil duinn
dhan dug mi mo loinn cho mòr;
dhùraiginn dhut pòg san anmoch
ged bhiodh càch ga sheanchas oirnn;
mo ghaol òigear a' chùil duinn
dhan dug mi mo loinn cho mòr.

Dhòmhnaill dhualaich 'ic Gillìosa,
bha thu uair a bha thu strì rium,
ach on thàinig an tighearn' Ìleach
sguiridh mi gad bhrìodal beòil:

mo ghaol òigear a' chùil duinn
dhan dug mi mo loinn cho mòr.

Gura mise tha gu h-uallach
on a thàinig an duin' uasal,
le mo ribinnean mun cuairt dhomh:
cumaidh iad mo ghruag air dòigh;

mo ghaol òigear a' chùil duinn
dhan dug mi mo loinn cho mòr.

Cha dèan mi sùgradh ri gillean,
chan fhaod iad bhith rium a' mire;
on tha 'n Caimbeulach gam shireadh
chan fhaigh iad tuilleadh nam chòir:

mo ghaol òigear a' chùil duinn
dhan dug mi mo loinn cho mòr.

Mo ghaol òigear a' chùil duinn, St Kilda song attributed to Marion
Gillies

My darling is the brown-haired young man

My darling is the brown-haired young man
With whom I fell so completely in love;
I'd kiss you late at night

148

Even if everyone gossiped about us –
My darling is the brown-haired young man
With whom I fell so completely in love.

Curly-haired Donald Gillies,
You were trying to win me once,
But since the noble Islay-man came
I no longer dally with you:

My darling is the brown-haired young man
With whom I fell so completely in love.

I've been feeling so pleased with myself
Since this gentleman visited,
With my ribbons all about me:
They keep my hair in order;

My darling is the brown-haired young man
With whom I fell so completely in love.

I won't flirt with mere lads,
They are not allowed to play around with me;
Since the Campbell sought me out
They don't get near me any more:

My darling is the brown-haired young man
With whom I fell so completely in love.

My darling is the brown-haired young man, St Kilda song, attributed to Marion Gillies (Anne Lorne Gillies, *Songs of Gaelic Scotland*, 2005)

Whether a besotted Marion Gillies wrote that song about *Iain òg Ìle* or not, John Francis Campbell was very unusual among Highland aristocrats, as John Murdoch noted.

The landlord if born at all among his people, is carefully removed from the reach of their Celtic influences and educated so as to have a language and a mode of thinking quite foreign to the sphere in which he is destined to act the most important parts in the serious drama of life. One consequence is that not one landlord in a hundred is capable of communicating directly with the great bulk of his people. There is thus an impenetrable barrier raised between him and them.

John Murdoch rightly deserves his reputation as a Highland radical. Deeply influenced by the Irish Land League, he campaigned for land reform and the Gaelic language, and launched a newspaper, *The Highlander*, to support these causes.

Words poured from Murdoch's pen – articles, pamphlets and an unpublished autobiography. The editors of this anthology are indebted to Dr James Hunter, author of *For the People's Cause*, a deft distillation of the best of Murdoch's writings published in 1986, the centenary of the Crofters Act, by HMSO Books.

Although John Murdoch was born in the crofting hamlet of Ardclach, in Nairnshire, his family moved to Islay when he was a child, and he spent his formative years and part of his adulthood there. When asked about his identity, he replied: 'I feel myself as if I were an Islay man.'

Our removal from Perthshire to the island of Islay took place in the year 1827. I remember our staying for a night in Perth, also the steep and narrow bridge at Stirling – but not much else along the way to Glasgow. I do remember Tarbert, then a very small place. And well do I remember the voyage on a small sloop to Port Askaig on the Sound of Islay. The steamer *Maid of Islay* was off the station; and, there being no wind, we were at the mercy of tides for I do not know how long. It was summer when we reached 'The Queen of the Hebrides'. But I do not feel as if I caught the enthusiasm which this destination should have kindled. Coming as we did from a richly wooded district, I at once felt the absence of trees. No doubt the island was elevated to the rank of Queen on account of its superior fertility – not on account of its beauty.

John Murdoch, unpublished autobiography, 1889–1898

His father became both a tenant of, and a gamekeeper to, Walter Frederick Campbell. The Murdochs lived at a small farm at Claggan about a mile from the impressive Campbell mansion, and the young Murdoch became friends with the laird's young son, John Francis Campbell.

But while John Francis attended Eton and Edinburgh University, Murdoch received an elementary education. He was, however, a voracious reader. Murdoch became an exciseman, and his duties took him to Lancashire, where his now widowed mother came to stay.

In Lancashire I was very nearly married to an attractive, nice young girl. But my mother coming spoiled that project. My mother had got into hot water with William Webster, the factor, in Islay. He wished to victimise her and to secure to himself some effects which my father had left. She lost Claggan and it was thought well that she should come and live with me . . .

However, a vacancy occurring at Bridgend in Islay, I asked for the Ride and was sent there. Thus we got back to Islay in the Autumn of 1845 – and after knocking about, took up our abode in Bowmore. John MacLachlan was settled in Claggan and we could not get back there. Had we done so it is not improbable that I should have stuck to the farm and left the excise.

Murdoch later regretted that he had not made better use of these years on Islay.

Of course, it was not for many years afterwards that John Francis Campbell gave an impetus to the movement for saving folklore. Had he begun at this time, I could have rendered him immense help and saved many tales which have since been lost beyond all recovery.

Instead, Murdoch made friends with a group of progressive young islanders, who met to discuss science, history, poetry, theology and politics.

After so many years, I confess that if we had divided the island between us at that time and made a point of collecting all the lore then existing, we should have done ten times the good we did.

We spent the time mostly in each other's houses – the society sweetened by the presence of young ladies of whom there were a good many in the island at the time. We had at Bridgend a little gathering at which papers were read and subjects discussed. What these subjects were, I do not remember. But I know the land question, was under discussion in the autumn if 1847 when the laird of Islay failed.

The bankruptcy of Walter Frederick Campbell left Islay entirely in the hands of factors.

The laird was now away. The trustees were in Edinburgh. And Webster was more master in the island than ever. He had not even a co-factor, as he had previously in Mr Cheyne, and he drove things pretty well as he chose. The case as between himself and the laird was remarkable in that the master went bankrupt – while the servant had nearly all the best lands in the island in his hands.

He had got himself planted in the best house in the island when he came at first. And now that things were getting into a state of dissolution he was taking farms in every direction – until I remember old Sandy Campbell and myself making up one day that he had farms which had been held by 37 substantial farmers in former times. It was observed, too, that when any men who came about could be turned to account, he encouraged them. And then, when they were no longer likely to be of service to him, he threw them aside and let them sink.

The failing of Walter Frederick Campbell came as a great blow to many a one. For all his extravagance and passionateness, he possessed all the natural elements of popularity. He was a fine looking man with a ruddy complexion and brown hair. He was strong and active, too, and took much delight in promoting manly sport. To the folly of shooting and game preservation, however, he was devoted to an excessive degree. He carried this craze so far that there was no offence so great, in his eyes, as to meddle with game and salmon.

John Murdoch, unpublished autobiography, 1889–1898

Although Murdoch admired Campbell as a man, he condemned him as a landlord. For a Dublin magazine, he assumes the role of an Irishman visiting Islay for the first time. Here he describes land cleared by Campbell to make way for a Lowland farmer, George White.

The people are kept poor, the land waste; and from the community generally is withheld the wealth which this land and this labour are capable of yielding. Nor is Kilchoman at all peculiar in this respect. After exploring many miles in Islay we can declare, from the marks of cultivation with which we met, that in times past nature was taken at her word in this matter and beginnings were made to bring the wastes into subjection to the will and wellbeing of man.

In some places we found the ruins of the humble husbandman's cottage; in others there remained nothing to tell where a human habitation had been but the nettle; whilst ridges, and even fences, could in many places be discerned far away in the interior of wild regions now left to the undisputed dominion of heather and wildfowl. The now prevalent notion that it is only by a system of high and large farming that the most can be made of the soil, and another notion in

The cross at Kilchoman, a fourteenth-century masterpiece with ancient folk traditions. (Photographer: Archibald Cameron)

Kildalton Chapel, one of many ancient Christian sites on Islay. Kildalton dates from the thirteenth century. (Archibald Cameron)

Port Askaig and the Paps of Jura. (Archibald Cameron)

Bruichladdich from across Lochindaal. Ships took refuge from storms here and the loch's name may be derived from the Gaelic for Loch of Delay. (Archibald Cameron)

Rhinns lighthouse on the tiny island of Orsay, opposite Port Wemyss. It was Islay's first lighthouse, built by Robert Louis Stevenson's grandfather, Robert, and completed in 1825. (Archibald Cameron)

Port Charlotte and Lochindaal, with Laggan Point and the Mull of Oa in the background.
(Archibald Cameron)

Port Ellen, one of the planned villages created by Walter Frederick Campbell.
(Archibald Cameron)

Islay House was built by generations of Campbell and Morrison landlords from between 1677 and 1911. Locals called it Tigh Bàn, *the White House.* (Archibald Cameron)

Machrie Strand, Kilchoman. (Archibald Cameron)

Mount Zion on Machrie Golf Course. (Archibald Cameron)

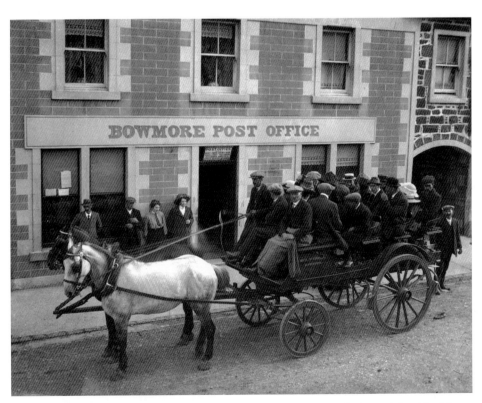

Bowmore Post Office around 1910. Regular communications with the mainland had been established by the Stent Committee which, in 1771, imposed a tax of just over £32 to run a mail boat between Islay and Tarbert. (Archibald Cameron)

Bowmore around 1910, seen from the pier and looking up Main Street to the Round Church. The first house on the right is an inn where the Stent Committee had once met.
(Archibald Cameron)

Portnahaven – a fishing community on the far west point of the Rhinns of Islay.
(Archibald Cameron)

Stacking peats for Laphroaig Distillery. Peat gives the distinctive smoky flavour to most Islay malt whisky. (Unknown photographer, courtesy of the Museum of Islay Life)

Lagavulin Distillery. In the eighteenth century the bay was a notorious centre of illicit distilling. (Archibald Cameron)

Workers at Caol Ila Distillery. (Unknown photographer, courtesy of the Museum of Islay Life)

Workers at Port Ellen Distillery. Once they produced 140,000 gallons annually. Today it is one of Scotland's 'lost distilleries'. (Archibald Cameron)

Mending creels at Caol Ila. Crab and lobster fishing has traditionally been – and remains – an important industry on Islay. (Archibald Cameron)

The Council Road Crew at Blue Houses, on Lochindaal. Previously, local cottars and labourers were drafted in to build and repair Islay's roads. (Photograph courtesy of George Rhind.)

The quarry at Carnain around 1910. Alistair MacEwan collecting stones for the building of roads. (Archibald Cameron)

Workers at the harvest on Claddach Farm in the 1920s. They are Neil McKinnon, Donald Murdoch, Angus Ferguson, Donald McFadyen and Ian MacArthur.
(Unknown photographer, courtesy of the Museum of Islay Life)

Funeral of Tuscania *victims at Kilnaughton, February 1918.* (Archibald Cameron)

'The Wild West', Lossit, Rhinns of Islay. The rugged coast made the west of Islay a fatal shore for many ships, including the troopship Otranto. (Archibald Cameron)

Funeral of Otranto *victims at Kilchoman, October 1918.* (Archibald Cameron)

Survivors of the Otranto *treat their rescuers to afternoon tea at the Bridgend Hotel. One of the survivors wears a tea-cosy as a hat, while another has borrowed the bonnet of Private Woodrow of the Seaforth Highlanders, who had played his bagpipes at the* Otranto *funerals.* (American Red Cross photograph)

*The American Monument on the Mull of Oa – built to commemorate more than 500
American soldiers who died when two British troopships sank off Islay in 1918.*
(Archibald Cameron)

Horses carrying seaweed. Seaweed, along with Islay's natural limestone, has been used as fertiliser for centuries. (Archibald Cameron)

Finlaggan – the island on this freshwater loch was the seat of the great Medieval rulers, the Lords of the Isles. (Archibald Cameron)

Duncan MacNiven who, with his brother, Charles, were known as the Kilchoman Bards.
(Photograph courtesy of Etta Shaw)

Islay's first school bus, operated by D. & N. MacKenzie, in 1932. This photograph was donated to the Museum of Islay Life by Moira MacLaren, whose mother, Katie Ferguson, is in the front row, fifth from the right.
(Unknown photographer, courtesy of the Museum of Islay Life)

pursuance of which men are banished to make a solitude for game, have in too many instances in Scotland interfered with the obvious designs of nature. And, as a great and melancholy result, we find the land in a state of wild unproductiveness while the people who ought to be cultivating it are wanderers in strange lands.

Instead of pursuing a south-eastern course from Kilchoman, we turned westward, by a road which crosses the Rinns of Islay diagonally, and made our way towards another of those spots favored alike by nature and by man – and thus selected by the primitive missionaries as camps for themselves, places of worship for their followers and resting places for the dead. This was Kilchiaran. Here we found a very snug looking farmhouse situated on the bosom of a fertile slope facing the western ocean and curving towards the head of a deep gullet in the rocks below.

On every side there were to be found rich fields, some extending a considerable distance into the interior where they were surrounded by the heathy moorland. About a stone's throw from the dwellinghouse was a suit of outhouses for the accommodation of the stock of an extensive and well laid-out farm. And a little further off still was an old thatched and soot stained house bearing every mark of belonging to another age and another order of things. The old and the new stood side by side in a goodly place where, one would suppose, either could well have thrived. And yet there was no sign of that animation and that prosperity which one is apt to associate with an improved modern Scotch farm steading. The old had lost the life which had at one time pertained to it. And it was hard to say whether the new had ever possessed any life or not. The fine, large farm of Kilchiaran was, in short, without a tenant. And one could imagine the old, begrimed and condemned house of the peasant farmer, who held possession there before the new house was dreamt of, taking to himself some consolation from seeing the more imposing edifice provided for the favoured Saxon now forsaken and yielding to the dissolving elements.

This old house is the only one now remaining of the homes of 25 families which, about 30 years ago, lived in this one farm or townland of Kilchiaran. Of these families, six were those of regular farmers who held the land from the proprietor – the rest being cottars who had houses, and enjoyed certain privileges, from the chief tenants.

John Murdoch, Manuscript (National Library of Scotland), 1858

After describing the day-to-day life of this little community, which Murdoch points out was like thousands of others in the Highlands, he describes its downfall.

> But by false and foolish council the proprietor was induced to break up this prosperous little community. A Fifeshire farmer, supposed to be wealthy, came to the country to look for a farm. Kilchiaran was the one he coveted. The landlord, desirous of introducing the light of Lowland farming among his people, agreed to let the stranger have the land – even before the expiration of the leases by which the natives held it. He offered these natives farms elsewhere – an offer which some accepted. But whether they accepted or not, they were all turned out and dispersed and the Fifeshire man installed – not exactly in their place but in the new house and steading which were prepared for him.
>
> Some of the old tenants went to the law with the landlord and were ruined. Some went to America. One man, whom we met on our tour, is a miserable pauper in the country. And one, in his extremity, stole a few turnips from a field belonging to the proprietor, was imprisoned for the felony and died of disgrace and a broken heart. As a natural consequence, the humble cottars were scattered to the four winds of heaven. And not one stone remains upon another to tell where their cosy hearths once blazed – excepting what we saw in the one old sooty house of which mention has already been made.

Murdoch then tells us that the Fifeshire man's lowland methods were ridiculed by the deposed farmer and cottars – and failed amid the weather and landscape of Islay.

> In three or four years he threw the farm, the new house and the costly steading on the landlord's hands and left the place for ever.
>
> A curse seems to have hung over it ever since. It is now more than 30 years since the deed of wrong was perpetrated. And from that day to this, no one – landlord or tenant – has been able to make anything of it. One or two Lowland tenants have since made an attempt to turn the place to account – but with even worse results than those which attended the first man's essay and with still additional losses to the landlord who, not to speak of the increased rent which he might naturally have expected, lost all the capital which he sank in the new buildings.

But these results surprised no one who at all was imbued with the spirit of the ancient polity of the native Celtic people. The power of the landlord was unjustly exercised to gratify the covetousness of the stranger. Both sowed iniquity and they reaped simply the fruit of their own doings. In short, the case of Kilchiaran is but one among thousands which can be quoted by the thoughtful Highlander to show that it is not only wrong to take land from under another man's feet, but that wrong cannot be perpetuated without bringing its own visible punishment.

Walter Frederick Campbell, who was an MP, argued to a Parliamentary committee that the 'redundant' population of the Highlands should be subsidised to emigrate.

The proprietors, instead of receiving rents, are in times of scarcity, obliged to support the population; but if they were removed, farms might be enlarged instead of divided; for, at present, a farmer having sixty or a hundred acres of arable land, will give to each of his three or four sons, when they marry, a portion of his farm. These sons again divide, till the produce of the farm is insufficient to support the families living on it. The Proprietors have, indeed, the power of preventing sub-letting, and Mr Campbell has strictly forbidden it; but when the proprietors are not resident, divisions are more particularly carried on.

There is a sort of affection in that country between landlord and tenant that would prevent the former from contributing for the removal of the latter, notwithstanding the inconvenience, unless it were clearly for his advantage. But if the redundant population were once removed, the landlords have suffered too much to admit of subdivision of the future. He has relieved himself by persuading them to give up their land and reside in villages with enough land for potatoes and a cow's grass; but some refuse to give up their lands: in such cases he would have been glad to have got them to emigrate, and would have advanced a moderate sum of money for the purpose, providing the bonus held out to them was advantageous, how much he could not say; in some instances he might have given 3/- each; but his situation is more favorable than that of many other proprietors, who would be induced to give more than he had. The disposition of many of the people is toward emigration, they would, in many instances, move heaven and earth to scrape the money together, if the landlord did not . . .

... There is at present a certain degree of prejudice against emigration, as some had emigrated to America under speculators who took their little property from them, and having nothing to begin upon, could nether get land nor money, and returned completely beggars; but if the bonus held out to them was such that they had a chance of being made comfortable by their own labour, they would receive it as a very great boon. – By the term bonus, I mean receiving land and work.

Report of the Select Committee on Emigration, 1826

Islay's history of ownership, and the continuing poverty of the people, made dismal reading for progressive commentators.

In reading over what has been written there is a melancholy reflection which will present itself to the thoughtful, viz., that almost all is taken up with the deeds of the great, the people being lost sight of almost entirely, excepting as so many passive creatures, fit for war or fit for the payment of rent, and responsible to no authority but that of the owners of the soil. As the Island passed from one Lord to another, it did so with its unwitting complement of serfs, called tenants, almost as completely and virtually as a South Carolina plantation does with its pack of negro "servants." The apologists of British slavery may say that Tenants are at liberty to leave their country, whereas American slaves are not. True; and they are also at liberty to perish for want of food whilst the land lies waste, because they cannot pay an exorbitant price for liberty to till God's earth at home! There is hope, however, that a better fate awaits Islay yet. Let the Plan proposed in the accompanying Essay be carried out, and whosoever has the writing of Islay's History in 1950 will have a much more pleasant task to perform in recording the peaceful endeavors of a free and industrious people after true, rational, and moral greatness.

William MacDonald, *Sketches of Islay*, 1850

The accompanying essay that was attached to Dr MacDonald's *Sketches* was an alternative plan, by John Murdoch, for the disposal of Walter Frederick Campbell's sequestrated Islay Estate. Murdoch summed up his scheme in his autobiography.

It was while the Islay estates were in the hands of trustees that I drew up a plan for the sale of the properties. I had in view the setting up of a peasant proprietary in Islay and leaving, after all the debts were paid, 20,000 acres to the late laird – of the annual value of £2000 or £3000. The population which was to be provided for then was 15,000. So I proposed that 120,000 acres out of the 140,000 should be laid out in 3000 lots averaging 28 acres – of which 12 should be arable . . .

. . . I founded my scheme for the sale of a large part of the island on the supposition that men would buy small portions of land and be able in time to pay the price.

John Murdoch, unpublished autobiography, 1889–1898

Unsurprisingly, John Murdoch's radical plans were never adopted. Campbell's Islay was simply sold as a job lot to the highest bidder.

After a short bidding war with the Lanarkshire industrialist, James Baird, James Morrison, a London merchant banker and former Member of Parliament, bought Campbell's Islay estate for £451,000. Entry was at Martinmas, 11 November, 1853. When Campbell of Shawfield had purchased Islay 130 years earlier the price had been £12,000.

Emigration

Under the ownership of James Morrison, who may have been the richest commoner in Britain, the many chimneys of Islay House smoked again. But, elsewhere on the island, hundreds of fires had already been extinguished.

> We are informed from the western isles, that upwards of 500 souls from Islay, and the adjacent islands, prepare to migrate next summer to America, under the conduct of a gentleman of wealth and merit . . .
>
> *Scots Magazine*, Summer 1771

One commentator recognised a 'brain drain' from Islay – with the brightest and best being the ones to emigrate.

> In 1841 the population was 18,071, whilst in 1831 it was 19,700; shewing a considerable falling off in numbers. Emigration has not only drained away numbers, but actually the choice of the people, who now seek in other countries the success which did not seem to attend the possession and exercise of energy, skill, intelligence and generosity; but which meet with their reward wherever else the genuine Islayman gets a footing. The full character of the real Islay people can scarcely now be ascertained; as the present population consists chiefly of remnants of emigrated families, and immigrants from other parts of the Highlands and Lowlands, and also from Ireland.
>
> William MacDonald, *Sketches of Islay*, 1850

> . . . alas! alas! the "evictor" has been at work in Islay, for all around are seen the ruins of many cottages and farmhouses. I was told that where there were at one time fifty or sixty families resident, one shepherd now is only required to look after his woolly subjects. In bygone times that which was a splendid recruiting ground for the British Army is gone, the marks of cultivation are fast disappearing, and what were once fertile fields are now being obliterated; sheep and sport are more to some lairds than human beings, for the bold

and hardy peasantry are no longer considered necessary. The men who in olden times were the pride of the country are now gone to strengthen distant lands, but where'er they be, their hearts yearn with a tender regard for the isle of their nativity and,

"To the old thatch cottage on Western Island,
With its heather-clad mountains surrounded by seas,
Though our eyes cannot see our old home in the Highlands,
Yet in dreams we are carried to the dear Hebrides.

"Our youth was spent in climbing thy mountains
Or sailing along thy western seas,
Again we would smell the bloom of thy heather,
Islay, ever verdant, Queen of the Hebrides."

Robert Thomson, *A Cruise in the Western Hebrides or a Week on Board the SS Hebridean*, 1891

By the last census, (April 1881) the population of the Island was 7526. During the last decade there has been a decrease of 613; the most of whom have become the bone and sinew of the great iron manufactories of Glasgow and Greenock. The decrease, however, can scarcely be looked upon as a calamity; in fact, the material comfort of those who have gone and those who have remained has been increased.

Robert Oliphant, *The Tourist's Guide to Islay, The Queen of the Hebrides*, 1881

To walk, *to-day*, among the glens of the Oa or to wander through the meadows beyond Ballygrant is like following in the wake of a ravaging army; like viewing the devastation of a plague. To-day the sheep graze round the deserted clachan, and the nettle grows rank among the crumbling ruins. An adder, the only tenant, glides under the wall and the grim skeleton of what was once called by the sacred name of *home* lifts its naked gables to heaven as if in protest – a sermon in stones, a monument and a sign. It was that Celtic hero Galgacus who, in the first century, used the words which might to-day be written over many a landscape up and down this Scotland of ours, "They have made a solitude and they call it peace."

L. MacNeill Weir, *Guide to Islay*, 1911

But what of those left behind? One splenetic Victorian tourist – who described Islay women as 'slatternly' and Islay men as knowing of nothing 'excepting whisky and potatoes' – put the blame for the islanders' many ills squarely on the shoulders of the landlords.

> They are the characteristics of an enslaved people, and the consequence of a state of serfdom . . . Ground down by a landed aristocracy who treated them like dogs, they have gradually increased in poverty and misery.
>
> Seeing none on earth, they place all their hope on heaven, and possessed of a strange mixture of superstition and religion, through a life of labour, immorality and devotion, pass wearily to the grave.

> W.A. Smith, *Off the Chain*, 1868

The 1870s and '80s saw an outbreak of agitation in the Highlands and Islands that has come to be known as the Crofters' War. People were rebelling against rising rents and lack of tenure and access to land. Their weapons were rent strikes and land raids. John Murdoch's newspaper, *The Highlander*, valiantly supported the cause.

This agitation, and the disquiet of the landlords, prompted the Liberal Government of Prime Minister Gladstone to do what Governments do. It set up a public inquiry.

Lord Francis Napier's commission took evidence from hundreds of crofters and cottars. Although Napier's recommendations did not directly shape the Crofters' Act that followed in 1886, it played a huge part in informing the public about the lamentable state of the rural powerless and poor, and sharpened the appetite for change.

As well as describing the hard lives of crofters, the transcripts of the evidence give remarkable insights into the social and political attitudes of the late Victorian era.

While Napier and his five colleagues travelled extensively through the Highlands and Islands – they were almost shipwrecked and drowned off Stornoway – they also took evidence in Glasgow. On the 19th and 20th of October, 1883, the Commissioners interviewed Islay men there.

Islay-born Free Kirk minister, John McNeill, prefixed his evidence by reading out a letter from a landlord who refused to confirm that no action who be taken against any of her tenants who gave evidence.

The Chairman.
Have you got a written statement to make?

— Yes. Before I read the written statement, will you allow me to make reference to two letters which I have got here, bearing on the delegates who have come with me from Islay. The delegates are from two different estates. Two are from the estate of Mr Morrison of Islay and three from the estate, of Mrs Baker of Liverpool. I wrote to Mr Morrison's factor about the men from Mr Morrison's estate, and he says: *'I can assure you that no action will be taken against the delegates from Port Wemyss on account of any evidence by them before the Commission in Glasgow on the twentieth.'*

The other letter is from Mrs Baker, the proprietrix of Cladach and Port-na-haven, to the following effect: *'I am favoured with your letter this morning. I distinctly refuse to bind myself by any such terms as you ask for. I hope your delegates are not losing their brave spirits, and beginning to show the white feather. They shall have all the credit of their bravery, and shall not give evidence under shelter of any promise of protection from me. Your representatives seem to be chosen from the worst specimens in the village'* —they are here before you — *'but I should not like to put much faith in the Highlanders, as I am afraid they are a little treacherous.'*

Was this letter intended to be read here by the lady who wrote it?

—That is what I meant when I wrote to her. I asked such a promise, and she distinctly refuses.

Yes, but you might have stated the fact without reading the letter.

—I mean not particularly with reference to the assurance, but with reference to the character she gives of the delegates. Do you think the lady, when she wrote the letter, wished and understood that you were to read the letter aloud in so far as the character of the delegates is concerned? Do you think the lady would like that?

—I don't know that.

Do you think she intended that letter to be read aloud in a public assembly or not?

—Well, she did not desire me not to read it.

Perhaps she could not anticipate you would read it. However, it is read now, and I cannot help it. I am bound to say I regret it was read, because I think you could have communicated the fact. The only important thing to us was that this lady refused to give any assurance. I think you might have stated that fact without reading the letter, another portion of which is apt to destroy the confidence or kindly feeling between the lady and her tenants, and which she did not probably expect to be read. You have now a written statement to make?

—Yes.

The Reverend McNeill's written statement has a contemporary edge to it. Lamenting the plight of the 'wretchedly poor', and quoting a plethora of statistics about acreage and rents, he argued that Islay's problem was not a lack of land or wealth, but the unfair distribution of it.

These statistics clearly prove that Islay is not over-populated, but contrariwise that there is in it enough of land and to spare for a population fully twice as large as its present number. There is therefore no necessity in reason, nor in policy, for the adoption of a compulsory scheme of emigration with reference to Islay. If there are centres of congested population in the island, they are entirely restricted to badly planned villages, the receptacles into which have been unwisely compressed the capriciously evicted crofters, the helpless remnants of emigrated families. The cruel process of eviction commenced in Islay in the year 1831, under the so-called mild administration of the Campbells, whose ancestor, Mr Daniel Campbell of Shawfield, bought it one hundred years before that for £6080, sold at £450,000. This silent system of depopulation and consequent deportation was vigorously prosecuted all over Islay during the decennium terminating at census 1841. During the currency of that period a few emigrant vessels left Lochindaal, on board one of these were packed off 402 souls.

During this decade from 1831 to 1841, 1300 emigrants sadly departed from the fertile shores of green and grassy Islay. The beautiful glens and the sunny bens were ruthlessly denuded of over 1200 native peasantry during the decennium ending with 1851. The two successive census periods of 1861 and 1871 show the hitherto unprecedented decrease of 4176 in the rural population of Islay. The census of 1881 exhibits a further decrease of 613. Fifty years ago the population of the island was 14,992, now it is only 7526. The family dispersal policy, begun by the Campbells, was bitterly intensified under their trustees, and was consummately perpetuated under the succeeding landlords till within a recent date.

The Reverend McNeill described conditions in his own parish.

The village of Port-na-haven was formed on exposed, bare, barren rocks in the year 1818 by Captain Walter Campbell of Sunderland, Islay. It contains a population of 361 souls. The original idea was to make it a fishing village, but practically it has been a haven of refuge for the migratory individuals of rural families who had been dispossessed of their homes. They were allowed to erect one-storied dwelling houses, consisting of one room and kitchen as a rule, on the following co-operative principle – site for house and small plot of ground for garden, annual rent 13s., the tenant to build a house according to proprietor's plan, the tenant to furnish all the building material at his own expense, except the wood and slates, which were furnished by the proprietor at 7½ per cent. per annum during the currency of the lease, a period of ninety-nine years. The tenant at the same time was bound to keep the roof in sufficient repair at his own expense, besides paying 7½ per cent. yearly on the outlay on roof, amounting to sums varying from 19s. and 27s. in the case of each tenant who agreed to build on this principle.

McNeill reported that the cost of paying for their roofs caused some tenants to fall into arrears and lose their homes. In Portnahaven even that traditional Hebridean 'perk' – driftwood – was denied.

. . . a vessel with a cargo of wood was wrecked in the immediate vicinity of this village, and no person was allowed to buy a log of it save the superior, who secured it all, and gave the use of it to the tenants on the above most unreasonable terms.

McNeill stated that there were twenty-two inhabitants without crofts:

Twelve of these have neither croft, boat, cow, nor house of their own. They are all in deep poverty.

A further seventy-five families had inadequately small crofts. And on this peat-rich island, cooking and keeping warm meant paying the landlord.

The people who formerly could secure peats on their own lots have now to cut them on a neighbouring farm, each family paying annually for a bad and insufficient supply from 5s. to 10s. The superior gets this money, but the people at their own expense have to keep the peat ground from being flooded with water, because having been in some cases cut twice and thrice it is irregularly hollowed out, and much water lodges on it.

The fishing, which has been a comparative failure for some years, cannot be prosecuted under existing conditions for more than four months in the year; and as there are neither public works, agricultural industries, nor any other local remunerative employment, the ill-used, able-bodied fishermen, to keep the wolf from the door, are compelled to seek work outside the island. Some go to sea, others go to centres of trade and commerce, such as Greenock and Glasgow. I know the islands well from the Butt of Lewis to the Rhinns of Islay, and independently of their earnings outside Islay, the villagers of Port-na-haven are the poorest class of fishing crofters ever I saw. Those of them who have neither crofts nor cows are constantly on the verge of starvation.

As the landlords take little interest in them, were it not for their proximity to the Clyde shipbuilding yards, where they get work in winter, they would absolutely perish with hunger on a productive wealthy island. A district called Balmeanach, with a goodly number of comfortable and thriving crofters and cottars, was cleared out by Captain Walter Campbell, although none of the crofters were in arrears of rent. This township was added to a neighbouring farm, and the capriciously removed families sought shelter in the neighbouring villages.

Professor Mackinnon.

What is the minimum croft, of those you know yourself, where a family could be reared by hard work; what is about the rent of such a croft, as you know them yourself, in Islay just now?

—I should think thirty acres.

What would be about the rent?

—Over £20.

Do you think a croft under £20 of rent, as rents go there just now, could not bring up a family?

—Not very well.

What is the average number of a family taking them all overhead?

—About five.

Well, supposing the place was rearranged as you would wish it in crofts from £20 upwards, do you think that the island could support more than its present population?

—I think it could.

It has been stated to us often that it might have been better for the fisherman to be a fisherman and the crofter to be a crofter; would you agree with that view, looking to the state of matters in Port-na-haven?

—I don't think that would suit Port-na-haven. The people cannot prosecute the fishing all the year round, and they would require something to support their families over and above the fishing. The coast is so rough and the current so strong that when a succession of storms comes in winter they cannot go to sea, and unless they have some land to support their families they must leave the island to earn money.

Where is the fishing ground off Port-na-haven?

—They go to Barra to fish.

But at home?

—A good distance from the shore.

Right out?

—Yes.

Mr Fraser-Mackintosh.

Have you occasion yourself to observe, in the performance of your ministerial duties, a deal of poverty in that beautiful and naturally fertile island?

—Yes. Sometimes on a Saturday night, if it is a stormy week, if there is a fisherman who depends entirely on the fishing and has no croft, we have to send him what will tide him over the Sabbath or a day or two after that. That has been done by myself.

Really a case of living from hand to mouth?

—Yes.

And you, as a native of the island, no doubt feel very deeply the position of your fellow islesmen?

—Yes.

> *Report of Her Majesty's Commissioners of Inquiry into the Condition of the Crofters.* Rev. John M'Neill, Minister of the Free Church, Port-na-haven, Islay, 1883

Two years before the poverty of the Highlands and Islands prompted the setting up of the Napier Commission, Glasgow publisher, Wilson and M'Cormick, issued a handy guidebook to Islay, priced sixpence. We have already quoted from it at length. However some of its content should be taken with enough salt to preserve a barrel of Portnahaven saithe.

> On the left of Greag-a'-gheòidh, a fine lofty situation, though rather exposed, stands the Free Church Manse, where the Rev. John George MacNeill the pastor has been eminently successful in many ways amongst his people.
>
> The adjacent village of Port-Wemyss, on the Islay Estate, Mr Morrison's property, consists almost wholly of fishermen. The population by the last Census is 263. A number of whom have lots of good land which they diligently cultivate. John Barleycorn keeps at a respectful distance – fancy pictures the good people living in peace, plenty and primeval felicity.

> Robert Oliphant, *The Tourist's Guide to Islay, The Queen of the Hebrides*, 1881

Lots of good land? Primeval felicity? This is the same community that, according to the Rev. McNeill whom Oliphant mentioned, told the Napier Commission two years later that the people were 'wretchedly poor', 'all in deep poverty', and threatened with 'the cruel process of eviction'.

Oliphant's guide book brilliantly – if unconsciously – skewers the class system of the era. Here he is, describing the Duich Lots near Torra Farm:

> About a mile further on, an eminence is gained, from which, the minor holdings called the "Lots" are to be seen – the tenants are of aboriginal descent – their kind landlord, Mr. Ramsay of Kildalton governs them on patriarchal lines, and they are a happy and innocent people.

The author of this guide was Robert Oliphant, who is described as a Bowmore man. He may be the 'Robert Oliphant, accountant' listed as living in Bowmore in the directory at the end of the guidebook. Whoever Oliphant was, he was clearly cast from the same mould as the hymnist who wrote in *All Things Bright and Beautiful*:

> The rich man in his castle, the poor man at his gate,
> God made them, high or lowly, and ordered their estate.

Oliphant is at his most patronising when he describes the half-yearly sittings of the Sheriff Court in Bowmore.

> This half-yearly Assize is one of the few events which occur throughout the course of the year to break the monotony of this sea-girt isle; and generally speaking, it causes a little stir, as being a time, when, as some say, all that's wrong is now set right; while others declare –
>
> > "It's a very good Island to live in –
> > To spend, to lend, or to give in;
> > But to beg, or to borrow, or ask for one's own,
> > It's the very worst Island that ever was known."

> The examination of the witnesses affords some amusement at times, especially the testimony of those whose English is rather faulty. Not unfrequently, it is quite impossible to induce some of them to have the oath administered in English, and give their evidence in that language; and when a dilemma of this kind occurs, many are the pitying and imploring looks cast towards the venerable Clerk, Mr Chisholm, in order that he may come to the rescue.

How quaint these Islay aboriginals are! Fortunately, thanks to the Napier Commission, there are other accounts of conditions on Islay at this period.

JAMES M'NAB, Crofter and Fisherman, Port Wemyss, Islay (50)

The Chairman.
Will you be so good as to make a verbal statement?

—I have only to state that we are in a poor condition; that we have too little land, and that little is not good. The fishing has done very little good to us for the last twenty years. If we had more land we think we would be better off. We are paying interest for drain money for the last thirty-two years, and we would like that remitted. There are twelve families in the village who built new houses, and they have no land at all. The park that we have to graze our cattle is not good. It is small – too small to pasture a cow if each had a cow, and then it is bad, so bad that the cows require to be hand-fed, and the getting of that hand-feeding takes up the services of one to look after the cow, when one has a cow. Mr M'Neill has said everything else that is necessary to be said.

Mr Cameron.
What size of croft have you?

—Two acres. Some of it is very rocky. Probably about one-third of it is rocky. Some of it is very, very bad ground – ground where the peats have been cut off the surface, and where the people themselves have worked, and it is very unprofitable.

What estate are you on?

—Mr Morrison's estate, Port Wemyss.

Do the two acres you talk of represent the whole ground, or have you any pasture ground besides?

—This is the arable ground. There is a common park in which those of us graze our cows who have cows, and we pay separately for that park.

What do you pay for the two acres and the right to graze the cattle in the park?

—I pay 34s. for the two acres, and £1 for my share of the park.

What beasts do you keep in the park?

—A cow and a calf. The calf is allowed with the cow till it is about a year old; but we pay 8s. for the calf. It is 34s. for the arable ground, £1 for the cow, and 8s. for the calf.

And you sell the calf at what age?

—We sell the calf when it is a year old, and if we keep it longer we pay a higher rate for it.

Are they black cattle you keep?

—We are going into the Ayrshire cattle for the last few years. It used to be black cattle.

How many crofters are in the same position as you yourself?

—There are thirty-eight who have land, and each of them has the right to send a cow to the park, but they have not all cows, and if they all had cows the park would not feed them all.

Do you think that, putting aside the cow and the park, 34s. is too dear a rent for two acres of such arable ground ?

—I think it is too dear.

By how much?

—The first rent was £1. Then the late Mr Webster raised the rent by 14s. This addition was not known for two years, and it came upon the people in a lump sum, which bore rather hard upon them. I think that the original rent is quite sufficiently high, if not too high.

When was the rent altered from £1 to 34s.?

—About forty years ago.

Have not a good many changes occurred in the value of agricultural produce in forty years?

—That is the case in some places, but it is the reverse in ours.

In any case, the rent has not been altered or raised for forty years?

—No, except interest for drain money.

What interest do you pay on the drain money?

—Five per cent.

Do you think you have paid it long enough?

—Yes, we think we have paid it too long. We were told we would only have to pay it for twenty-one years, but now we have paid it for eleven years more than that.

Are the drains in working order now?

—Some of them are; many are not.

The Chairman.
You stated you have about two acres of ground, and that you keep one cow and a calf, and pay £1, 14s. for the arable . . . does the £1, 14s. include the rent of the house?

—We pay additional for the house. We pay a feu duty of 15s. Our lease is for sixty years.

How much do you pay for the site of the house?

—15s.

So your whole rent is £2, 9s?

—Yes.

Who built your house; did your family build it themselves?

—My father bought it from the man who built it.

Can you tell me how much he paid for it?

—£30.

How do you dispose of the two areas of ground; how much have you under potatoes?

—About half an acre under potatoes. We plant about four or five barrels.

And the other half in corn?

—Oats.

Is there any general complaint in the place that the soil is becoming less productive?

—That is the general complaint, and the general belief among the people. It is a very rocky place, and constant cropping has made the soil lighter and thinner upon it, so that the pieces beside the bare rock, although sown, are very seldom reaped.

Mr Fraser-Mackintosh.

Mr M'Neill mentioned there was a great deal of land once under cultivation which is now lying untitled under sheep; do you know that to be true of your own observation?

—Yes, I know that.

In other places we have been told that after lands have been in that position for a certain time the very pasture becomes deteriorated; have you observed that?

—Yes. That is the case in Islay. It is getting under rushes for want of being ploughed up again.

Is that going on and extending from year to year?

—Year after year, every year.

Have you any relatives who emigrated or were sent away in former times?

—Yes, I have relatives in America.

Do you hear from them?

—Yes. There are some of them dead, but their families write now and again.

Are their circumstances good?

—Yes; they write that they are pretty well off.

Is there a disinclination on the part of yourself and others like you to leave the country so long as there is any land that you might cultivate with advantage?

—Yes, they are all of that opinion. There is a backwardness to emigration. They think that if they got the chance they might make a living in their own land without being asked to go to foreign lands.

Report of Her Majesty's Commissioners of Inquiry into the Condition of the Crofters, 1883.

John Murdoch, the land reform campaigner, had been asked to represent the people of Islay by the Islay Association of Glasgow.

Mr Fraser-Mackintosh.

You are a native of Islay?

—No, I am a native of the north country. My father was one of the aliens who were introduced into Islay.

But you have a great attachment to that country?

—Yes, I feel myself as if I were an Islay man.

Murdoch's written statement included a stinging attack on landlord John Ramsay of Kildalton. Ramsay was a Stirling-born merchant who had acquired the Port Ellen distillery. When Walter Frederick Campbell's estate was sold in 1853 to England's richest commoner, James Morrison, some of the land was then sold on to Ramsay. Ramsay then went on to purchase the Oa.

> In the division of the estate called Oa, and which is outside entirely of the wretched village of Port Ellen, there are only fifteen farmers and twenty-three cottars, where there were ninety-seven farmers and sixty-six cottars; thirty-eight families where there were 163. Angus M'Cuaig, blacksmith at Gleann a Mhuiluin, told me that in one of the little townships he shod thirty-six horses where now he shoes four. And it is not merely that this land is not inhabited, but there is a covering of rushes on it which renders it incapable of supporting the stock which should be available for the feeding of the people elsewhere. It is not tilled, and the grazing, as elsewhere, is becoming too bad for sheep and cattle; and the chief use I saw it put to was yielding rushes with which to thatch the corn stacks of Cornabus and Lag a Mhuilinn.

Murdoch describes the building of two of Islay's planned villages, Port Ellen and Port Charlotte. These had been created by Walter Frederick Campbell, and named after his first wife and his mother respectively. But Murdoch points out that it was sweat, not capital, that built the homes.

> In 1821 the village of Port Ellen was projected, and 130 houses were built on the promises of 57 years' leases; two-acre lots in case of one-story houses and four acres for two-story houses, together with peat mosses and grazing for cows. Port Charlotte started in 1828, and eighty houses were built on similar expectations. Before giving an idea of their present condition, I will direct attention to what the fact of the erection of the villages demonstrates with regard to the condition of the population when it was twice what it is now. In these two villages there were 210 houses erected in a very few years, and if we estimate them over head at only £80 apiece, we have £16,800 . . .
>   . . .The most of the 210 houses were built without money by small farmers, joiners, masons, weavers, shoemakers, &c. These people jumped at the prospect of having a permanent hold of even two to four acres of land that they could call their own; and they left us proof to demonstration of what can be done with next to no capital,

173

when there is a fair prospect of fruition before the workers. You will ask how on earth they could do such things without capital. First, they could do it all the better when the people were numerous in the island, and when 60 per cent. of them at least were of the farming class, and when even the cottars were possessed of some stock and had access to some land; and where the people are, as now in Lewis, in battalions, we see similar work in hand.

The mason built for the joiner, and vice versa, and both built for the slater; and, meanwhile, numbers of them went to the homes of their parents nightly or weekly, as the case might be, and got their share of what was going. Self-reliance, self-sacrifice, hope, co-operation, on the part of 210 persons without capital produced what would to-day be worth more than £22,000 of property in these two villages. This is my matter-of-fact answer to much of the speculation as to how the landless people are to stock the land and provide houses when the chance is given them.

While admiring the spirit of self-reliance which had built the villages, Murdoch argued that they had been a mistake, and that homes were no use to Ileachs without land to go with them. He claimed that scattered houses, built on little patches of fertile land, and with long leases, would have better supported a growing population and stemmed the flood of emigration. As access to land declined, so too did the planned villages of Port Ellen and Port Charlotte.

The villages could not but decay and go to ruin as the surrounding population lost possession of the land and left the country. The time before last that I was in Port Ellen I counted thirty houses utterly unfit for occupation, and at the present moment, out of the 130 village cottars, there are only 14 who have lots, the possessions of the rest having been consolidated into parks and farms for a few persons. Bad and all as the county is, offers have been made to repair the houses; but the proprietor, Mr Ramsay, refuses leases, and the cancer eats its way into the wretched framework of the village. And so bad are the houses in every way that the wonder is that one-third of them are not deserted. Some of the poor people have been praying to be allowed more room; but they have been refused; and, not long ago, fever broke out in a house in which two families occupied one room apiece. One of these consisted of six members and the other of ten. Flora Logan in the one room and

James Mackintosh in the other—the two bread-winners among the sixteen—were carried off. Eight years ago things were so bad that the schoolhouse had to be closed repeatedly in consequence of the breaking out of epidemics.

Evidence continued the next day.

The Chairman.

You would like to do away with landlordism?

—Decidedly.

And in the Highlands as well as in Ireland?

—Decidedly.

Going back to Islay, the condition of the whole island of Islay is something like this, is it not, that the population has very much decreased, the rental has very much increased, but there remains a considerable deal of poverty; is that the state of matters ?

—Yes, there is far more actual poverty in Islay to-day with 7500 people than there was when there were 15,000.

Such poverty was the engine that drove generations of Islay men and women to seek opportunities on the mainland, or abroad. From his adopted home in Glasgow, the poet William Livingston lamented the depopulation of native Islay. Here are the last four stanzas of his poem, *A Message to the Bard (Duncan's Wife's Song).*

> *Fios chun a' bhàird (Òran bean Dhonnchaidh)*
>
> Ged a thogar feachd na h-Alb',
> As cliùiteach ainm air faich' an àir,
> bidh bratach fhraoich nan Ìleach
> gun dol sìos ga dìon le càch:
> sgap mì-rùn iad thar na fairge
> 's gun ach ainmh'ean balbh nan àit'
> mar a fhuair 's a chunnaic mise –
> thoir am fios seo chun a' bhàird.

175

Tha taighean seilbh na dh'fhàg sinn
feadh an fhuinn nan càrnan fuar':
dh'fhalbh 's cha till na Gaidheil,
stad an t-àiteach, cur is buain;
tha stèidh nan làrach tiamhaidh
a' toirt fianais air 's ràdh
'Mar a fhuair 's a chunnaic mise –
thoir am fios seo chun a' bhàird.

Cha chluinnear luinneag òighean,
sèist nan òran air a' chlèith,
is chan fhaicear seòid mar b' àbhaist
a' cur bàir air faiche rèidh;
thug ainneart fògraidh bhuainn iad,
's leis na coimhich buaidh mar 's àill:
Leis na fhuair 's chunnaic mise
thoir am fios seo chun a' bhàird.

Chan fhaigh an dèirceach fasgadh,
no 'm fear astair fois o sgìos,
no soisgeulach luchd-èisteachd,
bhuadhaich eucoir, Goill is cìs;
tha an nathair bhreac na lùban
air na h-ùrlair far 'n do dh'fhàs
na fir mhòra chunnaic mise –
thoir am fios seo chun a' bhàird.

Uilleam Mac Dhùnlèibhe, *Fios chun a' bhàird (Òran bean Dhon-nchaidh)*, 1863

A Message to the Bard (Duncan's Wife's Song)

Though the army of Scotland is raised,
of famed renown on the battle-field,
the heather badge of the Islaymen
will not be there to protect her with the rest;
malice scattered them over the sea
leaving only dumb animals in their place,
as I found out, as I saw –
take this message to the bard.

The houses that we owned are where we left them
throughout the land – cold heaps of stone –
the Gaels have gone and will not return,
cultivation has ceased, sowing and reaping;
the foundations of the dismal ruins
bear witness to it, and say
'As I found out, as I saw –
Take this message to the bard.'

Maidens are not heard singing
choral refrains around the waulking-frame,
no more are seen the heroes who used to
aim at goals on the level playing-field;
the brutality of eviction took them from us,
and the outsiders got their way:
with all the things I've found out and seen
take this message to the bard.

The beggar will get no shelter
nor the weary traveller rest,
the missionary will get no listeners;
the only winners are injustice, foreigners and taxes;
the spotted adder now coils
on the floors where once there grew
the great men that I used to see –
take this message to the bard.

William Livingston, *A Message to the Bard (Duncan's Wife's Song)*, 1863

The Bards

Canain àigh nam buadhan òirdhearc,
A b'fharsuing cliù air feadh na h-Eòrpa;
Bithidh I fatast mar a thòisich,
Os ceann gach cainnt 'na h-iuchair eòlais.

Strange mystic powers lie in that tongue,
Whose praise through Europe wide has rung;
As 'twas of yore in school and college,
It shall be first – the key of knowledge.

William Livingston, 1808-70

The creations of Islay's bards are part of the warp and weft of their island's culture and history. We have already encountered William Livingston through his lament about emigration and his imagined description of the warlike Vikings preparing to do battle as their longships lay in Lochindaal, but this fascinating man deserves to be further described.

Uilleam Ileach, William the Islayman, was one of the island's most cantankerous sons. He was born in 1808 at Gartmain, near Bowmore. His father, a carpenter, insisted that his son learn a trade, and the young William became apprenticed to a tailor.

> The master and his apprentice would take up their abode in the house of their employers, until all who needed new suits in the family were provided for. On these occasions the house in which the tailor wrought was generally the centre of attraction on the hamlet. Thither all the young people, and sometimes old as well, went to spend the evening at a friendly *céilidh*. Song and repartee, story and legend, guesses and conundrums, helped to make the time pass lightly and merrily. We may safely assume that the apprentice boy's tongue was not the most silent at those gatherings, nor his answers the least witty. Although this was not the best school to teach a young boy discretion and self-control, doubtless a certain rude education was given. The witty answers helped to quicken the faculties, and the many tales of the olden time awakened in the Bard's mind that love of country, and that fondness for its early history which to the last were

so characteristic of him. According to his own account he was at this time wild, tricky and full of mischief; a great favourite in the houses where his master wrought, and much sought after in social gatherings.

Coming home one Hallowe'en night from some merrymaking, he had the misfortune to overturn a creel that was on his master's kitchen floor, under which a young pig was confined. The door being open, the pig escaped, and was lost in the darkness. The master was furious; there and then he turned his apprentice to the door, and William had his revenge by composing the song entitled "An t-Oircein" . . .

This adventure put an abrupt termination to the apprenticeship. He resolved to seek his fortune in the Low Country, and left his native island with a light purse but a resolute heart.

Robert Blair, *William Livingston – A Memoir*, 1882

Blair included Livingston's youthful poetic account of the incident in his anthology of the bard's work.

An T-Oircean

This seems to be but a fragment. Those who heard the Bard reciting it say that there were a greater number of verses. The following stanzas are all that can be found among the manuscripts of the poet.

> Oidhche Shamhna nan Uruisg,
> Bha, mar a chualas ùr is sean,
> Glaisrig, Sac-bàn is Caointeach,
> 'S bodaich an t-saoghail fear, is fear,
>
> A mach à uamhachan 's fmgan
> 'S iad fiaclach, crògach, glas,
> 'S am feusagan calgach, ròmach,
> Mar sguab eòrna slàn o'n dias,
>
> 'S iad ag iarraidh balach an Tàilleir
> Seo mar bha 's mar chaidh e às,
> 'S an ruaig air gu lag an dùnain
> 'S a chòmhla dùinte 's i fo ghlais.
>
> Chuireadh cliabh 's a bheul ri ùrlar
> Bha 'n Torc beag 's e dùinte steach

ISLAY VOICES

'Nuair a chuir e le gnosan na grùide
Bun os ceann a lùchairt shlat.

Dh'fhalbh e gun fios duinn fhàgail
C'àit' an robh e dol gu stad
Oircein bhig chlis nan àmhuilt
Chuir thu mis an càs gu grad.

Sin' thuirt Dòmhnall 's e glaodhaich
'S iomadh saothair a fhuair mi riut
Tog ort a-nis is fàg mo theaghlach
Chaill mi t-fhoineis a' mhuc.

Le sèideadh gaoith an iar is clàdain
'S dealanach a' deàrrsadh bras
Bha m' fheòil air chrith air mo chnàmhan
'Nuair a ghlaoidh an tàillear, 'Bi mach'.

Chaidh gach bruach is gleann is alld
A rannsachadh le siubhal chas
'S ma 'f fior 's an t-oircean gun fhaotainn,
Thòisich caoineadh 's greadadh bhas.

Poems of William Livingston, edited by Robert Blair, 1882

On Hallowe'en, night of bogles,
as both young and old have heard,
there came hag, white sack[1] and banshee,
and the old men of the world, one by one,

Out from caves and crevices,
pale, with fangs and great big paws,
with their bushy, bristly beards
like a sheaf of barley after flailing,

In pursuit of the tailor's lad –
this is how it happened and how he got away
when he was chased to the hollow of the fort
and found the door closed and locked.

1. The Sac Bàn 'White Sack' was a being known around the shores of Loch Creran who would bring men down by entangling their legs in a piece of sackcloth or luman and then murder them.

A creel had been upturned on the floor
with the Wee Boar trapped inside
when, with his gungy snout,
he overturned his palace of wattles.

He set off, leaving us no word
where it was he planned to stop;
Oh, clever, little, wily piglet,
see how you dropped me in it!

This is what Donald said, yelling,
'You've given me a lot of grief,
get out now and leave my household:
thanks to your nonsense, I've lost the pig'.

With the blowing of western wind and snow
and fork-lightning blazing bright,
my flesh was jittering on my bones
when the tailor yelled, 'Get out!'

Every brae and glen and burn
was minutely searched on foot
and as the piglet was really lost
lamenting started and the beating of palms.

(Translation by Meg Bateman)

We come now to the men who kept alive, and are still keeping alive, the fervour of the Celtic lyre in these latest days, when red-tape and centralisation and Examination Boards seem conspiring to chase all nationality, all freshness of original colour, and all interesting variety of type out of the country. The first on this most recent roll is LIVINGSTON, or, as he insisted on writing his name in Gaelic, MacDhunleibhe, not Mac-an-Leighe . . .

Livingston was a native of Islay, born in 1808, and saw with his own eyes the sorrow of the passage of the land from its hereditary lords into the hands of new men, with the consequences, always disagreeable to the old inhabitants, which accompany a new dynasty. Whether anything was done in the way of clearance in that time harsh or impolitic, I do not know; but Livingston, as a poet and a patriot, naturally thought so, and he poured forth his wail for the

181

country of his love in verses that will long echo in the ears of the
islanders: –

> "Though the sun is shining brightly,
>   And bright flow'rets gem the lea,
> And a thousand sheep are feeding
>   On the land so dear to me;
> Though the shag-haired nolt are browsing
>   On the brae and in the glen,
> I have seen, and I will sing it,
>   Islay, thou hast lost thy MEN!"

Home, history and local tradition are the natural food of the poetic
mind. So Livingston devoted himself with all the ardour of the poetic temperament to the study of Scottish history, as it is recorded in
Fordun and other ancient annalists.

John Stuart Blackie, *Language and Literature of the Scottish Highlands*, 1876

Livingston's friend, the Dunoon-born minister, Robert Blair, admired the
poet immensely. But Blair was under no illusions about the Bard's temperament, and the extreme views which his study of Scottish history had
instilled in him.

He was particularly well acquainted with the early history of Scotland
and with the legends and monkish stories of these far off times, all of
which William believed as veritable history, provided they reflected
any honour upon old Scotland. Indeed he lived so entirely in those
rude times that he imbibed a spirit of the most intense hatred towards
England and everything English. No Irish Home Ruler ever hated
the Saxons more than the Bard did. This blind hatred of England
and all her belongings rendered him incapable of taking an impartial
view of history and marred very considerably his reliability as Guide
and Historian.

Blair adds that Livingston also took a pretty dim view of most of his fellow
Scots.

Naturally he was of a distrustful suspicious nature, and the hardships he
had to strive against did not tend to lessen this disposition. He could

182

hardly brook a co-worker, not to say a rival in any field whatever. Hence he was perpetually at war with his fellow Celts, who made any attempt to cultivate Gaelic literature.

Robert Blair, *William Livingston – A Memoir*, 1882

For Scottish Gaels, following the 'Clearances' and other forms of population displacement in the century after 1760, the last quarter of the nineteenth century became a time of renewal, which witnessed the struggle for crofters' rights and ultimately the passing of the *Crofters' Holdings (Scotland) Act* of 1886. In preparing hearts and minds for the fight, Livingston's poems may have been of some significance. Even in the twenty-first century, if we can rid ourselves of the 'difficult' baggage of battles and warfare that these poems deposit unceremoniously at our feet, we may be able to appreciate their deeper resonances, and we may find Uilleam Ileach a surprisingly congenial companion. This is because Gaels and Gaelic still require to be defended, and the example of the 'ancestral struggle' for 'the things that matter' retains an inspirational power.

Donald Meek, *A Land That Lies Westward*, 2009

Sheas na Gàidheil gun bhristeadh
Mar a chleachd iad, 's nach cualas riamh
An iarrtas stìochdidh an talamh nam beò;
Còir a thug nàdar dhaibh 's gach linn,
Cha toir ùine dhinne i,
A chlann nam fear ud!

The Gaels stood without breaking
As was their wont, and never was heard
Their desire to yield while still in the land of the living;
A right that nature gave them in every generation,
Time will not take away from us,
O children of those men!

William Livingston, *Blar Shumadail*

Charles and Duncan MacNiven (born in 1874 and 1880) were bachelor brothers who worked as cattlemen most of their adult lives at Rockside near Kinchoman, although Duncan served in the Navy during the First World War. As farmhands they could have led useful, but unremarkable lives. But what went on in their (now demolished) cottage and in their heads was extraordinary.

The MacNiven brothers were knowledgeable and well-read, and were talented poets both in Gaelic and English. Both competed regularly in local and national Mods. They wrote love poems to local ladies and laments for the fallen of two world wars, and Duncan even translated Goethe's supernatural poem *Der Erlkönig* – a grimmer take on *Tam o' Shanter* – from German into Gaelic. But it is for their depiction of ordinary Islay life and society that they are best loved. Today Charles and Duncan are remembered and revered on Islay as 'The Kilchoman Bards'.

Their primarily relevance as poets is as *'Bard Baile'* recording the minutiae of rural life in an agricultural community and recounting tittle-tattle tales of real people. Often comic, the poems are witty, sometimes caustic and extremely well observed. The local anecdotal focus of the poetry does not decrease its relevance; by focusing on small scale events, the brothers create humorous and quirky pen-pictures, social commentaries that tell us much about the nature of such communities, and of the human condition. Today *Bard Baile* are becoming an increasingly respected genre for their work in documenting social mores and conditions in rural communities which are fast disappearing.

MacNìmhein C. agus MacNìmhein D. – Poets of Place, Bòrd na Gàidhlig leaflet, 2012

Here is a poem by Charles about not being invited to a wedding.

Òran Bainnse

Siud a dh 'fhàg mi 'n-diugh gun sunnd,
  Air mo dhìochuimhneachadh sa chabhaig;
Siud a dh 'fhàg mi 'n-diugh gun sunnd
  Chionn nach d'fhuair mi thun na banais.

Bha sùil agam ri cuireadh fialaidh,
  Gun rachadh m' iarraidh thun na banais
'S gum faighinn cearc le forc is sgian
  Gu bhith ga h-ialladh – biadh ro bhlasta.

Gun do reamhraich mi 'n gèadh mór
  Le min phònair thàin á Glaschu

'S nan do chuir me e gu margadh
    Chuireadh e airgead dhomh am banca.

Cheannaich mi tiodhlaic a bha fiachail,
    Deagh leab' iarainn a chuid Shasainn,
Ach gun chuireadh mar bu mhiann leam
    Chaill iad fiachan nach bu mhaith leo!

Fhuair mi cùrainn a bha crùn,
    Air son flùr gun phàigh mi tastan –
Fhuair mi siud is casag chaol,
    Sgoltadh bha 'na cùl san fhasan.

Gléidhidh mi 'n tiodhlac nis domh fhéin
    'S cuiridh mise feum oirr' fhathast
Nuair a gheibh mi bean dhomh fhéin –
    Ach s ainmig iadsan gheibh gu m' bhanais!

Bu lìonmhor ann na daoine mòra
    Le 'n cuid charbad 's paidhir each annt',
Ach a' chuid aig nach robh carbad,
    Fhuair iad coingheal o Mhac Artair.

Cha robh 'n coisiche gu stàth ann
    'S cha robh ann ach sàr nam marcaich –
Ach ged bha 'bhanais ud cho stràiceil
Se 'm biadh fhuair pàirt buntàta 's sgadan.

Bidh mi tighinn gu ceann le m' òran,
    A fhleasgaich òig, thoir thus' an aire,
Cuimhnich nuair a bhios thu pòsadh
    Gun iarr thu mo sheòras thun do bhanais.

      Tearlach MacNìmhein

Wedding Song

That's what left me sad today,
    Being forgotten in the rush;
That's what's left me sad today,
    Not getting to the wedding.

ISLAY VOICES

I expected a generous invitation,
    That I'd be asked to the wedding,
That I'd get chicken with a fork and knife
    To pick it up with – delicious food.

So I fattened the big gander
    With bean meal from Glasgow,
And if I'd sent it to market
    I'd have money in the bank.

I bought a valuable present,
    A good iron bed made in England,
But without the invitation I'd have liked
    They lost possessions they'll regret!

I bought clothes that cost a crown,
    For a flower I paid a shilling –
All that and a tailored coat,
    With the split behind that's in fashion.

Now I'll keep the gift for myself
    And I'll make use of it eventually
When I find myself a wife –
    Though *they're* unlikely to be at my wedding!

There were plenty of toffs there
    With their carriages and pairs,
While those without a carriage
    Got a loan from Macarthur.

Arriving on foot was inadequate
    And no-one was there but equestrians –
Yet despite the wedding being so swanky,
    Some were given tatties and herring!

I'll be bringing my song to a finish,
    But young bachelor, you be careful,
Don't forget when you get married
    To invite my sort to your wedding.

Charles MacNiven (translated by Ronnie Black)

Weddings were important Islay social gatherings. Here is Charles' none too serious description of one.

Banais Chòrsabuil

B'i siud a' bhanais urramach a chruinnich ann an Còrsabol,
S iomahd aon fhuair cuireadh bha urramach ro mhòr ann;
Dh'fhàg iad mis' am' aonarach is shaoilinn nach bu chòir
    dhaibh,
Cha robh mi idir cianalach 's mi trang a' dèanamh òrain.

Bha gu leòir de bhiadh ac', oir fhuair iad fiadh á Pròaig,
Chuir iad molt á Sanaig agus gamhainn ás an Otha,
'S mun robh 'n dìnneir seachad ac' bha fallas air gach còcair' –
Loisg iad tunna guail rithe, 's mo thruaigh' a' chruach mhòna.

Bha corr is dusan fidhleir ann, bha trì dhiubh á Dùn Éideann,
Ach thachair nì bha mìothlachdail, dhìochuimhnich iad na
    teudan,
'S dh'ith a' mhuc am pìobaire 's e seinn, mas fior an sgeula –
Se 'n dòig a rinn iad dannsadh a bhith canntaireachd ri chéile.

Bha dà fhichead òg-bhean ann 's gillean òg' do réir sin,
Gach aon dhiubh 's cearc 'na achlais a' tarraing chum na féiste;
Bha cuid aig an robh tunnag dhiubh, sann bha cearc-ghuir aig
    té dhiubh,
'S bha fear ann a thug coileach leis, ach ghoideadh e á Gréineil.

Ach guidheam do an chàraid sin buan shlàint' 'nan laigh' 's
    'nan éirigh,
Sìth, sonas dhaibh, is àghalachd, seadh ge b'e àit an téid iad;
Tha 'm pòsadh dhìth san rìoghachd seo, se sin aon nì tha
    dearbhte,
Tha feum air tuille shaighdearan chum oillt chur air a' Ghear-
    mailt.

Tearlach MacNìmhein

The Wedding at Corsapol

What a grand wedding party it was that gathered in Corsapol,
Many folk were invited who were most honourable guests;

They left me by myself and I thought they really shouldn't have,
But I didn't mind a bit as I was working hard on a song.

They had plenty of food, as they'd got a deer from Proaig,
They'd sent a wedder from Sanaig and a stirk from the Oa,
And before the meal was over every cook was in a sweat –
They burned a ton of coal on it, and I'm sorry for the peatstack.

There were over twelve fiddlers, with three of them from
    Edinburgh,
But an unfortunate thing happened, they forgot the strings,
And the pig ate the piper as he played, or so I'm told –
But they managed to dance by singing mouth tunes at each
    other.

There were forty young women there with enough young
    men to match them,
Each one arriving at the feast with a chicken in his oxter;
There were some that brought a duck, one girl a broody hen,
And one man brought a cockerel, but it was stolen from
    Greineil.

I wish that couple lifelong health both in going to bed and rising,
Peace, happiness, prosperity, yes wherever they may go;
This country's short of marriages, that's one thing that's shown
    for certain,
For more soldiers are essential now for frightening the Germans.

Charles MacNiven (translated by Ronnie Black)

Duncan was the more prolific, and more thematically wide-ranging, of the
MacNiven brother bards. Here is a First World War lament Duncan wrote
for a young Islay man killed at the front.

Do Alasdair Mac Fhearghais, a thuit anns an Fhraing, 14 October, 1915.
    Air fonn – 'Anns a' ghleann 'san robh mi òg'.

      Ged a rùisgeadh mais' na coille
      Air a lomadh leis an stoirm;
      Ged a shearg gach luibh is doire
      Rùisgte leis an doinionn bhorb;

Bheir an Samhradh iad mu'n cuairt
Sgaoilidh iad gu nuadh 'nan glòir,
Ach cha till, cha till, mo ghaol-sa
Thuit 'r-son saorsa na Roinn Eorp
Thuit 'r-son saorsa na Roinn Eorp', etc.

'S truagh a ghaoil nach robh mi làimh riut,
Air a' bhlàr 'nuair chaidh do leòn;
O! nach d' fhuair mi féin am bàs leat
'S mór gu'm b'fhearr dhomh na bhi beò.
Mi air m' fhàgail 'n so leam fhìn,
Le cridhe briste, tùrsach, breòit',
Oir cha till, cha till, mo ghaol-sa
Thuit 'r-son saorsa na Roinn Eorp',
Thuit 'r-son, etc.

'S ann mu ghlinn ghorm Chille-chomain,
'Ghaoil, a thogadh thu bho t'òig,
Far an tric a rinn mi coinneamh
Riut an coille dhlùth nan cnò;
Bidh na smuaintean sin, a rùin,
A chaoidh ag ùrachadh mo bhròin,
Oir cha till, cha till, mo ghaol-sa
Thuit 'r-son saorsa na Roinn Eorp',
Thuit 'r-son, etc.

'Na mo chodal no 'nam dhùsgadh
'S tu mo smuaintean dh' oidhch' 's a lò;
'S tric mi féin leat ann am bruadar
Feadh nan cluanag buain nan ròs;
'S ann a thà thu fada bhuam,
Far nach dùisg do chluan ri m' cheol,
Oir cha till, cha till, mo ghaol-sa
Thuit 'r-son saorsa na Roinn Eorp',
Thuit 'r-son, etc.

Dhealaich thu an teas a' ghaoil rium;
Spìonadh thu bho m' thaobh ro òg,
Chi mi féin ar leam, a rùin thu
Air an raon gun lùths gun treòir,

ISLAY VOICES

Sinte 'n cadal trom na h-ùir,
Thuit thu ann an tùs do ghlòir
'S O! cha till, cha till, thu ghaol rium
Thuit 'r-son saorsa na Roinn Eorp',
Thuit 'r-son, etc.

Donnchadh MacNìmhein

*In Memory of Pte. Alexander Ferguson, youngest son of Donald and Marion
Ferguson, Kilchoman, Islay, who fell in action in France, 14th October, 1915.*
Air: 'In the Glen where I was young'.

Though the beauties of the forest
In the winter's blast are shed,
Though from every twig and flower
Summer's bloom ere now has sped,
With the genial breath of spring,
Their former glory will return;
But from me my darling's parted:
Ever more for him I mourn.
Ever more for him I mourn.

O! that I was with my darling
On the field where he was slain,
O! that with you I had fallen,
And in death beside you lain.
I am now, alas, alone,
Broken-hearted, daily mourn;
For from me my darling's parted,
Never more will he return,
Never more will he return.

In the glen near Cille Chomain,
There it was your youth was passed,
Where I often, in the gloaming,
In your arms was fondly clasped,
With the mem'ries of these times,
Now my heart within me mourns,
For he fell in Europe's combat,
And to me no more returns,
And to me no more returns.

In my sleeping hours and waking,
You're my thoughts by night and day,
Oft in dreams with you I wander
'Mong the verdant fields in May.
Ah! but now you're far away,
And your bed awaits no morn;
For you fell among the bravest,
Fighting for an age unborn,
Fighting for an age unborn.

Almost ere our love has blossomed,
You were hurried from my side,
And methinks I now can see you,
Where your blood the daisies dyed,
In your glorious youth and manhood,
You were from my bosom torn,
Now for me there's nought to live for;
Ever more for you I mourn,
Ever more for you I mourn.

Duncan MacNiven

This is Duncan's song in memory of his mother.

Mar Chuimhneachan Air Ealasaid Nic Dhomhnuill, Bartrach Ghilleas-
buig Mac Nimhein, Maighstir Sgoile, a chaochail an Ile (Rockside).
Air an dara la fichead de'n Lùghnasdal, 1916.

Gur muladach a tà mi
'S mo chridhe 'n impis sgàineadh,
'S mi fada bho an àite
Rinn m' àrach 's mi òg;
Ged 's iomadh là o'n dh'fhàg mi,
A chaoidh bidh agam blàths ris;
An sin 's ann tha mo mhàthair
Ag cnàmh fo an fhòid.

Bidh cuimhn' agam gu bràth air
A' mhaduinn sin a dh' fhàg mi,
Nuair ghlac i teann air làimh mi
Cho faillineach aosd,

191

'S le osnadh thùrsaich bhreòite,
'S ann ghlac i mi 'g am phògadh,
Is bhruchd i mach ag caoineadh,
'S na deoir air a sùil.

Ach O! bu bheag mo dhùil ris,
Nach fhaicinn tuille ghnùis sin;
'S e so ceann-fath mo thùrsa,
'S mo smuain dh' oidhche' 's a là
Cha bhiodh mo chridh' cho brùite,
Ar leam, na 'n robh mi dlùth dhi,
'S gu'm faca mi an t-sùil sin
'Ga dùnadh 'sa bhàs.

Tha fhios a' m gu'm b'e dùrachd
'San àm, gu'n robh mi dlùth dhi;
Ach cha robh agam saorsa
'S chan fhaodainn bhi ann,
Bho cheangal teann mo dhùthcha,
Le càbhlach nan crann lùghmhor,
Air bharraibh nan tonn dùbhghorm
An taobh so de'n Fhraing.

Is ged tha 'n dachaidh làthair
Chan 'eil i mar a bhà i:
Tha 'n teallach fuar gun mhàthair,
Tha 'n fhàrdach gun aoibh.
Ged thillinn féin gun dàil ann,
Chan fhaigh mi 'n aoibh a b'àbhaist,
An cridh' aig an robh gràdh dhomh,
Ag cnàmh anns a' chill.

'S m' ùrnuigh ris an Ard-Righ,
Gu'n criochnaich mo làithean
'San eilean a rinn m' àrach,
Le càirdean mo ghaoil,
Is taobh ri taobh ri m' mhàthair,
'Sa chill ri taobh na tragha
Gu'n teid an sin mo chàireadh
Gu bràth fo an ùir.

Song in memory of Elizabeth McDonald, widow of the late Archibald MacNiven,
Schoolmaster who died at Rockside, Islay on 22nd August 1916.
Air: 'Highland Mary'.

I'm sad and sorrow laden,
My heart is like to fail me,
I'm far, far away from the land where I was born,
Though long I've been away, still
Fast mem'ries are unfading.
For yonder one is laid low – my mother from me torn.

And long my mind keeps guard o'er
That morning when we parted,
How close she held my hand in her own, so old and frail,
And how, with sighs and moaning,
She embraced me in the gloaming,
And wept upon my shoulder, and bathed me in her tears.

But oh, could I conceive that
I ne'er again would see her.
My loss and sore bereavement, and my thoughts night and day,
If only I were nigh her,
To hear that voice so kindly,
And in life to see those eyes, and to dry away her tears.

I know that her desire was
That I should be beside her,
But duty's call had tied me, and there I could not be.
For we wait the savage foeman
Upon the surging ocean,
On our ship of surest motion, patrolling Gallia's seas.

I've still that home to go to,
Though not as I have known it,
To me the hearth is cold, and the house is full of gloom,
And though the war was over,
And I prepared to go there,
Her heart, so warm of old, now lies mould'ring in the tomb.

Now 'tis my daily prayer,

ISLAY VOICES

When at an end my days are,
That in the Isle that reared me I lay me down to die,
That by my mother's side,
'Neath the sod near ocean's tide,
Till yon morning, to abide, in peaceful rest I lie.

(Translated from the Gaelic by Eachann MacDhughaill.)

Around 1947, Duncan had a leg amputated after contracting gangrene. The new National Health Service had difficulty in providing him with an artificial leg that fitted – and found itself at the sharp end of a poet's pen.

If there's a place on earth I hate,
That place's in Sauchiehall Street,
I visited that place of late –
The gates of Hell I call it
A well-known name above the door,
"The Ministry of Pensions",
While every rogue within its walls
Should be in detentions.

I went a poor and limbless man,
To have a leg adjusted,
They kept me waiting for a year
And now the leg is rusted;
In there they seemed like fiends from Hell,
Their faces even twisted:
They call them servants of the Crown –
Such men should ne'er be trusted.

The greatest wretch among them all,
He calls himself a Doctor,
His nose as red as any rose,
More like a well-boiled lobster.
I think poor soul he's always dry
He likes his gin and shandy –
But well I know he would prefer
Good Cognac, pure strong brandy.

My thousand curses on their heads,
They'll never taste salvation,

194

O' how I long to see them dead
And smothered to damnation.
With pen and ink I write in verse
A tribute from a poet,
An epitaph to mark their heads –
And ages yet shall know it.

Duncan MacNiven never got a satisfactory leg, but continued to take his daily walk around Loch Gorm on his crutches. He died in 1955 having outlived Charles by eleven years.

Duncan Johnston – '*Am Bàrd*' – was born in 1881 and raised at Lagavulin. Much of his work can be sung and can often be heard at Islay gatherings.

Throughout his lifetime Duncan Johnston's love of his native Islay and its native folklore influenced his poems and songs with themes ranging from love songs, songs of longing, song dealing with historic themes based on local legends and pipe tunes. He competed at the National Mod many times and was crowned as Bard in 1929.

Bòrd na Gàidhlig leaflet, 2012

During the First World War Johnston served in Islay's local regiment, the Argyll and Sutherland Highlanders, and was gassed in the trenches and invalided out of the Army in 1916.

It is perhaps for his two works dealing with the First World War – *Sine Bhàn* and *Tuireadhn nan Treun* (especially so as they have been prescribed National Mod pieces) that Johnston will best be remembered.

Bòrd na Gàidhlig leaflet, 2012

Sine Bhàn is a song of parting, as a young man leaves his 'fair Sheena' to go to war. Sheena is an anglicised version of the Gaelic *Sine*, which itself is the Scots Gaelic version of Jane or – in Scots – Jean.

Sine Bhàn

Blàth nan cailin, Sìne Bhàn
Reul nan nighean, dìleas òg,
Cuspair dìomhair i dom dhàn,
Gràdh mo chridh', an rìbhinn òg.

Àros sona bh' againn thall
Àirigh mhonaidh, innis bhò,
Sgaoil ar sonas uainn air ball,
Mar roinneas gaoth nam fuar-bheann ceò.

Bruaillean cogaidh anns an tìr,
Faic an long a' togail sheòl,
Cluinn an druma 's fuaim na pìob
Faic na suinn a' dol air bòrd!

Feumaidh mise triall gun dàil,
Chi mi 'm bàrr a croinne, sròl.
M' eudail bhàn, o soraidh slàn!
Na caoin a luaidh, na sil na deòir.

Cha ghaoir-cath' no toirm a' chàs'
Dh'fhàg mi-n dràsd' fo gheilt is bròn
'S è na dh' fhàg mi air an träigh,
Sìne Bhàn a rinn mo leòn.

Sìnte 'n seo air achadh blàir,
'S duine 'mhàin cha tig 'nam chòir
O! 's nach robh mi anns an Aird
Le Sine Bhàn a' ruith nam bò!

Ma tha e 'n dàn mi bhi slàn
Stadaidh ràn nan gunnan mór
Am Baile Mhonaidh nì mi tàmh
Le Sìne Bhàn, mo rìbhinn òg.

Fair Sheena

Flower of maidens, Sheena fair,
Star of damsels, young and braw,
Secret theme of all my lays,
Dearest fair; my sweetest all.

Happy days among the kye,
In yonder shieling by the vale,
Time too soon went fleeting by,
Like mountain mist before the gale.

The Bards

Noise of war is in the land,
See the ships along the shore,
Hear the drums and piping bands,
See the heroes going aboard!

Parting time is drawing nigh
Flags are waving at masthead,
Darling child, O do not sigh!
Do not cry, my lovely maid!

It isn't war or cannon's roar
Unmans me now and makes me mourn,
My heart is left on yonder shore,
My lonesome lass; my sweet, forlorn.

Stricken low on battle's plain,
With none to cheer the dragging hour,
Would I were in mossy vale,
With Sheena fair; my bonny flower.

If fate decrees that I should see,
Coming peace; war flags to furl,
Homeward I will hie with glee,
And never leave my bonny girl.

Duncan Johnson

Duncan Muir is a gifted contemporary Islay poet. He is a young man with a wide view of the world (he speaks Chinese!), but this next poem has deep roots in the physical and imagined landscape of his childhood. Written in memory of a poet, scholar and lover of Celtic lore and literature, this work has echoes the work of Islay's traditional bards and the folklore of John Francis Campbell.

In Search of Magic, or
The Wizard's Apprentice (i.m. Edmund Cusick), 2014

In school, I was told that all of the magic
had left the world before I was born
and that in its stead we have logic and religion,
as if these might make up for magic's loss.

ISLAY VOICES

Our farm stood a quarter-mile
from Emeraconart, the dragon's lair,
but the dragon lay dead in the loch,
turned to stone more moons

ago than anyone could count
or know. Nearby grew The Golden
Tree, whose curse had twisted its roots
and branches, and the three brothers of a family

who once lived in our house,
how long ago? Before the magic died,
of course. I was taken to The Toothache Stone
sprouting its crop of rusted nails;

to The Kildalton Cross where my mother says
she saw some pellucid, blue-white girl
walking, melancholy, upon the hill;
and to The Magic Well, where we cast

quartz wishes into a sparkling pool.
I was warned away from The Fairy Hill
because the daoine sìdh are the worst of all.
But still, they said, there is no magic.

At university, I met a modest, awkward man
in whose office a desk was under threat
from an avalanche of books and papers and Tolkien
action-figures. He took me to The Fairy Glen

and gave me a wooden tourney sword
and when I broke it in battle, he gave me steel.
He introduced me to a pack of wolves,
and in the forest, at dusk, he taught me

levitation and the Pictish secrets of invisibility,
how to see that which is behind me,
how to interpret dreams and harness chi.
I was instructed to create my own language,

which I did, though no one else could understand,
and a map of an uncharted land where monsters
still haunt the sea. But the greatest gifts,
I think, he gave to me were poetry

and the knowledge, though he never said it,
that the magic never really went away.

Duncan Stewart Muir

The unusual dandling song below may be useful to those, who like
the Editor, are sometimes exasperated beyond endurance by an in-
somniac infant.

Refrain:

Hóbhan óbhan óran hailig thu
Criomaidh na luchaigh thu,
ithidh na radian thu,
Hóbhan óbhan óran hailig thu

Thig armachd nan tonn
Le targaidhean òir
Le srannsa, le sròl
Gu Tràigh a' Mhachaire

Hóbhan óbhan óran hailig u
The mice will nibble you,
the rats will eat you,
Hóbhan óbhan óran hailig u.

The host of the waves will come
With golden targes,
With [?rattling of ?] silk banners,
To Machrie Beach.

School of Scottish Studies Archives, University of Edinburgh,
recorded from Alasdair Hay, Portnahaven, Islay, by Mary
MacDonald in November 1969. Published in *Tocher* 4, 1971

Our final selection of Islay verse is a piece of ever-popular doggerel that
nevertheless has interesting roots. Some people claim it to be Islay's 'national

anthem'. Call it sentimental, or even schmaltzy, but heartfelt renditions of *Westering Home* can be heard crooned by teetotal grannies at ceilidhs and belted out by well-lubricated local football teams on ferry journeys home from mainland matches.

It shares its tune with *Trasna na dTonnta* (Across the Waves), an Irish song about a wanderer's return, but the Islay lyric was written in 1920 by Sir Hugh Roberton, the brilliant choral master who founded and led the famous Glasgow Orpheus Choir, and also wrote *Mairi's Wedding*.

Westering Home

Chorus:

Westering home and a song in the air,
Light in the eye and its goodbye to care,
Laughter o' love and a welcoming there,
Isle o' my heart, my own one.

Tell me o' lands o' the Orient gay,
Speak o' the riches and joys o' Cathay,
Aye, but its grand to be wakin' each day,
To find yourself nearer to Islay.

Where are the folk like the folk o' the West,
Cantie and couthie and kindly, the best,
There I would hie me and there I would rest,
At hame wi' my ain folk in Islay.

The Tourist Trail

Today, it is hard to imagine Islay without tourists. Some come for the whisky, others for the beaches, golf, fishing, the peace and quiet of its landscape, or the wildlife (either to watch it or shoot it). But it was not always so.

> There is no Corner of Europe, so little known even to the Inhabitants of Britain, as the Islands which are here described. We have long had more Information concerning the Islands of Asia; and it is likely will soon be better acquainted with those in the far distant parts of the Southern Hemisphere; than we are with the Islands adjacent to our own Coasts, and which make part of the Kingdom.
>
> The Rev. John Walker, *Report on the Hebrides*, 1764

By the late nineteenth century technology had revolutionised travel, and tourists discovered Islay. The writers of guide books were quick to spot an opportunity.

> Its difficulty of access, in time gone by, has no doubt prevented its thorough exploration by the outer world, and may thus account for its having being looked upon with some degree of disfavour; but since the happy advent of steam and electricity, annihilators of time and space; and since the very excellent and satisfactory communication with the great centre of population has been established by our enterprising and indefatigable steam-ship owner, Mr David M'Brayne of Glasgow, and his worthy predecessors, leaving it optional either to go round by the Mull of Kintyre in the fast sea-going Steamer "Islay" or by Tarbert with the magnificent floating palace, "Columba" of the same line, the Island has been altogether held in very different estimation with the general public.
>
> Robert Oliphant, *The Tourist's Guide to Islay, The Queen of the Hebrides*, 1881

There are two routes by which a passenger can get to Islay. A tourist intending to take either one or the other of these can have all up-to-date information by applying to Mr. David MacBrayne, 119 Hope St., Glasgow.

One route is by the Royal Mail steamer, with passengers only, which sails from Bridge Wharf, Glasgow, daily (Sunday excepted), at 7.00 a.m., for Islay, *via* East Tarbert; thence a journey of two miles to West Tarbert, where another steamer is waiting to carry passengers across to Islay. The steamer takes about three hours to cross to Islay. In connection with the daily steamer from Glasgow to Islay trains leave Glasgow, Central Station, at 8.30 a.m. for Gourock; St Enoch Station at 8.5 a.m. for Princes Pier; Queen Street Station at 8.10 a.m., *via* Craigendoran Pier, joining the steamer at Dunoon. A steamer leaves Islay daily at 8.30 for Glasgow, *via* Tarbert.

The other route is by the steamer Islay, from Shed 40, Lancefield Quay, Glasgow, *via* the Mull of Kintyre, for Port Ellen, Islay, every Monday and Thursday at 12.00 noon. Train, Central Station, to Greenock, at 3.42 p.m. To Port Askaig and Jura every Thursday; to Bruichladdich Pier, weather permitting, every Monday.

J. G. MacNeill, *Islay*, 1899

Why go to Islay? It had the 'healthiest weather in Europe', claimed one writer.

The climate is conducive to health and longevity. The Registrars state, that by the census of April, 1881, the ages of the population range from one to 104 years. With but little frost or snow during the last three winters of storm and disaster, a perfect immunity was enjoyed in Islay. From indisputable meteorological authorities and personal experience, we are able to say, that in Islay, we have had the best and healthiest weather in Europe.

Robert Oliphant, *The Tourist's Guide to Islay, The Queen of the Hebrides*, 1881

The country round Port Ellen, Ardbeg, Bridge-End, Bowmore, and Port Askaig is interesting to the geologist, the historian and the antiquarian as well as to the tourist, for the land in summer is all aglow with yellow broom and purple heather, and the hills rise clear and blue in the distant landscape. There are several beautiful bays with white silvery sand where bathing can be indulged in, and enjoyed in the clear, pure, cool, invigorating waves of the great Atlantic. To those who long for a quiet retreat at holiday time, they will find here all they desire, for this lovely island is easy to get at and cheap to live in, and the hotel accommodation is very comfortable. Walks are plentiful and there seems no restriction placed on those who wish to explore any part, as the visitor can wander hither and thither as he listeth. The roads are good for driving or cycling and no beggars torment the stranger.

Robert Thomson, *A Cruise in the Western Hebrides or a Week on Board the SS Hebridean*, 1891

Dr Johnson, that 'pot of flat porter', as Heine called him, visited the Western Isles in 1713. *Gruamach* that he was he found many things to complain of and one of these was that he was '20 miles from a lemon.' Needless to say, Johnson never was in Islay. Nowadays no such complaint could be justified. The daily packet and the semi-weekly steamer place the utmost resources of civilisation at the disposal of the visitor.

L. MacNeill Weir, *Guide to Islay*, 1911

Weir clearly believed that Islay didn't miss much in not being graced by Johnson and Boswell's company during their tour of the Hebrides. The Gaelic word *Gruamach* is a splendidly onomatopoeic description someone who is sulky, sour, peevish, surly or moody. Weir goes on to assure late nineteenth-century visitors that there was plenty of suitable accommodation for them on Islay. More than a century later, some of these establishments are still flourishing – although not the Temperance Hotels.

Port Ellen – MacCuig's White Hart Hotel is an old-established, comfortable hotel, and commands a fine view of Port Ellen Bay. Every comfort can be had in MacLeod's Islay Hotel, and in Bell's and M'Fadyen's Temperance Hotels.

Bowmore – First-class accommodation can be had in Kirk's Hotel, and in Joss's Temperance Hotel. There is also Dunne's Black Bull Inn and Jamieson's Sea View Hotel. Bowmore is 10½ miles from Port Ellen.

Bridgend – The hotel in this central place is one of the best-appointed in the island. It is about eleven miles from Port Ellen, and three from Bowmore.

Port Askaig – In this well-sheltered and convenient port on the Sound of Islay, about twenty miles from Port Ellen, there is a commodious and comfortable hotel.

Port Charlotte – Dick's Hotel here is good and comfortable. It affords a fascinating view of Lochindaal. There is also Maclachlan's Inn.

Bruichladdich – From this homely hotel one gets a view of sea and land which, for scenic grandeur, can hardly be surpassed.

Portnahaven – Here there is an inn with limited accommodation.

Machrie – Here there is an excellent Boarding House, ably managed by Miss Mackay.

J. G. MacNeill, *Islay*, 1899

One of the attractions of Islay was its plentiful game.

In an article on the sporting estates of Scotland, *Rod and Gun* says: "Islay is the most fertile of the more important islands of the Hebridean group, and is a happy combination of Highland and Lowland scenery. Passing along the richly wooded banks of the Sorn, as it winds through Islay House grounds, were it not for the stern bare summits of Ben Bhain and the other hills towering over the trees to the south, one might well fancy himself in the heart of England's fairest meadow-land. It is to this mixture of moor and pasture, of rich cornfields and desolate hill sides, that the variety of sport to be obtained on the shooting is due. A mixed bag is the inevitable result of a day's shooting . . .

The shootings are over 46,000 acres, about two thirds of which is moor. The covers extend for some miles in both directions – up the valley of the Sorn and along the shore – and are fairly well stocked with pheasants, for which there is ample room. The various tenants have hitherto been in the habit of rearing hundreds of pheasants; but the lands, which have never been fully stocked, would carry at least four times as much game as they usually contain. In an ordinary year the bag of pheasants would be about 500. There are many clearings in the covers where corn could easily be sown, and once such clearing has been thus utilised. In these covers there are many rabbits, the yearly bag of which, shot and trapped, is between

5000 and 6000. For woodcock, Islay House shooting is surpassed by none in Scotland.

J. G. MacNeill, *Islay*, 1899

There are many rural retreats in Islay where the enthusiastic Waltonian may enjoy this health-giving sport; and he can be at no loss at any time for information on the subject, as at the various Hotels throughout the Island he can obtain this. His chief requisites, besides his fishing equipments, are a good stock of sandwiches and a flask of the "real Islay" – the latter, over and above serving for his own necessity and comfort, is a pretty passport in any case of trespass or other emergency.

The principal Rivers are the "Laggan" and the "Sorn" . . . salmon abound in both Rivers, but more especially in the Laggan.

Robert Oliphant, *The Tourist's Guide to Islay, The Queen of the Hebrides*, 1881

One 'enthusiastic Waltonian' fished the Sorn on a visit to Islay House.

We ourselves felt very anxious to retain a few of the finny inhabitants of the glittering waters, of which the delightful murmur had long been music to our ears, and which we could discern at intervals stretching in fine alternate streams and pools between the umbrageous banks. It was a mild sweet morning in the "leafy month of June" (the 28th), and as the river bears a good character both for trout and salmon, we were not without the hope of sport. The supply of water, however, had been for some time before extremely small, it had rained in torrents during the preceding night both over hill and dale, and the immediate result was that opaque of muddy flow so unpropitious to the angler's art. If there were fish in the river they were occupied with their own concerns, and declined to come ashore, for all we got was a few small trout. But we greatly enjoyed our ramble, rod in hand, along these sylvan banks, to which each successive year will add increase of beauty.

Indeed, the river side already exhibits for a long way upwards from its mouth, rather the features of an English landscape than such as usually characterise the Western Isles.

James Wilson, *A Voyage Round the Coast of Scotland*, 1842

Loch Finlaggen, the most interesting loch on the island, is about three miles in circumference, and belongs to Charles Morrison. Esq., of Islay, who lets it with the shootings. The loch contains salmon and trout, the latter running two to a pound, and fifteen pounds is a fair basket. Best months – May, June, July and August.

The Laggan, which is the largest stream in Islay, is capricious, but if in ply yields capital sport, both salmon and sea-trout. There are eight miles of it, and the spring months are best.

J. G. MacNeill, *Islay*, 1899

The writers of guide books extolled Islay for its scenery. In the following purple passage the view looking east from the road just above Port Askaig across the Sound of Jura is described.

The view here is one of surpassing beauty – the quiet loveliness of the placid waters of the Sound of Islay – the imposing majesty of the gigantic paps of Jura, hoary sentinels, towering like ancient pyramids of the desert or the vast Cuchullins of Skye, often capped with misty mantles, the degree of whose density or tenuity is almost a never failing prognostication of the weather and prospective, to all within range of their horizon.

Descending a rather steep road, the tourist finds himself at the comfortable Hotel of Mrs Bankier, situated in one of the most ro-mantic spots it is possible to look upon – close to the edge of the waters of the Sound, the surface of which at full tide oft appears like a lake in the midst of the mountains – a lovely spot where to enjoy a season of perfect rest.

Robert Oliphant, *The Tourist's Guide to Islay, The Queen of the Hebrides*, 1881

But Port Askaig was not always a place for 'perfect rest', and some travellers were irked by the persistence of local people carrying out their occupations of farming and fishing.

Port Askaig is not an exciting place to stay at; so there are few visitors and no 'handsomely furnished lodgings' to tempt them. Once a week a steamer arrives here from Glasgow, bringing passengers and goods, and makes a stir which is not always agreeable. The appointed hour is

11.00 o'clock at night, and the hour of departure 8 o'clock the next morning. A large proportion of the population of the surrounding hamlets assemble to receive their friends, to overlook the landing of their goods, or to get their letters. The quay is noisily occupied all night by porters, sailors, carters, and drovers, many of whom find their way to the inn, and while discussing their whisky, scream and scold in Gaelic; or, if more harmoniously disposed, join in a Gaelic chorus, accompanied sometimes by a bagpipe or Jew's-harp, but having the melody less marked than the time – the latter being loudly, if not accurately preserved, by a diligent thumping with sticks on the table. Among the melodists is to be found one individual who, when the drink has begun to take effect, indulges in a fit of weeping and sobbing for the loss of his mother, who, he tells those who understand him, 'died eleven years since.'

Once or twice a week a half-decked sailing-boat arrives from the neighbouring island of Colonsay, bringing the mail-bags, a few boxes of herrings, and perhaps a passenger or two, who, as the weather has been wet and stormy of late, look drenched and dismal. More frequently, small fishing-boats, each with a crew of two or three men, come in with a cargo of lobsters, which are counted over, and duly consigned to the steam-packet agent, to be deposited in boxes and let down into the water off the quay until the next arrival of the steamer. Many hundreds of dozens annually find their way from this obscure port to the principal cities of Scotland and England

Sir Smith Child, *Three Weeks on Islay*, 1861

In the Sound lies the Hebrides' first port of call, Portaskaig. The green-bordered islands of Islay and Jura narrow the waters of the Sound until one appears to be sailing up the centre of a rapid-running stream, when, without warning, Portaskaig jumps into sight from behind an unobtrusive headland.

On a late autumn trip my wife and I walked into the village, through the village, and returned through the village without meeting a soul. Then while admiring the withered remains of giant sunflowers, who should we meet but the genial proprietor of the cosy hotel. It seemed remarkable that these giants of garden flowers should be able to grow here, without being blown and broken by the fierce winds, which must often strain their stems to the utmost. The luxurious growth of trees and bushes on steep surrounding sides of the bluff in which Portaskaig shelters is wonderful, and every variety of shade of green is seen in the leaves.

A short walk to the solitary shop and we passed the time of day with its proprietor. Then a walk to the top of the bluff that overlooks this secluded portion of earthly paradise. Here one obtains a fine view of the Sound to the north and south.

Perhaps a word to the amateur photographers would not be out of place. No doubt you will take with you plenty of films. Decide on the number of negatives you want to take. Then double the number of film spools to take that number of photographs. If you do so you will not come back disappointed. On such a trip as this, excepting at Oban, it is as easy a matter to get fresh and suitable films as it is to take photographs without them.

If you want a charming photograph of Portaskaig, turn past the hotel on to the projecting point of land. From that point you will obtain a most charming picture of the village.

Iain F. Anderson, *To Introduce the Hebrides*, 1933

A visit to the Mull of Oa will full repay the tourist for all his labour. Many are the interesting sights to be witnessed – the expansive waters of the Atlantic – the bold and rugged rocks – fantastic pillars and subterranean labyrinths – the curious caves where turmoil waters ceaseless roar, and where in the days of yore we are wont to be told, that dusky hobgoblins had their dark abode.

Robert Oliphant, *The Tourist's Guide to Islay, The Queen of the Hebrides*, 1881

Most of the visitors who come to Islay, however, come to golf. The strenuous enthusiasts go to Machrie, the others to Geisgeir or Gartmain. There is nothing dilettante about Machrie golf. It demands the wholehearted homage of a devotee, relegating the fickle attentions of the dabbler to the crowded courses of the mainland. If your business, say the facetious, interferes with your golf, give up your business. Indeed, the oft-told tale of the Scots minister has been more than once associated with Machrie.

Emerging after a hot and unhallowed strife in an exasperating bunker, he exclaimed bitterly: –

"Ah maun gi'e it up! Ah maun gi'e it up!"

"What!" cries his partner, in consternation, "gi'e up gowf?"
"Na," he replies, with sublime scorn, "gi'e up the ministry."

L. MacNeill Weir, *Guide to Islay*, 1911

Lauchlin MacNeill Weir was the son of Port Ellen man. He studied at Glasgow University, became a journalist and, after unsuccessfully fighting the Argyll constituency, became the Labour MP for Clackmannan and East Stirlingshire in 1922. He was Parliamentary Private Secretary to Ramsay MacDonald for seven years, and published a controversial book about him, *The Tragedy of Ramsay MacDonald*.

. . . During his life Mr Weir delighted to visit Islay. He was long a member of the Glasgow-Islay Association, serving for a time as one of the directors. In 1931 he presided at the annual gathering of the association. He rendered useful service to Islay with his pen in a well-informed guide book extolling the beauties of the island and inaugurating what was a form of "Come to Islay" movement.

The Glasgow Herald, obituary, 19 August, 1939

Chief among those that Weir encouraged to 'come to Islay' were golfers.

All good golfers, they say, go to St Andrews when they die. We grudge not St Andrews the ghostly company so be it they come to Islay while they live, and thus compensate for a Valhalla *in Fife*.

L. MacNeill Weir, *Guide to Islay*, 1911

Is there not plenty of room on the attractive links of Machrie for a ladies' golf course? It is high time the lords of creation emerged from their selfish exclusiveness to show chivalrous devotion to their help-meets, whose influence so unmistakably tends to elevate and refine man's nature. Neither ladies nor gentlemen need take cart-loads of changes of apparel with them when they go to Machrie, for one of its chief claims is its perfect freedom from restraint – its absolute un-conventionality. When the great end in view is the improvement of health, a daily round on the beautiful links of Machrie is an exhilarating and absorbing pastime which engages one's attention.

J. G. MacNeill, *Islay*, 1899

The Machrie takes its name from the Gaelic word machair, which means the links. Set in the dunes of Islay, and designed in 1891 by Willie Campbell, it is the traditional Scottish links.

Planet Golf rates The Machrie as a strong candidate to join its list of the top 100 courses on Earth. And says its magnificent Hebridean bay is one of the most beautiful locations in world golf.

The Machrie withstands the ultimate test, the test of time.

Walk in the footsteps of the golfing gods.

Play The Machrie.

Play it twice and fall in love!

Machrie Golf Links website, 2015

Today's owners of Machrie have made changes to the course, but will be hoping that future golfers share MacNeill's enthusiasm for it.

It is a fine sight after a westerly gale to see the great rollers coming on in unbroken smoothness till their curly crests, many feet in height, dash themselves in white foam on the sullenly resistant sands, or are broken among the rocks at Kintra into inland hurrying spray. Close to these rocks is one of the most notable holes in the links, No. 17, Mount Zion, it is called. It is over 400 yards in length, has many pitfalls for the unwary on the way, and its approaches are guarded on all sides. The green itself is of good size and turf, and is placed on an elevated tableland. Two things are difficult – first to get your ball onto this height; and second, when there, to get it to stay. Should you overrun it, you may find yourself in rather bad lies on the beach. Fabulous scores have been run up here, and if you manage to hole out in five, then you may pat yourself on the back in self-congratulation. Another grand hole is No. 5, The Scots Maiden. You tee your ball, grasp your club, look for the line of direction, and lo! rising sheer in front of you is a yawing sand bunker, whose outstretched brownness distinctly cries out, Come. Woe betide the golfer who gets into the arms of this siren, if you lose your head to her, sure as fate your heart will follow, and you are undone. In a game of strokes these two holes are apt to be terribly accumulative, and many a card has mysteriously disappeared at these places.

J. G. MacNeill, *Islay*, 1899

The annual migration to Islay of bird-watchers and shooters got pawky and poetic treatment from the *Ileach's* regular versifier, Jim Mitchell. The doctor referred to is 'Doc' Tait, a much admired Islay G.P. and keen ornithologist.

> Though the feathered population
> Doesn't worry in the least,
> The genus, Ornithologist
> Has very much increased.
>
> They come to watch the sea-birds,
> To look and mark and learn,
> The intimate life details
> Of gannet and of tern.
>
> From cares of town and city,
> Awhile they gain release,
> Sneaking up upon the chough,
> And numbering the geese.
>
> The birdies they scan closely,
> Each in its natural state,
> Then ascertain the species by
> Consulting Dr. ★★★★!
>
> But there are other sub-types
> Of homo sapiens,
> Whose interest is not confined
> To watching through a lens.
>
> In Autumn come the shooters,
> Intent upon the game,
> With double-barrelled shot-gun,
> And double-hyphen barrelled name.
>
> For the grouse and for the pheasant,
> One sometimes feels a pang,
> As their world comes to an end with
> Not a whimper but a bang.

ISLAY VOICES

Hail to thee, blithe spirits!
The moral would appear,
Just suffer the bird-watchers,
And of the shots keep clear.

J.S. Mitchell, *The Ileach*, August, 1974

Wildlife

Ther are many fresh water lochs in Ila, full of big trouts and a great many eels. Loch na Breck upon the top of Benlargi mountain is famous for many trouts, though no springs run to it nor come fra it.

Upon the banks of Loch Grennord, many selchs haunt, which are slain with dogs bred for that sport.

Donald Monro, *Description of the Western Isles of Scotland*, written around 1563

Martin Martin describes seals being killed in the Hebrides for their flesh, skins and blubber but, according to one prominent folklorist and naturalist, the hunting technique noted by Monro was unique to Islay.

I have not heard elsewhere of dogs being used to kill seals.

Seton Gordon, *Highways and Byways in the West Highlands*, 1936

The quadrupeds of this island are stoats, weasels, otters and hares: the last small, dark coloured, and bad runners. The birds are eagles, peregrine falcons, black and red game; and a very few ptarmigans. Red-breasted goosanders breed on the shore among the loose stones, wild gees in the moors. Herons in the island in Loch Guirm. The fish are plaice, smeardab, large dabs, mullets, ballan, lumpfish, black goby, greater dragonet, and that rare fish the lepadogaster★ of M. Gouan.

Thomas Pennant, *A Tour in Scotland and Voyage to the Hebrides*, 1772

In this and some of the neighbouring islands, multitudes of adders infest the heath. Many people retain still the vulgar error, that they sting with their forked tongue; and prescribe many ridiculous cures for their bite.

On the north-west side of the island is the cave of *Sanegmore*, which is a grotto, divided into a number of far winding passages, sometimes

★A species of Atlantic fish, described by French zoologist, Antoine Gouan.

opening into fine expanses; again closing for a long space into galleries, and forming a curious subterranean labyrinth. Beside this there are many other caverns, the haunt of numerous wild pigeons. The goats that feed among the rocks are so wild, that their owners are obliged to shoot them like deer.

Robert Heron, *Scotland Delineated, or a Geographical Description of Every Shire in Scotland*, 1799

The game on Islay is abundant. Besides roe, and occasional red-deer which come across from Jura, fallow-deer exist almost in a state of nature. Rabbits are numerous, and hares are said to be of two kinds, – one of them probably identical with *Lepus Hibernicus*. Vermin (with the exception of rats) are not particularly troublesome, and neither foxes or badgers, nor wild cats, exist upon the island, though otters are of course well known. Feathered game is likewise plentiful, – pheasants, partridges, grouse, black game, and, in their season wood-cocks in great abundance. Mr Campbell has brought in thirty-nine of the latter to his own gun in one day, although he has in vain attempted to achieve the twenty brace.

James Wilson, *A Voyage Round the Coast of Scotland*, 1842

In the rivers and streams, are to be found trout and salmon of delightful relish. The game consists of the usual varieties, with neither fox, fumart★ or wild cat to molest them.

Robert Oliphant, *The Tourist's Guide to Islay, The Queen of the Hebrides*, 1881

Islay's earliest settlers were attracted by the island's natural resources – not least its wildlife. Today, many of the islanders still have a keen interest in and knowledge of the flora and fauna that surrounds them, and the island has RSPB sites at Loch Gruinart and the Oa, and The Natural History Trust in Port Charlotte. Birdwatchers play an important role in Islay's tourist industry.

Islay's ornithological and other natural history riches arise from a combination of its geographical position in the Gulf Stream, giving a mild climate with little or no snow and few frosts, plus ample, but

★Polecat.

not excessive rainfall, and a great diversity of different habitats. The latter include fertile farmland, mature woodland as well as broadleaved and coniferous plantations, extensive dunes, sea cliffs, long sandy and rocky coasts, moorland, hills, more than 200 freshwater lochs, and two shallow and sheltered sea lochs, both with extensive inter-tidal mudflats and saltmarsh. Over 100 different bird species breed on the island and an additional 70 to 90 winter or visit as migrants. Islay is the British wintering headquarters for Barnacle (c.35,000) and Greenland White-fronted (c.5,000) Geese and holds 80% of the Scottish population of the Chough. Groups such as divers, freshwater and sea ducks, waders, raptors and gulls and terns are all well represented. Being an island restricts the total of flowering plants to just under 1,000, but the dune flowers can be spectacular complete with carpets of orchids, the latter also common in areas of old pasture. A nationally rare butterfly, the Marsh Fritillary, is widespread across the island and, in some years, abundant.

Malcolm Ogilvie, *The Birds of Islay*, 1992

Choughs are a 'must see' species for bird watchers coming to Islay, but their survival has been touch-and-go, as one of Scotland's most eminent biologists recounts.

The chough faced the blast of nineteenth-century game preservation and went under. Whether it was truly inimical to game is highly questionable, but it was one of the crow tribe and therefore must be bad. (Similarly the shag still suffers for the sins of the cormorant. Lovers of cheap shooting, and coastal fish and game preservers have never taken the trouble to ascertain the harmless food habits of the shag.) By the middle of the nineteenth century choughs had gone from inland districts of Scotland and were to be found only on the wilder coasts. Then they had to be cleared from these fastnesses. Graham mentions three pairs breeding on Iona in 1852, where they were left alone, but there are none there today. Skye lost its last chough by 1900 and no one knows how few were left on the cliffs of Islay when at last their rarity made them birds to be protected (and equally birds to have their eggs stolen). However, there has been a distinct increase in recent years on South-West Highland coasts. The bird is breeding regularly on Jura and has been seen on the forbidding cliffs of Ardmeanach in Mull. It was in Eigg till 1886 and this island is a likely station for a new colonization if the egg-collectors allow the bird to increase. The Northern Irish island of Rathlin must have been a reservoir which helped to stock Islay and made possible the spread from practical extinction, but for some years now Rathlin has been systematically sacked by British collectors. Nevertheless, if we can achieve some effective protection for our wild life in the future, the chough is in the way of coming back. The bird has one serious enemy in the peregrine falcon, particularly serious at the stage of low numbers of the chough. But peregrines have had a thinning time in the second German war as far as numbers are concerned, for they have had to be shot because of their depredations on carrier pigeons, on the safety of which birds the safety of aircraft crews might depend. There is probably no time more propitious than the present for the chough to increase – if man will but allow it.

F. Fraser Darling, *Natural History in the Highlands and Islands*, 1947

Islay is as green as the best of Ireland, except in the rugged north and south-east, which have more the look of Jura and share the same quartzite formation. Sanaigmore in the extreme north-west is one of my favourite places. The view stretches uninterruptedly to Colonsay and the Ross of Mull, with eastwards the Garvellachs and Seil Island. Here, too, are fine bird cliffs where, if you have a head for heights, you can traverse airy ledges on sound rock and almost rub noses with razorbills who merely turn inquiring heads, seldom moving off to reveal the single pointed egg which seems too large for such a small bird. No nest, just a spotted egg on a bare rock, a top-storey for quiet birds with noisy neighbours below in screaming kittiwakes and 'gurring' guillemots.

The special bird of this place and other sea cliffs of Islay is the chough whose sound is an explosive 'tee-ah', more dynamic than the sound of any jackdaw and a flight to match: powerful down-strokes and sudden dives as the wings are thrown back to bullet down, then spread out the brakes and soar up again. One I watched did a vertical dive of 200ft, suddenly flattening out to adhere a moment on a ledge then it was off again. But in that second I saw another chough dart to it, take food from its red curved beak and scramble back again into a hole.

Strange that the chough stronghold should be here when it has disappeared from the rest of the British coast. Yet perhaps not so strange when Ireland is only 23 miles across the water and there are good colonies of choughs in Donegal. Gordon Booth, a resident ornithologist, tells me the Islay population is holding its own very nicely, and long may it continue.

Tom Weir, *The Western Highlands*, 1973

Islay is a world-class birdwatching site, and the winter home to about 70% of the world's barnacle, and about 40% of the Greenland white geese. Between forty and fifty thousand of the two species descend on the island around October, congregating mostly at Loch Gruinart.

I have studied barnacle geese in Greenland and I have had the thrill of seeing them in their wintering grounds on Islay on other occasions. It is a thrill which never fades, for nowhere else in the world can so many barnacle geese be seen in one place at one time as here. Motoring along the green bowl of the flats we were surrounded by them, like mobile grey rugs edging away from us whenever we stopped the car. Glad to record, for the farmers' sakes, that they were nicely shared out over the best grazing acres. In fact the geese can be prevented from being a nuisance by merely breaking up their packs with a dog.

The massive edging-away movements became alarm when we got down from the car and the few dog-like yelps became one clamouring wave of high-pitched sound as thousands of birds took the air. All we needed was the sun to break from the obscuring clouds, and we got it, a flash to light the snow-white cheeks of the barnacles and show off the ebony chests and dove-grey back of birds on the ground and in the air. By contrast the Greenland white fronts showed off their zebra stripes and patch of facial snow round the base of the bill. Farms, cattle, water hollows, reed beds and green hills shone as we edged along slowly in the car, stopping to listen to the piping of golden plover mingling with curlew cries.

Tom Weir, *The Western Highlands*, 1973

The seas off Islay's 130 miles of coastline also teemed with life, and with opportunities to make a living or a profit.

Fish abound on the Islay coast, although there is but one ostensible fishing station, namely, Port-na-haven, whose athletic and fearless inhabitants derive their subsistence from the mighty deep. Of late years Lobster and Salmon fishing has been carried on by adventurers from Ireland, whose praiseworthy exertions have been rewarded with success.

William MacDonald, *Sketches of Islay*, 1850

Basking sharks, the largest fish in Scottish waters, were once hunted by Islay fishers, who referred to them as 'cairbin' or 'cairban', derivatives of the Gaelic, *cearban*.

> . . . in February 1777 Daniel Campbell of Islay was granted £200 by the Commissioners for the Annexed Estates to buy a vessel suitable for fishing 'for herring, for cod, and for cairban, which come on at different seasons'.

Traditionally, small whales like pilot whales had been simply driven by men in boats into shallow waters where they would be dispatched with spears, but the technique of harpooning at sea had reached Scotland.

> To obtain harpoons and lines (ropes) suitable for the basking shark hunt, a Scot would have to look no further than a ships chandler in the nearest sizable port because by the early 1750s ships were regularly setting out for the Arctic whaling from the Scottish ports . . .
> . . . In 1778 the accounts rendered to the Commissioners of the Annexed Estates by Walter Campbell of Islay in respect of the *Nancy* include a payment to a Daniel McGibbon of Greenock of £24 '. . . for Salt, Harpoons, whale lines etc.'

A basking shark could yield up to eight barrels of oil, and could keep cruisies on Islay burning a long time.

> While it seems that the dead shark was sometimes butchered alongside a boat, when the liver was cut out and the carcass abandoned, it is more likely that the usual practice was to tow the fish to a convenient beach for this operation, as the gutting of the liver could be done unhampered by rough seas. The oil extraction process was simple, with chunks of the liver just being boiled in an iron cauldron and the oil skimmed off. The flesh . . . was utilised on occasion as a food for the poor in hard times.

> Denis Fairfax, *Species History in Scotland: Man and the Basking Shark*, 1997

Whisky

Compton MacKenzie's most popular book was *Whisky Galore* (interestingly, both the words *whisky* and *galore* are derived from Gaelic words). Macken-zie based his novel on the true story of the *SS Politician* which sank off the Outer Hebridean island of Eriskay in 1941 and had its cargo – much of it whisky – 'salvaged' by the enterprising people of Barra. Islay's own *Whisky Galore* happened more than eighty years earlier, when a wooden ship came to grief off Kilchoman on a voyage from Glasgow to New Brunswick with a cargo of pig iron and spirits.

The brig *Mary Ann*, of Greenock, now lying a wreck at Kilchoman Bay, Islay, is fast breaking up, and portions of the cargo, floating ashore. Up to Saturday there had been about 200 boxes saved, con-taining bottled brandy, whisky and gin, and upwards of six puncheons of whisky, brandy, and wine; but the wildest scenes of drunkenness and riot that can be imagined took place.

Hundreds of people flocked from all parts of the neighbourhood, especially the Portnahaven fishermen, who turned out to a man. Boxes were seized as soon as landed, broken up, and the contents carried away and drunk. Numbers could be seen here and there lying amongst the rocks, unable to move, while others were fighting like savages. Sergeant Kennedy and Constable Chisholm, of the County Police, were in attendance, and used every means in their power to put a stop to the work of pillage.

They succeeded in keeping some order during the day of Thurs-day, but when night came on the natives showed evident symptoms of their disapproval of the police being there at all, and on the latter preventing a fellow from knocking the end out of a puncheon, in order, as he said to 'treat all hands', they were immediately seized upon by the mob, and a hand to hand fight ensued, which lasted half an hour, and ended in the defeat of the police, of whom there were only two against from 30 to 40 of the natives.

The police beat a retreat to Cuil Farm – about a mile from the scene of the action – closely pursued by about 30 of the natives, yell-ing like savages. Mrs Simpson, of Cuil, on seeing the state of matters, took the police into the house and secured the doors, at the same time placing arms at their disposal for their protection. The mob yelled two or three times round the house, but learning that the police had got fire-arms, they left and returned to the beach.

Next morning the scene presented was still more frightful to contemplate. In one place there lay stretched the dead body of a large and powerful man, Donald M'Phadyen, a fisherman from Portnahaven, who was considered the strongest man in Islay; but the brandy proved to be still stronger. He has left a wife and family. Others apparently in a dying state were being conveyed to the nearest houses, where every means were used to save life. Mrs Simpson, who is a very kind and humane person, supplied every remedy, but there was no medical man within fifteen or sixteen miles of the place. Mr James Simpson got a coffin made for M'Phadyen, and had him interred on Friday. At the time when the corpse was being taken away, some groups could be seen fighting, others dancing, and others craving for drink, in order, as they said, to bury the man decently. Up to Saturday there was only one death, but on Monday it was reported that two more had died.

The Argyllshire Herald, 27 May 1859

In Compton Mackenzie's *Whisky Galore!*, Barra was his 'tight little island' (as the film based on it was named in the USA). But Islay is the Hebridean island that really lives up to that name. Islay malts are international bestsellers and draw enthusiastic whisky 'pilgrims' to the island. But in the past, travellers to Islay often deplored the islanders' habit of turning grain into spirit.

The 'bere' referred to here is an ancient form of barley that was probably introduced by the Vikings, and is still grown in parts of Scotland.

The produce is corn of different kinds; such as bere, which sometimes yields eleven-fold; and oats six-fold: a ruinous distillation prevails here; insomuch that it is supposed that more of the bere is drank in form of whisky than eaten in the shape of bannocks.

Thomas Pennant, *A Tour in Scotland and Voyage to the Hebrides*, 1772

Historically, the spirit produced in the Hebrides was much stronger than the whisky sold today.

Their plenty of corn was such, as dispos'd the Natives to brew several sorts of Liquors, as common *Usquebaugh*, another called *Trestarig, i.e., Aqua-vita*, three times distill'd, which is strong and hot; a third sort is four times distill'd, and this by the Natives is call'd Usquebaugh-baul, i.e. Usqyebaugh, which at first taste effects all the Members of the Body: two spoonfuls of this last Liquor is a sufficient dose; and if any Man exceeds this, it would presently stop his Breath, and endanger his Life.

Martin Martin, *A Description of the Western Islands of Scotland,*
2nd edition 1716

To keep the natives sober, and to conserve grain for food, a 1795 Act of Parliament prohibited all distillation, and remained in force for two years. The collector of excise on Islay confiscated stills with which people had been producing legal and taxable whisky. What happened during prohibition in America, happened on Islay – the booze business was forced underground, with the Ileachs adopting Robert Burns' dictum that 'Freedom and Whisky gang thegither'.

After these Stills were taken up by Mr Campbell, from the distillers, and lodged in his own house, the distillers got over from Ireland tinkers, who fitted up for them cauldrons and boilers as Stills; between 90 and 100 of which, some of them upwards of 100 gallons, were seized by the Excise officers during the prohibition. After the prohibition was removed, Mr Campbell's lease of the Excise revenue of Islay was not renewed; and the people of the island, finding that they were not to get licences for a trifling sum, as before, were much displeased, and resolved not to take out licences, but they made no resolution not to distil. Mr Ross says, they are distilling perhaps to a greater extent than ever, sending their Spirits to Argyllshire, Inverness-shire, Mull and even to Lewis, to Galloway, and Ireland, but there has not been a licence taken out for distilling Spirits, nor has a shilling of Excise revenue been paid in Islay since the prohibition.

Report from the Committee upon the Distilleries of Scotland, House of Commons, 1798

Apart from the loss of revenue to the state, the home-distillation whisky was having dire social consequences. Islay clergymen – recruited to provide the information for a survey of the land, people and wealth of Scotland – saw the results first-hand.

ISLAY VOICES

Peculiar Privilege, and Consequences –

This island hath the liberty of brewing whisky, without being under the necessity of paying the usual excise duty to government. We have not an excise officer in the whole island. The quantity therefore of whisky made here is very great; and the evil, that follows drinking to excess of this liquor, is very visible in this island. This is one chief cause of our poverty; for the barley, that should support the family of the poor tenant, is sold to a brewer for 17s the boll; and the same farmer is often obliged to buy meal at £1. 3s. Sterling, in order to keep his family from starving.

When a brewer knows that a poor man is at a loss for money, he advances him a trifle, on condition that he makes him sure of his barley at the above price; and it is often bought by the brewers even at a lower rate; while those who are not obliged to ask for money until they deliver their barley, receive 20s. or more for it.

This evil, of distilling as much barley as might maintain many families, it is hoped, by some means or other, will soon be abolished. It may take some time, however, to prevent the people from drinking to excess; for bad habits are not easily overcome: but there would surely be some hopes of a gradual reformation, if spirituous liquors were not so abundant, and so easily purchased.

Statistical Account, 1791–1799
Parish of Kildalton, Rev. Mr. Archibald Robertson

Islay's 'local Parliament' of Gentlemen weighed in to stop the bootleggers.

The meeting considered the great Exertions of the Legislature in Suppressing the Distilling of Spirits and the great revenue given up by Ministry for the purpose of providing a sufficiency of Grain for the use of the nation, which in many parts is threaten'd with a Famine, and Considering that great Exertions have already been made in suppressing the Distilling in the Island, This Meeting unanimously Resolve Individually and Collectively to exert themselves in putting a total stop to the said Illegal Practices, in case they hear or know of any person within the Island attempting to Distill privately after this date. And they further resolve that they will not only give Information to the Capt' or Officers of Vol(unteers) of any person they know or hear of private Distilling, But that they will themselves assist personally in Suppressing the same.

The Stent Book of Islay, 1796

It was competition from commercial – and legal – distilleries on Islay that finally put an end to large-scale illicit whisky production.

> We believe that the moral and industrial habits of the people are also much ameliorated since the erection of legalised distilleries, and the consequent cessation of the illicit trade in whisky. Whatever may be the general effect of ardent spirits (and they are often sufficiently obvious), there can be no doubt that the payment of duties, amounting to a yearly revenue of upwards of £30,000 to Government, must be useful in its way.
>
> James Wilson, *A Voyage Round the Coast of Scotland*, 1842

But whether whisky was taxed or not, many believed its influence was evil. Among them was John McNeill, the Free Kirk minister at Portnahaven, who railed against whisky production to the Napier Commission.

> The only village industries are whisky distillation, a kind of unsteady work which has a most ruinous influence upon the community. Another prolific source of poverty and misery are the insanitary distillery taps, the village dramshops, to whose pernicious effects the villagers are constantly exposed.
>
> *Report of Her Majesty's Commissioners of Inquiry into the Condition of the Crofters*, 1884.

Even the shortage of food caused by the potato famines didn't stop the flow of barley away from hungry families to Islay's distilleries.

> In the years 1782, 1807, 1817, 1836 and 1837 there was a scarcity of foodstuffs which almost amounted to a famine; but in 1846-7 the continual scarcity, due to the ever-lessening area of soil under cereal cultivation, was aggravated by a potato blight, and there ensued a destitution and a starvation from the effects of which our peasantry has never rallied. In Brocodale, and in Barra, people died of actual hunger; one-third of the population of South Uist were in actual starvation. In Islay, the parish minister of Kilmeny reported: Oatmeal was poor in quality, and the best of the barley was ordered off to the distilleries for the landlord's rent, while "5000 souls" wasted away in hunger.
>
> Thomas Johnston, *The History of the Working Classes in Scotland*, 1920

While the distillation, and consumption, of whisky caused problems on Islay, the product was increasingly becoming synonymous with the island. Writing for an Irish magazine in 1859, John Murdoch reported:

The chief visible support of Port Ellen would seem to be a distillery which is carried on there by one of the present proprietors of the island. The support of the place is no doubt considerably augmented by the traffic occasioned by the calling of the steamer, the chief of this traffic being with four other distilleries in the neighbourhood. Indeed, it may be said that Islay's chief manufacture and most famous product is whisky – Islay whisky being about as well known as Dublin stout.

In this small island there are at present no fewer than nine or 10 distilleries busily engaged in the manufacture of the mountain dew for the delectation and refreshment of the thirsty Saxons of the Lowlands and England. A few years ago there were even more, perhaps as many as 15 in all. But the smaller of them have been gradually allowed to fall into decay and there, as in other places, although the taste seems to be in favour of the product of the smaller still, it is only the larger concern which can be worked at a profit.

John Murdoch, unpublished autobiography, 1889–1898

The habits of the population, with respect to industry and sobriety, are of late years materially improved. The nefarious and morally de-structive trade of illicit distillation used to be carried on among them to a very great extent; but the introduction of legal distilleries, and the steady discountenance which this traffic has received from the late and present proprietors, have well-nigh put an end to it, and with it to many of its injurious consequences.

George Anderson and Peter Anderson, *Guide to the Highlands and Western Islands of Scotland*, 1863

Of the state of morals in the Highlands and Islands I received the following proof, lamentable enough, but cheering:

"A great moral improvement has already taken place among the people. When Mr. W. Campbell arrived fourteen years ago, they were wild, savage and averse to reformation; and indeed, in some parts of the island, as we have seen, they still remain in an uncivilised state. Illicit distillation of spirits, smuggling, and shore-hunting *i.e.* plundering wrecks, were much practised, producing the necessary demoralising effects. It is only lately that the last of these habits has been abandoned, and in no small degree in consequence of the cessation of wrecks, resulting from the erection of the lighthouse. Five years ago Mr. W. Campbell committed some persons, two of them sons of a principal inhabitant of the island, for this offence, and they were transported for seven years. The legal distilleries now absorb all the grain requisite, and have here, as elsewhere, seconded the efforts of the landed proprietors to diminish the baneful practice of smuggling. The removal of these two incentives to vicious conduct has already produced salutary effects, though the people are still represented as idle and disorderly, and given to drinking, and consequently sometimes to fighting at markets, and fairs, funerals, weddings and other occasions of public assemblage."

Lord Teignmouth, *Reminiscences of Many Years*, 1878

It is a fact worth noticing, that the existing distilleries in Islay are all close to the sea. Formerly, there were a number of small distilleries inland, but none of them are now worked, it having been found, that proximity to the sea, favours the various processes of malting, brewing and distilling – especially is this apparent in the cooling and fermentation of the worts, most important items in the operations, which are particularly favoured by the fresh sea breezes, never wanting at a place like this.

Bowmore Distillery receives a splendid supply of the purest water in Islay, from the Laggan, the best and largest river in the island; it gives permanent employment to a considerable number of men, and a great amount of work to many in discharging cargoes of barley, landing coals, shipping whisky, cutting peats, &c. The quantity of peats consumed is very great, nothing else being used in the drying of the malt. The farmers, for miles round, and the villagers find the draff and pot ale most useful for cattle-feeding, and a perfect boon in winter when fodder is scarce. To those in any way interested in the process of malting, brewing and distilling, the stranger is ever sure to receive a kindly welcome from Captain James Mutter, the local acting member of the firm, who is at all times glad to show the premises.

Robert Oliphant, *The Tourist's Guide to Islay, The Queen of the Hebrides*, 1881

Few of the whisky pilgrims who come to Islay today have the passion and commitment of Alfred Barnard. Between the years 1885 and 1917 he visited all 162 working distilleries in the British Isles, 129 of them in Scotland. The result was a monumental book on *uisge beatha*. As well as being encyclopedic, his book was a remarkable physical achievement. Barnard's description of his visit to Islay is full of incident and stories of the rigours of travel at this time. But the travelling and the tippling seemed to have suited Barnard – he lived till he was 81.

> Upon due arrival at West Tarbert we boarded the steamer bound for Port Ellen, a journey occupying some hours, yet withal rendered pleasant by weather that was all that could be desired. Tired and hungry after our long day we were glad to reach our destination, and immediately on landing proceeded to the "White Hart Inn" where for several days we took up our quarters, and found the accommodation excellent and the attendants obliging.

Next morning, after 'a substantial breakfast', Barnard and his party set to work.

Ardbeg Distillery, Islay

The Ardbeg distillery is situated on the south-east coast of the island, in a lonely spot on the very verge of the sea, and its isolation tends to heighten the romantic sense of its position. It was established in the year 1815, but long previous to that date it was a noted haunt of smugglers. For many years the supervisors had been searching for this nest of illicit traffickers without success; most of the band were known by sight, and endeavours had long been made to catch them when out in their boats. At length the spot where they carried on their nefarious practices was discovered, but the band was too strong for an open attack; however, one day, when the party was absent with a cargo of whisky, a raid was made and the place destroyed after a seizure of a large amount of the illicit spirit. As it was impossible to procure other vessels, and finding their occupation gone, the whole band was scattered, and most of them migrated to the Kintyre shores. The site of their operations was shortly after occupied by the founders of Ardbeg distillery who chose it on account of the water, the chief characteristics of which are its softness and purity; it is obtained from Lochs Arinambeast and Uigidale . . .

Lagavulin Distillery, Islay

From Ardbeg our route homeward lay through the beautiful village of Lagganmhouillin or Lagavulin, "the Mill in the Valley." And no prettier or more romantic spot could have been chosen for a distillery. We trotted merrily along. The horse apparently knowing that its face was stable-ward, and the driver, evidently anticipating another "wee drappie" at our next halting place, occasionally broke out into song, but as it was in Gaelic we were none the wiser, and his command of the English language so limited, that he could not favour us with a translation. As we rounded the ridge of one of the hills we came in sight of the historical ruin of Dun-naomhaig Castle, which stands on a large peninsular rock, protected on the land side by a thick earthen mound opposite the village of Lagavulin.

Barnard worked for *Harper's Weekly Gazette*, a magazine apparently dedicated to the wine and spirit trade. He knew a good story when he heard one, and smugglers make a good story.

Lagavulin is said to be one of the oldest distilleries in Islay, the business to a certain extent having been founded in 1742. At that period it consisted of ten small and separate smuggling bothies for the manu-facture of "moonlight," which when working presented anything but a true picture of "still life," and were all subsequently absorbed into one establishment, the whole work not making more than a few thousand gallons per annum. The term "moonlight" used always to be applied to illicit Whisky in contradiction to that which paid duty, which was termed "daylight." A century ago smuggling was the chief employment of the crofters and fishermen, more especially during the winter, and many were the encounters which took place between them and the Government officers. Up to the year 1821 smuggling was a lucrative trade in Islay, and large families were supported by it. In those days every smuggler could clear at least ten shillings a day, and keep a horse and cow. Early in the century the buildings were converted into a legal Distillery, and in the year 1835 they came into possession of the present firm, who repaired the place and made considerable additions and improvements.

Laphroaig Distillery, Islay

The Whisky made at Laphroaig is of an exceptional character, being largely sought after for blending purposes, and is a thick and pungent spirit of a peculiar "peat reek" flavour. The small output renders it of high value in the market; and although the Distillery is of small dimensions, the proprietors would not attempt to disturb the present arrangements, as thereby the character of the Whisky might be entirely lost. The distilling of whisky is greatly aided by circumstances that cannot be accounted for, and even the most experienced distillers are unable to change its character, which is largely influenced by accidents of locality, water and position. No better instance of this can be given than the case of the Lagavulin and Laphroaig Distilleries, which, although situated within a short distance of one another, each produce Whisky of a distinct and varied type.

Port Ellen is one of Scotland's 'lost' distilleries. It ceased whisky production in 1983. Barnard's description of the distillery serves as an example of the precision of his observation.

Port Ellen Distillery, Islay

The Port Ellen Distillery is planted on the seashore, about half a mile from the village. The works cover three acres, and were built in the year 1825, but since that time several important additions have been made. In the absence of the manager, to whom we had letters of introduction, the distiller conducted us over the premises. We were first taken to the three spacious Barley Lofts, well lighted and ventilated, of the following dimensions, No 1 is 100 feet long and 36 wide; No 2, 110 feet by 52; No 3, 135 by 30. The three Malting Floors are of the same size, each having the usual Steeps; in close proximity are two Kilns, floored with wire cloth, one 52 feet by 26, the other 36 feet square. A flight of steps leads into the Malt Store, off which is the Mill Room, containing a pair of malt rollers; and in the adjoining room is the Mash Tun, 14 feet in diameter by 5 feet deep, a Wash Charger containing 5,000 gallons, two heating tanks, etc.

From this department we proceeded to the Tun Room, which contains seven Fermenting-backs, of an average capacity of 7,000 gallons each. Passing from here we came to the Still House, containing two old Pot Stills, one holding 3,500 gallons and the other 2,100, also two Receivers, 1,400 and 1,600 gallons respectively. In a line with the Distillery are six handsome Warehouses, containing at the time of our visit 3,700 casks, holding 240,000 gallons of Whisky of different ages. We may here remark that only peat which is dug in the district is used in the drying, and the water comes from two lochs in the hills; the principal one used for distilling purposes is noted in the locality for its clearness and purity, the other is used for driving purposes. Elevators are used all over the works; there is a Cooperage and Seasoning House for casks, a fine Spirit Store, and one of Morton's Refrigerators. The Whisky is Islay Malt, and the annual output 140,000 gallons.

Bowmore Distillery, Bowmore, Islay

We found the coach drive from Port Ellen to Bowmore one of the most uninteresting that we had ever experienced. During the journey for four hours we saw but two or three habitations, and scarcely any trees; in all our wanderings we have never travelled by such a dismal and lonely road. Fortunately we were a large party and a merry one, or we should have wearied of this dismal track long before we reached our destination. Sandy, our aged coachman, was a character and drove us at about a rate of four miles an hour. We continually remonstrated with him, but to no purpose, and plied him with nips of Whisky to induce him to urge his steeds along, but no persuasion would induce him to trot his horse, except at those parts of the road where they were accustomed to increase their speed. Some of us walked many a mile, and were yet able to keep ahead of him.

Within a very short distance of our journey's end a most agreeable and surprising change came over the scene, and we found ourselves driving beneath trees whose thick branches met overhead, and passing through the well cultivated policies and rural retreats, which form the aristocratic village of Bridgend.

Today's direct route from Port Ellen to Bowmore hadn't been built in Barnard's day. He'd taken the higher road, which reaches Lochindaal at Bridgend. The next morning, he took the three mile road along the loch side to Bowmore, where the distillery was owned by the Mutter brothers, whose father had bought the business.

We were told a story of this gentleman which betrays a marked character of the Islay-men: When Mr. Mutter first came to the island, he was invited to dinner with Captain Walter Campbell, When the meal was over, the Gallant Captain proceeded to give Mr Mutter advice, and amongst other things warned him as a stranger not to accept a present from any of his neighbours; "for if they send you a lamb they will expect a cow in return, therefore always refuse the gift, or pay for it".

In the year 1880 the Distillery came into the possession of their descendants, James and William Mutter, who have since then made great improvements and alterations in the works. It is a noticeable fact that all the Distilleries in Islay are but on the seaboard. The Distillers say that proximity to the sea favours the various processes of malting, brewing and distilling. Bowmore Distillery is supplied with an unlimited quantity of splendid water from the Laggan, the best and largest river in the Island, and is favourably suitable for the disposal and sale of the draff and pot ale, both most useful for cattle feeding, and a perfect boon in the winter when fodder is scarce.

Lochindaal Distillery, Port Charlotte, Islay

As we drove along, the sea was smooth and calm as an inland lake; but here, after a gale the Atlantic waves break in most magnificent array, and it is a sight never to be forgotten. We next passed Bruichladdich Distillery, which lies on the side of the road. Two miles further along we reached Port Charlotte, a village of little importance and interest except for the large Distillery owned by Mr. Sheriff, which employs a number of the labouring class, and gives some little life to the locality. At the back of the Distillery the ground rises into hills, near the top of which are two beautiful lochs, the Garroch and Octomore, from whence the water supply to the Distillery is obtained. The works, which were built early in the century, cover about two acres of ground, and although old fashioned are very compact and conveniently arranged for the operations of the Distillery. We entered by a gateway which faces the sea; on the right are small offices and a residence for the Brewer, on the left the spacious Granaries and Malt Barns, and in the front the Distillery proper. The kiln is floored with German wire cloth, the first we have seen in the Island, and we were informed that it is very expensive. Peat only is used in drying the malt, fired in open *chauffeurs*. The old Mash-house, which is kept very clean and is whitewashed, contains a circular Mash Tun, the Underback, and two heating coppers. In the Tun-room there are eight Washbacks, with an average capacity of 10,000 gallons each. The Still-house, which is a neat building, well lighted, contains three old Pot Stills, and the usual Receivers and Chargers. On the opposite side of the road, in the sea shore, are several large bonded Warehouses, capable of holding 5,000 casks. The Whisky is pure Islay Malt, and part of it is shipped from Bruichladdich pier, the remaining floated out to the ships, ten casks being lashed together by iron pins and a chain called "dogs," and towed out by boatmen.

After a century of production, Lochindaal Distillery closed in 1929, although its warehouses are still used by Bruichladdich Distillery.

Bruichladdich Distillery, Islay

In the afternoon we returned to Bridgend, calling at Bruichladdich on our way, as previously arranged. When we neared the Lighthouse, which was built on the margins of the sea, about a mile from Port Charlotte, we obtained a fine view of Islay House, called by the natives the White House, surrounded by its magnificent policies and stately woods, also the ridge of low hills on both sides of Lochindaal, which are cultivated in fine arable slopes almost to the edge of the sea. Day by day, as we get better acquainted with this fertile and interesting part of the Island, we are convinced that it well deserves the appellation of the "Queen of the Hebrides." Bruichladdich is quite an aspiring and tastefully built village, and is planted on one of the finest and most healthy spots in Islay. The Distillery, which is two miles from Port Charlotte and six from Bridgend, was built in 1881, covers a little over two and a half acres of ground, and faces the sea. It is a solid handsome structure in the form of a square, and entered through an archway, over which is a fine stone-built residence for the use of the partners when staying on the island . . .

Caol Ila Distillery, Islay

We soon came in sight of the Distillery lying directly beneath us, and we wondered for a moment how to get down to it. Our driver, however, knew the road well, for often had he been here before, and turning sharp to the right, we commenced the descent through a little hamlet of houses. But the way is so steep and our nerves none of the best, that we insist on doing the remainder of the descent on foot, much to the disgust of the driver, who muttered strange words in Gaelic. His remarks, however, are lost upon us, that language not having formed part of our education. As we descended the hill we paused now and then to gaze upon the far-stretching view before us, and to rest. Presently we found ourselves at the object of our search, and within a few yards of the sea. Caol Ila Distillery stands in the wildest and most picturesque locality we have seen. It is situated on the Sound of Islay, and within a few yards of the sea, in a deep recess of the mountain, mostly cut out of the solid rock. The coast hereabouts is wild and broken, and detached pieces of rock lie here and there of such size that they form small islands.

Messers. Bulloch, Lade and Co. have built a fine pier at which vessels can load or unload at any state of the tide, and besides the chartered vessels, arriving with barley, &c., there are two David MacBrayne's steamers calling here twice a week for whisky . . .

The water used, said to be the finest in Islay, comes in the form of crystal stream from a lovely lake called Torrabus, nestling among the mountains, over which ever and anon the fragrant breeze from the myrtle and blooming heather is wafted. This lake yields a never failing supply of this most essential factor in Distillation. We need not describe the suitable Cooperage and artisan shops, which are all perfect. The engine and steam boiler powers are highly efficient, and are evidently planned with a view to future extension. Comfortable dwellings have been provided for the employees, forming quite a little village in themselves, and we envied the healthy life of these men and their families.

Bunnahabhain Distillery, Islay

Nothing but peat is used in the kilns, which is dug in the district, and is of exceptionally fine quality. A large quantity of peat is always kept stored, so that only that which has become thoroughly matured is used; this is a very important consideration in drying the malt, as well-seasoned peat is free from the sulphurous matter which it contains when newly dug . . .

Neat villas have been erected on the rising ground in the rear of the Distillery for the Excise Officers, and two large ranges of houses provide ample accommodation for the workmen. A Reading Room and School Room have likewise, with praiseworthy liberality, been provided by the Company, and in the latter the children of the workmen receive an elementary education. There are fifty to seventy hands employed throughout the season.

Alfred Barnard, *The Whisky Distilleries of the United Kingdom*, 1887

Today, the distillation of single malt whisky on Islay is a thriving industry that has won a vast international market. But it has not always been so.

Islay is famous for black cattle and whisky, though, regarding the latter commodity, I am sorry to say that it is not being manufactured in such quantities as in past years. Many of the distilleries are closed down. The quality I am assured is still according to standard, and if the old Gaelic proverb "When the natives leave Islay, farewell to the peace of Scotland" is true, I would hazard a guess that they must be no mean judges of their liquid export . . .

Near the northern exit of the Sound we pass Bonahaven Distillery, now, I believe, closed. Its snow-white walls along the seashore gives to its surroundings a cheerful appearance of brightness, in strong contrast to the drab tenantless moorland.

Iain F. Anderson, *To Introduce the Hebrides*, 1933

Unfortunately the easier access to markets has coincided with a marked decline in the whisky industry. Things have not been helped by the Chancellor of the Exchequer's insistence on seeing whisky as a luxury drink and taxing it accordingly, rather than as the very water of life which is implied in its Gaelic name – 'Uisge-beatha'.

This is a fact of life of which every Ileach is well aware. At present none of the distilleries is in full production, while some are producing token amounts of whisky each year. If the distilleries close, in ten years there will be nothing left in Islay but trees and geese, as a shepherd prophesied at Finlaggan, summarising the island's Golden Age and its apparently dismal future with a sweep of his hand. An exaggeration perhaps, but the omens at the moment are not auspicious.

Norman Newton, *Islay*, 1988

The dawn of the 21st century found Scotland's whisky industry in better shape, and the first new distillery in 124 years was built on Islay.

Kilchoman Distillery's first ever bottle of single malt from cask number one, filled in December 2005, was sold at auction for £5,400. The winning bid was made by Niels Ladefoged, originally from Denmark and who lives in the UK. The bottle of three-year-old single malt has a unique design and is the only one of its kind. All proceeds of the auction will go to Islay charities.

The bottle is contained in an exclusively designed, attractive wooden presentation box which was hand-made by Howard Proctor, a member of Kilchoman's production team, and features a watercolour on the label, painted by Nicola Wilks, an artist with three generations of family connections with Islay. The auction took place at Kilchoman Distillery's Open Day, Thursday 28th May at 12.30pm during Feis Ile, Islay's festival of Malt and Music. Anthony Wills, Founder and Managing Director of Kilchoman Distillery said:

"We are delighted with the winning bid and a huge congratulations to Niels Ladefoged. Our thanks go to all those, both local and international, who made their bids for such a wonderful piece of whisky history. We look forward to an exciting year ahead and the launch this September of our very first single malt."

The Ileach, 6 June 2009

Islay people are rightly proud of the world-class whisky produced on the island, and jealous of its reputation. But the fact that the vast majority of production is owned by multinational corporations can lead to unease and the suspicion that what is good for the distillers is not necessarily good for Islay.

In December 2003, Diageo provoked a storm in the Scotch whisky industry over its decision to change its Cardhu brand from a single malt to a vatted malt (also known as a pure malt) whilst retaining the original name and bottle style. Diageo took this action because it did not have sufficient reserves to meet demand in the Spanish market, where Cardhu had been successful. They were eventually forced to back down after a fierce campaign led by whisky independent William Grant and Sons.

On Islay, the noted drinks journalist Andrew Jefford pointed out in his book *Peat Smoke and Spirit* that: 'The vast majority of the whisky in every bottle of Lagavulin has been aged not on Islay, but on the Scottish mainland. Lagavulin and Caol Ila are the two big exceptions to the general principle that Islay whisky is aged on the island – and to the general belief that island-aging has a profound influence on the quality of the spirit.' To Diageo, these points are irrelevant. Why should it matter where Lagavulin is matured? Why should it matter that bottles of Cardhu are actually mostly filled with spirit from other distilleries? To Diageo, Smirnoff is just a brand – it does not necessarily mean vodka. Does the Diageo Board think the French, Spanish, American, Indian and Chinese markets care about the association of Johnnie Walker with Kilmarnock? In the world inhabited by the world's largest drinks company, the word 'Kilmarnock' represents nothing but an unnecessary overhead.

The logical conclusion of this approach is to ask, why should Diageo bother with individual distilleries at all? If you can hire a few of the right people, why not build one uber-efficient mega distillo-factory, where super-bright chemists can reproduce the flavours and nuances of the ancient whisky brands in the comfort of the laboratory and then programme the hi-tech megastills to deliver exactly the right spirit of exactly the right character in exactly the right amounts? The distillofactory could be promoted as super-green and ultra-sustainable. It could be located next to a major port for bringing in the malting barley from around the world – purchased from wherever the market is currently most favourable. It could be located next to a railhead from where colossal volumes of finished product could be efficiently distributed. Spirit exhibiting the character of every whisky region, indeed every distillery, in Scotland could all be produced in one environmentally sound, sustainable, drink-aware kind of place.

The Ileach, August 2009

The Fatal Shore

The west coast of Islay is exposed to the full force of the Atlantic. Such a power can bring everything from curiosities to disasters.

> I was also favoured with several of the nuts, commonly called Molucca beans, which are frequently found on the western shores of this and other Hebrides. They are the seeds of the *Dolichos urens, Guilandian Bonduc., G. Bonducetta,* and *Mimosa scandens* of Linnaeus, natives of Jamaica. The fifth is a seed called by Bauhin, *Fructus exot: orbicularis culcis nervisque quatuor,* whose place is unknown. The four first found in quantities on the steep banks of the rivers of Jamaica, and are generally supposed to drop into the water, and to be carried into the sea: from thence by tides and currents, and the predominancy of the east wind, to be forced through the Gulf of Florida, into the North American ocean, in the same manner as the Sargasso, a plant growing on the rocks in the seas of Jamaica. When arrived in that part of the Atlantic, they fall in with the westerly winds, which generally blow two-thirds of the year in that tract; which may help to convey them to the shores of the Hebrides and the Orkneys. I was for resolving this phenomenon into shipwrecks and supposing that they might have flung on these coasts out of some unhappy vessels: but this solution of mine is absolutely denied, from the frequency and regularity of the appearance of these seeds. American tortoises, or turtle, have more than once been taken alive on these coasts, tempest-driven from their warm seas; and part of the mast of the Tilbury man-of-war, burnt at Jamaica, was taken up on the western coast of Scotland; facts that give probability to the first opinion.
>
> Thomas Pennant, *A Tour in Scotland and Voyage to the Hebrides,* 1772

Islay's Atlantic weather and the tides and currents around its rugged reef-strewn coast conspire to create a perfect storm for shipwrecks. Untold numbers of vessels have perished in its waters. One of the most harrowing of losses was that of the *Exmouth*.

It was near Sanegmore that the tragical shipwreck of the emigrant brig Exmouth, from Londonderry for Quebec, occurred, on 27th April 1847, when all the passengers, 240 in number, with all the crew excepting three, found a watery grave. The appearance of the shore after the storm, strewed with fragments of wreck, and dead bodies, and mangled limbs, is described to have been appalling and heart-rendering beyond conception.

George Anderson and Peter Anderson, *Guide to the Highlands and Western Islands of Scotland*, 1863

On April 27th. 1847, the brig *Exmouth* was wrecked on the rocks at Sanaig and her unfortunate passengers, 240 Irish emigrants, were lost. They had set out a couple of days before from Londonderry, bound for Canada. But after clearing the coast of Ireland, they encountered a storm which compelled them to put back. And, according to the testimony of the three of the crew who escaped, the pilot mistook the Rinns of Islay light for that of Tory Island. They lost their course and, before morning the *Exmouth* was dashed against the rocks and her unfortunate cargo of living beings shared the fate of the thousands of other evicted Celts who were shipwrecked in rotten vessels to be out of the way of more highly favoured sheep and cattle.

The vessel was literally reduced to atoms – for she was an old craft only for the timber trade. She had, in fact, been chartered to bring a cargo of timber from Canada. But it was turning a double penny to take out a cargo of 'mere Irish'. Their passage money was paid. And though they and the ship went to destruction, the owners were no losers. And the landlord who cleared out the people thought no more about them than if they had gone quietly to rest in their beds. In Ireland they were in the great man's way. At the bottom of the sea they ceased to trouble him.

The first intimation of the catastrophe was given by those three sailors who scrambled over the rocks on which they had been cast from the mast of the vessel ere she was rent to pieces. They wandered inland and soon came upon the habitations of men by whom they were taken care of. But ere the country people reached the scene of the wreck, the vessel was beyond recognition. Not so much as would make a table held together of her. And the poor passengers were beyond the reach of aid or pity. There was nothing that could be rescued excepting the clothes of the doomed people which floated to the shore.

All that could be done was done, however. John Francis Campbell, Colin Campbell, Balinaby, and others, including myself, worked for days rescuing the bodies. These were carefully picked up and carried ashore. And I think about 160 of them were lapped up in the clothes of different kinds which were washed ashore and buried on a green slope facing the sea about half a mile to the south of where they met their death.

There they rest – well on to 200 of the millions missed in the Irish census of 1851. And when the day of reckoning and retribution comes, the loss of these people will be laid at the door of the supporters of the British feudal land system. And these supporters, coroneted and gartered though they may be, will be arraigned at the bar of justice for the murder of these poor Irish men, women and children.

John Murdoch, unpublished autobiography, 1889–1898

There was living at the time a little girl called Eleanora McIntyre. She found a doll on the shore and took it home with her. The owner of the doll, so the story goes, was buried nearby. That night Eleanora dreamed of a sad and tearful little girl crying for her doll, so the next day she buried the doll with its owner.

Another story, which was well known locally, told how one poor survivor, so weak and weary that he could not drag himself out of the water, appealed to someone on the land to help him out. He had his belt containing his money round his waist and offered it in return for help in saving him. The offer was accepted, but as soon as the belt was handed over he was pushed back into the water and was drowned.

Peggy Earl, *Tales of Islay*, 1980

There is other evidence that shipwreck survivors, washed up on Islay's shores, were not always kindly welcomed.

This Meeting, with every feeling of humanity for the distressed Sufferers, who have the misfortune to be shipwrecked on the coast of this Island, have to regret that numbers of the Country people, shaking off all fear of God, or regard to the laws, are in the constant practice against every rule of Christian charity, or hospitality, of resorting in numbers to the shores, where strangers have the Misfortunate of being shipwrecked, and that for the sole purpose of plunder; which practice this Meeting hold in the greatest abhorrence, and now declare their disapprobation of; and in order, as much as possible, to remedy the evil, this Meeting not only collectively, but individually pledge themselves to use their utmost exertions, not only for the preservation of the property of the individuals, who may have the misfortune to be wrecked on these coasts, but also for bringing to condign punishment all and every such person as may be found plundering from wrecks: And in order that this resolution of the Gentlemen of Islay may be made as public as possible, the Clerk is hereby required to send an Extract of this Minute to the Ministers of the different parishes of the Island, to be affixed on the Church doors, that none shall pretend ignorance, and it is hoped that the Ministers, for the sake of good order, will explain these resolutions to their parishioners from the pulpit,

The Stent Book of Islay, 1798

Untold numbers of ships perished off Islay – many of them smashed into the rocky cliffs of the Mull of Oa.

It is something very remarkable, that on this dangerous promontory where many a ship has been shattered to pieces, there is no Lighthouse or friendly beacon to guide the storm tossed mariner who is obliged to find his way as best he can in dark and stormy weather. Speaking of this part of the Islay coast, we may here mention, the total loss of a German vessel which took place here about two years ago – the most melancholy part of the sad catastrophe being, that part of the crew and the Captain's wife found a watery grave.

Robert Oliphant, *The Tourist's Guide to Islay, The Queen of the Hebrides*, 1881

A lighthouse was never built on the Oa, but elsewhere lighthouse engineers worked hard throughout the nineteenth century to make Islay's waters safer. Today, five major lights shine out from Islay's coast.

Beyond Kilnaughton a few minutes walk, is the road to the Lighthouse, which though not of a modern cast, but rather old fashioned, is nevertheless of great service in guiding vessels entering the bay. It was erected in 1832 by the late Walter F. Campbell of Islay, to the memory of his wife, Lady Ellinor. On a marble tablet facing the shore, is cut the following inscription – the poetical lines of which are very beautiful and appropriate:

ISLAY VOICES

1832

This tower is erected to the memory of Lady Ellinor Campbell by her husband.

Ye who 'mid storms and tempests stray
In danger's mid-night hour,
Behold, where shines this friendly ray
And hail its guardian power.

'Tis but faint emblem of her light,
My fond and faithful guide
Whose sweet example, meekly bright
Led through this world's eventful tide
My happy course alright.

And still my guiding star she lives
In realms of bliss above,
Still to my heart blest influence gives
And prompts to deeds of love.

'Tis she that bids me on the steep
Kindle the beacon's flame,
To light the wanderer o'er the deep,
Who, safe, shall bless her name.

So may sweet virtue lead your way
That when life's voyage is o'er
Secure like her, with her you may
Attain the heavenly shore.

Robert Oliphant, *The Tourist's Guide to Islay, The Queen of the Hebrides*, 1881

Walter Frederick Campbell's monument to his wife still shines out – as do the four Islay lights built by the Stevenson dynasty of engineers.

There is scarce a deep sea light from the Isle of Man to North Berwick, but one of my blood designed it. The Bell Rock stands monument for my grandfather, the Skerry Vhor for my Uncle Alan and when the lights come on at sundown along the shores of Scotland, I am proud to think they burn more brightly for the genius of my father.

Robert Louis Stevenson, *Memoirs of Himself* (written in 1880, published in 1912)

The first Islay light was the Rhinns Lighthouse, built by Robert Louis's grandfather, Robert, by 1825. It stands on the tiny island of Orsay, opposite Port Wemyss.

The Rhins, a promontory forming the south-western extremity of the island of Islay, is another position of importance for pointing out the northern side of the passage from the Atlantic to the Clyde and Irish Sea, between Islay and Bengore Head in Ireland. The Commissioners, at their meeting in the month of January 1823, having ordered a Light-house to be built at this station, it is accordingly progressing.

Robert Stevenson, *An Account of the Bell Rock Light-House*, 1824

On this island a lighthouse has been built and, perhaps no station on the whole coast of Scotland, if we except Cape Wrath, more loudly demanded this preservative measure to the shipping interests and to human life.

George Anderson and Peter Anderson, *Guide to the Highlands and Western Islands of Scotland*, 1863

Coming in sight of Portnahaven, the next prominent object in view, is the magnificent Lighthouse on Isle Oversay, built in the year 1824 and which guards this dangerous coast. The Lighthouse, one of the principal sights of Islay, ought not under any circumstance, be omitted in the tourist's programme – it is 96 feet from the ground and always open to visitors (Saturdays and Sundays excepted). The passage to it is by ferry, where a very strong current runs, but the Lighthouse ferrymen will take passengers to and fro in comfort, and perfect safety. The tourist having now landed on the little Island, which forms a snug and productive farm in the free occupation of the Light-house keeper, proceeds up a gentle knoll and enters the courtyard of the Lighthouse, when he begins his ascent of what at first sight seems to be an interminable turnpike stair. From the summit of the tower a most exquisite, varied and gorgeous view is obtained of Ireland and several of the Western Isles – the great and restless Atlantic, whose ceaseless murmur of its mighty billows, in their endless roll, is constantly heard, and not a little startle us, as they dash against the adamantine rocks of the surf-beaten coast. During storm and tempest, the sea at this point runs mountains high – is awfully grand, and can only be realized when seen in this condition.

Robert Oliphant, *The Tourist's Guide to Islay, The Queen of the Hebrides*, 1881

Rhuvaal lighthouse, at the north end of Islay – like MacArthur's Head – was built by Robert Louis' father, Thomas, and uncle, David. Completed in 1859, it was automated in 1983.

At the northern opening of the Sound on the north-west point of Islay stands the white-limed lighthouse, a cheering sight at all times. Lying at anchor close by is the yacht-like lighthouse supply ship, SS May. At our passing its deck seems quiet, though when I look at it through the "glass" I see a group of men all busily engaged in some task, from their movements no doubt requiring much exertion. I know no ships nor crews in the Hebrides I admire more in their excellent unfailing service than those of the Lighthouse Service.

Iain F. Anderson, *To Introduce the Hebrides*, 1933

Among the keepers who lived in remote Rhuvaal prior to automation was Billy Frazer. Billy was 90 when he was interviewed for a television documentary about the 'Lighthouse Stevensons'.

He'd served in World War Two as skipper of an RAF search and rescue launch, and then spent 38 years as a lighthouse keeper. Once out of training, his first posting was to Rhuvaal. Even today there is no road to it, only a very rough track from Bunnahabhain. For a Belfast city boy it was the back of beyond.

Billy – in a Belfast accent undiluted by seven decades in Scotland – begins by describing how he came to be a keeper after leaving the RAF.

I used to go down and have a jar or two with the boys, and then this day had come up and the wife's mother had the lunch ready, and I sat down at the table and she kept looking at me and I felt a wee bit sort of funny and I said, 'Is there something wrong?' And she says, 'Aye there is, is it no time you were thinking of getting a job?' So I decided then I would and I asked the brother-in-law who'd also been in the RAF. He was what they called an occasional keeper. I said, 'What do those fellas do up at that lighthouse?' 'Och,' he says, 'they always seem to be running about with brass buttons on, showing visitors around.' So I said, 'That'll do for me.' Well the Coastguard maybe would have suited me better, but their money was even worse than the lighthouses, and it was pathetic. There was no glamour in lighthouses or anything like that for me. What they were to me was a light at sea where I could take a bearing off, to check my position and stuff like that. They were purely an aid to navigation. So anyway, I wrote to Edinburgh and I went up there and I was accepted.

I then descended into the lighthouses. And coming from being a skipper of a up-to-date boat, and having the crew at my disposal, I entered the world of paraffin oil which was quite a shock. And that was the start. Believe you me, I wasn't greatly enamored with it, but there you were. I was in it for good or for worse with my wife. She was very good. She could cope with it, coming from a small village like Drummore in Galloway, where I'd been stationed in the RAF for a while. There was no love of going to a lighthouse but I accepted the fact that I was then going to be there for keeps more or less. And that was the reason for joining.

I was eventually, what we called, "appointed" to Rhuvaal in the north end of Islay, and that was quite an eye-opener. But my wife, coming from a village and being used to cooking herself although she was only 19 when we got married – I was just 20 – she coped with it all and we were at Rhuvaal about three years.

Q: So you say Rhuvaal was an eye-opener. In what way?

Well, we arrived there, we first went to Port Askaig. You'd three boat journeys, one from Gourock to East Loch Tarbert, and then from West Loch Tarbert to Port Askaig, and then an open boat about six mile up the Sound to Rhuvaal, and it was two days it took us to get there. The principal keeper was dying to meet us and they landed me and my wife and two or three sticks of furniture, nothing much because the houses were supposed to be partly furnished. But they were very nice, we were very lucky. They were an Orcadian couple and they was at the end of their service really, and I was starting, but they were really very nice and we were very happy with them.

But like prior to going there, I had a letter from the chap who was leaving to say that he'd some hens and two goats and would I like to buy them? Well I think he thought that we would eventually have a family, and have goats' milk for the kids, instead of tinned milk. So I bought them and when we got to Rhuvaal, the principal light-keeper, said, 'Would you like to see your goats?' I said I would, and I went down to the cliff a bit and we came to this house and here was two goats, Tilley and Bessie. But I kept looking at these goats and he said, 'Is there something wrong with the goats?' 'Well,' I said, 'I think I've been done.' He says, 'What are you talking about?'

Well, I'd come from down in Galloway where they were cows you know, plenty of cows everywhere, and I says, 'Well, a cow's four and these goats are only two.' He says, 'What are you talking about?' And I says, 'teats!' He said, 'For God's sake, man, goats have only got two.' I thought they were a wee bit more formed you see, but they were great goats and they were actually just like dogs, so tame and nice and all. And we had these Exchequer hens and there was a wee incident with them. Because we used to get 12 pints a day of milk from these two goats and we tried to make cheese, we tried to make butter, we weren't very successful. And then we fed it to these exchequer hens and they laid like machines with this goat's milk, and we had a mountain of eggs instead of a mountain of milk. And the boatmen, on the Saturday when they came, said to me, 'Tell your wife that the shop wifey in Port Askaig would buy those eggs off her.' And I says, 'All right.' So we started selling our eggs to this Port Askaig woman. And it was two or three shillings extra and they were beautiful eggs. And he said to me one day before he come up to the lighthouse, 'The wifey in Port Askaig said she would give you an extra sixpence a dozen if you could guarantee they're fertile.' And I said, 'That'll be no problem.' So I says, 'I'll ask my wife when you come up.' So he came into our house for a cup of coffee and I said to her, 'We're getting an extra sixpence a half dozen for these eggs if we can guarantee they're fertile,' and she said, 'Are you stupid?' And I said, 'No, but I've been known not to be too bright.' She said, 'We've got no cockerel.' So I said, 'I suppose that's something to do with it.' But I was completely ignorant of this type of thing you know.

Q: How remote was Rhuvaal?

Well, the only thing you did see was the boatmen from Port Askaig every Saturday with the mail and the rations. There was a sheep track to Bunnahabhain which was a distillery about six miles, but just a sheep track over the hills, and we sometimes would take that over to Bunnahabhain if we required urgent mail, we would phone Port Askaig and they would send it up to Bunnahabhain which still had a road, but it was very long, and then when you got there you had to walk all the way back again. But it was very isolated, there was nothing there. And looking just across from us was Colonsay and across the Firth was Jura. With the two of us like, four of us in the two cottages, that was all the people you saw. And the loneliness in a way must get to you because when we were there about a year or two when the principal keeper wanted me, he used to open our front door into the hallway and he'd shout 'are you in, Billy?' and I'd say 'come in'. That was just how things went. And this day we were sitting at our lunch, a lovely summer day and Mary had put the lunch out and I was starting to eat and suddenly there was a knock at the door and a sunlit afternoon and I said to her 'there's somebody at that door', she says 'away out and see'. She says 'I'm not going out.' And I says 'oh well, I'll have to go.' And I goes out and you know I just thought who in the whole world is going to knock our door and I finally opened the door very gingerly, and this big tall man was standing outside. And I said 'hello.' He said 'I'm the shepherd,' he said 'Calum Shaw, and I've been out feeding the tups. I'd some corn left and I put it in the trough to feed your hens with, just to let you know.' And I said 'thank you very much' but my heart was thumping. After going through a war, just a knock on my door, that was how lonely this got like.

Och, these things happened and when we finally, actually left there I really got my transfer then because I had terrible toothache and there was no dentist in Islay and the doctor was in a place called Bridgend and he was a great doctor and a very poor dentist. To get to him I had to go 6 miles on an open boat and 13 miles in a taxi, and I finished up there and when I came in I never heard a doctor swear like it, I was sort of shocked you know, with the language. And I always remember he was taking this tooth out, he said 'that's the best place to have a bloody Irishman,' he said 'at the end of a pair of forceps'!

That was island life you know. We sort of survived it. We were happy in our own way.

Billy Frazer, interviewed for TV documentary 'The Lighthouse Stevensons', 2011

Islay at War

Before the horrors of war, the pleasures of peace. In the following extract, we meet Ileachs enjoying good times a few years before the outbreak of World War One. The conflict would dramatically alter the lives of many people who attended the event reported here.

Double Marriage

The farm of Gartbreck was on Wednesday of last week the scene of a very rare and highly interesting event. On the invitation of Mr and Mrs Barr a large company of friends, neighbours and acquaintances assembled to witness the marriage at the same time of two daughters of that highly esteemed and much respected family. The nuptials were those of Mr James Kerr and Miss Jeannie Barr and of Mr Angus Mactaggart and Miss Helen Barr. Owing to the favourable nature of the weather, the wedding ceremony was arranged for in the garden; and a prettier sight was never behold in that trim, well-tended enclosure. The brides, who were beautifully robed, and each carried large bouquets of charming flowers, were led forward by their father, attended by their two sisters, Misses Maggie and Janet, as bridesmaids; whilst the two grooms were Messrs John Kerr and David Mactaggart, brothers of the respective bridegrooms. The ceremony was performed by the Rev. Mr Macgilchrist, Parish Church, assisted by Rev. Mr Maciver, United Free Church, Bowmore.

On the conclusion of the marriage ceremony, the happy couples were the recipients of the best wishes and hearty congratulations of their numerous friends. Thereafter the process of cutting the brides' cakes was successfully accomplished and the guests were entertained with a service of cake and wine customary on such auspicious occasions, after which the entire company sat down to a bountiful table elegantly and tastefully arranged in one of the farm buildings, which had been impressed to do the service for such a large gathering, and which the united energies of the Barr family had transformed for the time being into a spacious, artistic, and comfortable dining hall destined soon after to become a most satisfactory ballroom, with smoothly polished floor, gracefully draped walls, and abundant and well lighted air space.

When all had partaken heartily of the tempting viands that loaded the tables, the healths of the happy couples were, on the call of the Rev. Mr Macgilchrist, cordially pledged. The toast of the host and hostess was neatly given by Mr Wm. Mactaggart, and was warmly received. Later in the evening similar compliments were given by Mr Holmes and Mr R Cullen to Mr and Mrs Kerr, Corrary, and Mrs Mactaggart, Kilchearan, the parents of the bridegrooms.

Dancing was afterwards enjoyed by the younger guests; whilst the older and more sedate beguiled the time with social talk and happy reminiscences.

The departure of the young couples on the honeymoon was attended by showers of rice and confetti, and they carried with them the best wishes of all for their future happiness and prosperity.

Oban Times, Wednesday 2 June 1909

Today Islay has six war memorials, established initially to commemorate the island's dead of World War One. Many had served with the local regiment, the Argyll and Sutherland Highlanders, while some found themselves in other units recruited as far afield as Australia and Canada. Others served in the Royal Navy, the Royal Naval Reserve and the Merchant Navy.

Many of the Islay men who served in khaki had joined the part-time Territorial Army prior to the war. Among them, Port Ellen man, John McNab.

> C Coy
> 1/8 A and SH
> BEF
> 4th Oct 1915

Dear John

Thanks very much for your very welcome parcel which I received safely a few days ago. You should have written a few lines also. I daresay there is very little material for news in Islay meantime, but I will be glad to have a note from you soon. The Battalion is in the trenches just now and the CQMSs are up just behind the reserve trenches with the cookers etc. McIsaac is lodging with me we have a fairly good dug-out with a fire in it and a bed we made ourselves, we may be here for a fortnight yet.

We saw a British aviator taking down a German machine the other day. "Our Man" got above the Hun and opened fire with his machine gun. He soon got him and the German aeroplane fell like a wounded bird. It was an awful sight seeing the aeroplane dropping over 3,000ft.

Alick McLeod has been at the Base for over 3 months now. He is a CSM there. Neil Boyd is our CSM. I am sending you a photo of a group of us. You will likely recognise them all. Well John I think this is all just now. I hope your wife and little girl are well also yourself. Remember me to Forrest and D Logan.

I noticed in the Peoples Journal a photo of Capt Thomson who was awarded the DCM. This Capt was in "C" Coy having been transferred from "B" shortly before we left Bedford. He went to the miners when we came out here. You would likely hear that big George Ross was killed. You may remember him being in the officers' mess in Bedford. He had been promoted to Cpl latterly. John McLachlan is a CQMS in the 3rd Scottish Prov Btn and of course Matthews is QM of the 2/8 AandSH.

Mind and write soon now.

Kindest Regards
Yours Sincerely
John McNab

Letter from John McNab, Museum of Islay Life

News from Islay

It was with very great and genuine sorrow that the local community heard of the sudden death on 10th inst. of Coy. Quartermaster-Sergeant John McNab of the 8th Argyll and Sutherland Highlanders, at the age of 28 years, third son of the late John McNab of the Islay Hotel, Port Ellen. The deceased had to his credit a record of nine years and 253 days efficient service in the Territorials, which included close on two years in France. On his discharge over twelve months ago, owing to ill-health, he was accorded an illuminated memorial of his service from the Record Office, Perth, in which it is stated that he served with honour, was disabled in the great war, and relinquished the service with a high character. The funeral to Kilnaughton on fourteenth inst. was largely attended. Much sympathy goes out to his mother and other relatives of the gallant soldier, who had given of his best to the service of his country.

Oban Times, 17 June 1919

In August 1918, a 23-year-old Islay man won Britain's highest award for bravery – the Victoria Cross. David Lowe MacIntyre was a lieutenant in the Argyll and Sutherland Highlanders, but attached to the Highland Light Infantry. MacIntyre was the son of Portnahaven's United Free Church minister.

War Office, 26th October, 1918.

His Majesty the KING has been graciously pleased to approve of the award of the Victoria Cross to the undermentioned Officer, Non-commissioned Officers and Men: –

T./Lt. David Lowe MacIntyre, Arg. and Suth'd Highrs.

For most conspicuous bravery in attack when, acting as Adjutant of his battalion, he was constantly in evidence in the firing line, and by his coolness under most heavy shell and machine-gun fire inspired the confidence of all ranks.

Three days later he was in command of the firing line during an attack, and showed throughout most courageous and skillful leading in face of heavy machine-gun fire. When barbed wire was encountered, he personally reconnoitered it before leading his men forward. On one occasion, when extra strong entanglements were reached, he organised and took forward a party of men and, under heavy machine-gun fire, supervised the making of gaps.

Later, when the greater part of our line was definitely held up, Lt. MacIntyre rallied a small party, pushed forward through the enemy barrage in pursuit of an enemy machine-gun detachment, and ran them to earth in a "pill-box" a short distance ahead, killing three and capturing an officer, ten other ranks and five machine guns. In this redoubt he and his party raided three "pill-boxes" and disposed of the occupants, thus enabling the battalion to capture the redoubt.

When the battalion was ordered to take up a defensive position, Lt. MacIntyre, after he had been relieved of command of the firing line, reconnoitered the right flank which was exposed. When doing this an enemy machine gun opened fire close to him. Without any hesitation he rushed it singlehanded, put the team to flight and brought in the gun. On returning to the redoubt he continued to show splendid spirit while supervising consolidation.

The success of the advance was largely due to Lt. MacIntyre's fine leadership and initiative, and his gallantry and leading was an inspiring example to all.

Victoria Cross citation, *London Gazette*, 25 October, 1918

Letters from those serving abroad were treasured by loved ones at home. Some – like this one from Andrew Barr, a Bombardier (an artillery corporal) serving on the Salonica front, where Britain was supporting Serbia against Germany and her allies – are now preserved in the Museum of Islay Life. Barr was the brother of Jeannie and Helen Barr, whose double wedding at Gartbreck Farm had been one of the island's most enjoyable social events of 1909.

In the Field, Sunday 27th May 1917

My dear father and mother,

I was very pleased to get your parcel posted on 16 April. I got it on the 24th of May and the contents were highly appreciated. Don't bother please sending me any more chocolates or sweets as those things can easily be done without. I enjoy them alright you know, but biscuits or something more in the line of food is better such as some tinned stuffs. I am glad to say I am still keeping in very good health.

I am writing this at 5 this morning for if it keeps dry I am going to ask the day off to go and search for John Currie. We are each coming half roads and meeting at a place fixed on.

There is nothing to write about. The weather is a little better and getting nice and warm again, just something like one of our warmest at home. I hope you are both keeping very well. Have you been on holiday to the mainland? I am sure a trip would do you both the world of good. No doubt you will all be so busy at home just now. I often think of it out here and wonder how you are getting on but you two should only be superintending and leave the burden on the younger shoulders.

I hope to hear from you both by the next Blighty mail. One came up yesterday but no luck for me only the Peoples Friend, perhaps the remainder of that mail will be this afternoon. If so and I get letters I shall let you know by post.

Ta-ta just now

With my fondest love
Ever your loving son
Andrew

P.S. I wrote Isa a long letter on the 23rd.

Letter home from Andrew Barr

Dear Andrew,

I got your latest epistle all right and pleased to hear you are still "going strong". Letters are not so long in coming as I thought, considering the long distance, not very much longer than it takes for a reply coming from the mainland in these days of restricted travel.

Here we are into May again with the corn sown and preparing to get in the turnips. "Laggan" has completed sewing about 120 acres of corn, all (with the exception of a few acres sewn with the disc drill) being sewn by himself by hand, so he has been "hashin in" as our old friend and neighbour "Roaden" would put it. James (Murdoch) was rather a comical happy go lucky sort of chap with a most amusing way of swearing. He would be somewhat under 30 when he left Townhead and was a great hand for attending balls and parties in these days. My uncle said to him one night "Man, Roaden, it's a wonner you don't get mairret and no gang to sae mony balls, then he would hae a ball every nicht, eh Toonheid, te-he-he". My uncle asked him how Joe Hastings was getting on, a young chap he had who went to Roadend. Joe was not a hustler when there was any work on hand requiring strenuous effort. "Oh he's getting on a' richt, nae damt nonsense ????" was James' comment. He used to tell with great glee a story about aul' Archie Smith a man he had working. Archie had lost an arm and wore a "cleek". He had one or two little weaknesses, one of them being a partiality for mountain dew, another, he was very fond of the girls and he was very easy to knock down. One day the servant girl from Dykes, James' father's farm, came down to help with the threshing. Archie and she happened to be left alone in the barn, and Archie feeling frisky made catch at the girl and as she made to rush to get past him, the cleek caught in her skirt and down went Archie. She hauled him half across the barn floor and then a hook gave way and Archie was left, like Potiphar's wife, with the garment in his hand (or rather cleek) while the lassie shipped out in her bloomers.

The weather has been more unsettled of late with some rain. It was needed to bring away the grass and we could have done with more but it may come yet. It was one of the best seed times we have had for a long time and we hope to have a good season all through. Garden seeds were sewn a month earlier than usual and are coming away strong. There was a good touch of frost some nights and I believe that some of the earlier sewn potatoes got a check. We are just planting main crop potatoes this year at Laggan.

The cows are out all day now and the young cattle have been lying out for more than a month now. We were very lucky for young calves this year having 22 out of 29 calved, rather unusual with us. They are off a Netherton Bull and are mostly white, the best lot of calves we have had yet. We had Bobby and your sister from the Cottage over one night recently. As for Tom he might as well be out in Macedonia. I haven't seen him since he was here with you the last time you were here. He will be kept busy though and will not have much time for visiting. We got 3 sittings of white Leghorn Eggs and 1 sitting of Wyandottes from Gartbreck. Aunt set four hens with Leghorn Eggs, giving them 10 each, but two of them did not do well. We have about 20 chickens altogether and a lot of the others were crushed in the nest. One hen did not sit right on the eggs at first and Aunt said she felt inclined to give her a good thumping. None of her eggs came out in consequence. Aunt asked me what she should do with the hen, I said, throw her out and throw the eggs at her. My Uncle gave your little nieces from Duich a lift, coming from school and was greatly amused with them. Jeanie said "I've got 12 pandys★ since I went to school". Laggan "I bate you I ken whit you got them for – talking". Jeanie (nodding her head and laughing) "You're jist richt". Bessie said "It's fine weather we are having but we would be better of rain". Jeanie "Do you ken what she wants rain for, she has got a new coat and she wants to get it on". Then Jeanie showed him the neck of a bottle. "Do you see that, I was in the Mill Hoose the day, ha, ha, ha, but do you ken whit was in the bottle. It was milk". They are a most amusing pair and he got great fun with them. I suppose "Island" is leaving the Mill House and I think it better that he should do so. Bob is sampling too many brands at times and spoiling his complexion. There are great happenings in France just now and many a gallant fellow has "crossed the Border". It is an anxious time, yet I have hope in the future. Germany will have reached her maximum I think by now and time is on our side. Probably the greatest conflict is to come yet but I think there is no fear of the result. You would hear that young Walter MacKay is reported killed, but I understand that they have not got word from the War Office. It is a pity if it is true. Two of the McCuaigs who used to be at Laggan are "missing", Neil and John, nice boys they were. John Bland is here just now. He was in Italy and had only been three days in the trenches when he was hit in the eye by some shell splinters and has been in hospital

★Strokes on the hand with a tawse

since until recently. He is nearly better but has to wear glasses. He is a 2nd Lieut in the 5th Cheshires. Last night Laggan Bay was livened by the presence of 6 mine sweepers which spent the night there, anchored near the Big Strand. This is the season for Gulls eggs and the Bowmore boys are on the hunt for them Sundays and Saturdays. Farmers are going to be hit hard under the latest Budget, they have to pay taxes on double the rents. Laggan will have to tootle up to the tune of about £31-10/-. If Kaiser Bill has called the tune somebody has to "pay the piper" but folk are well off that have only got to pay instead of fighting. I am going to be hit this time not paying income tax, alas, but through the increased rates for postage, 1½ a go after 1st June. I must "huff" some of my "best girls" to save writing. With regard to writing oftener I would like to do so but I am not so keen on writing letters as I used to be and since the War began one has not so much pleasure in writing, everything being overshadowed by the "Great Adventure". Yet I would gladly do so, when you are so keen to hear news of the old country and of that particular "tight little island" out in the Atlantic. Yes, I wish you were back home again and may the day not be far distant. There is one day that stands out vividly in my mind, a day of "Golden Memory" in which I saw you, whizzing past in a motor car that day we were at Kildalton. I was glad to be among the trees again, it seemed like being among old friends. Laggan has beauties of its own, a grander, wilder type and yet it lacks one thing, trees to complete the picture. I have always been a keen admirer of the beauties of nature, and supreme among them of course "the ladies" and I think I can include a "friend and brither" admirer in the person of my "Aul freen Mackie" as Harry Lauder would put it. Well Andrew if we cannot see the Maids of Greece, yet we can, and do, admire the Maids of Islay. Here's to them and may you soon be back among them. I hope this finds you well and that you will have the best of luck. Glad to say we are all well here. My Aunt has been keeping well of late I am glad to say. I have lately had a pain down on the right side somewhere in the appendix region but it may only be muscular pain and nothing serious. We're a' John Tamsons bairns have all our share more or less of aches and pains. At times I am inclined to think that life is not worth living. But the summer is coming and the birds are singing and there is joy in being alive. In my pilgrimage through life I have made many friends and among them my good friend Andrew holds a special place and there is a joy in the thought that we have gone part of the way (short though it was) together. And Andrew I will ne're refine, "Tho' fate should drag thee 'South the line'", we'll ne'er forget the happy times we've had thegither. So here's my haun' for Aul' Lang Syne.

Your friend and brither Robert Smith.

Letter to Andrew Barr from Robert Smith, Laggan Farm, 5 May 1918

Andrew Barr survived the fighting – only to fall victim to the worldwide flu epidemic that raged in 1918/19.

Death on service – Mr Robert Barr, farmer, Gartbreck, received intimation from the War Office last week that his son, Bomb. Andrew Barr, 5th Mountain Battery, RGA, died on 14th December from influenza and pneumonia at a military hospital at Salonika. It was with very deep regret this news was circulated in the district and sincere sympathy is felt by all for the family thus bereaved. The deceased soldier, who was aged 29 years, was very well-known in Islay, and was extremely popular with all classes. For quite a number of years he served in the office of Mr M Mactaggart, solicitor, Bowmore, where he gained a capital training in the various duties pertaining to the work of Inspector of Poor, Clerk to Parish Council, School Board, District Committee of County Council, Registrar and Clerk to local Justice of Peace Court. These duties he discharged with zeal and intelligence. An enthusiastic poultry fancier, he was Secretary of the Islay Poultry Society, and to his organising skill much of the success of the shows was largely due. He voluntarily enlisted in 1915 in the Argyll and Bute Mountain Battery, and after completing his training was sent to the Balkans as one of the 5th Mountain Battery of the Royal Garrison Artillery. There he continued in active service without leave for nearly 2½ years, and passed through the hardships of that period unscathed. In recent letters to his friends he wrote brightly of the prospect of returning home on the conclusion of peace. Now he has fallen victim to the fell disease so prevalent throughout the world. He will long be remembered as a man of bright, cheerful, obliging disposition, willing at all times to help in everything that pertained to the good of the community in which he passed his life.

Obituary of Robert Barr, unidentified newspaper cutting, Museum of Islay Life

Throughout the war casualty lists, newspaper reports and letters from the trenches left Ileachs in no doubt to the dangers faced by their loved ones serving far from home. But on 5 February 1918 the war arrived on Islay's shores.

The Anchor liner *Tuscania* was torpedoed at night off the Irish Coast while carrying United States troops. The American troops numbered over 2,000 and the total complement on board with crew was 2,401. The number saved was 2,235 there being 166 missing.

The Oban Times, February 1918

The SS *Tuscania* had sailed from Hoboken, New Jersey, bound for Liverpool, as part of a convoy transporting American troops to the field of war. On board were her crew of 384 and over 2,000 American soldiers.

The German submarine, UB-77, commanded by Captain Wilhelm Meyer, had been cruising around the west coast of Scotland and Ireland and arrived in the North Channel between Islay and Northern Ireland early in the morning of 5 February.

With surprise and trembling at 4.50pm February 5th, in the West I noticed heavy clouds of smoke. Immediately the UB-77 was ordered swung around. We hurried toward these and soon made out a large convoy that was steering in a south-easterly direction toward the North Channel, evidently having taken the extreme north route across the Atlantic. . .

I cruised above water back and forth and in front of the advancing transports in order to determine the course and the speed of the Tuscania; and also to work out a suitable method of attack. We then awaited the convoy in attack position, holding a north easterly course close to Rathlin Island . . . At 6.05pm I made up my mind to attack. Visibility was poor, as now twilight had set in; I wished to make a water surface attack from the starboard side. Going in a course 60 degrees, our range abeam estimated 1,000 metres.

There was constant danger we might underestimate the speed of the ships and be run down in their path as in the meanwhile the vessels in the rear and a few destroyers had set themselves out on the starboard side of the large liner, beside which they now rode a parallel course. This formation surely made a U-Boat attack difficult. We were now with our submarine directly in front of those ships, set abreast of one another and the destroyers. I thought we had been detected as we could easily be seen by them as there still was a good deal of light. I therefore dived at 6.25pm and thereby our visibility was greatly made more difficult and I could perceive things only through the periscope. Our course was now 80 degrees – the convoy 140 degrees. I had taken a good look at the largest transport before submerging. My hand trembled as I move the sighting apparatus.

On account of darkness I could but with trouble find the Tuscania, upon which we had intentions. Our situation was somewhat uncomfortable as the oncoming ships and destroyers could easily run us down. The navigating warrant officer used the foremost periscope to observe the approaching vessels on the port side, while I endeavoured to pick up the liner with the main periscope. I only succeed in doing so by using a magnification-sighting mirror and after searching for a long time.

Finally do I see gliding into the periscope an indistinct, befogged shadow. Only until over this shadow, just as indistinct, a smoke-stack makes an appearance, do I recognise the sought for ship. Thereupon at 6.40pm I fire No 1 tube, which torpedo is aimed for just about the second funnel and immediately after the torpedo from No 2 is released. They are G-7 torpedoes.

At this moment a destroyer appears 150 metres away and heads for the submarine. We dive to 30 metres, the crew and I listen in suspense. One minute and ten seconds later a very violent explosion is felt and told us we hit the target.

Captain Wilhelm Meyer, letter to *Tuscania* survivor Leo V. Zimmerman, 1928

At the time of being torpedoed, the *Tuscania* was immediately wrapped in darkness. Speech to us on board was muffled for a time in fright. It felt like running into a sandbar, in addition to the roar of the explosion, the crashing of steel and timbers as also the racket of scattered breakables. In no uncertain terms we were appraised of what has happened. So we crowded to the deck.

Thus the *Tuscania* met her fatal blow, heeling over 8 to 10 degrees and swinging to starboard. This occurred seven miles north of Rathlin Island lighthouse, off the North coast of Ireland, in latitude 55 degrees 22 minutes North, longitude 6 degrees 13 minutes West.

The hatches were filled with soldiers adjusting lifebelts as they scrambled up to the forward deck. With overcoats on, it made quite a difficult task and some of us fell down on the slanting concrete floor. The steps leading to the promenade deck were crowded with a slowly moving line. Others were clambering up ropes dangling near . . .

Like a wounded bird of the flock, the *Tuscania* whistle incessantly shrieked its call of distress as if to give voice to its pain. Up into the sky, like two spurts of blood, climbed and quivered two red stars, submarine warning rocket signals.

No panic was apparent amongst the soldiers; they knew their stations from previous boat drill. Few words were spoken, all being intent upon the one object of securing their position in line of abandonment of the ship. There in the dusk they stood, counting off or repeating names, as they waited the launching of the lifeboats.

The night was clear, a slight wind blowing and visibility for about a mile. One line of auxiliary lights, like a diadem about the promenade deck were now visible, gradually meeting their reflection in the water as the ship sank. The stars in the wide firmament blinked sadly and the lighthouse on the treacherous high Scotland cliff many miles away beckoned us on, like a siren to destruction amongst its pounding breakers.

Leo V. Zimmerman, *Tuscania* Survivor, National *Tuscania* Survivors' Association pamphlet

CHEERY SOLDIERS

"Where are we going to now?" American soldiers sang the refrain of that comic song on learning that their vessel had been torpedoed. The music was quickly suppressed, however, on the advice of those in their neighbourhood, who remarked that the occasion was not one for the indulgence of singing.

A sergeant rescued said that after the crash came he and his comrades were immediately lined up and standing to attention began singing "The Star Spangled Banner" and "My country 'tis of thee", the ship's crew singing the British National Anthem.

The men are very proud of the behaviour of the only two women aboard. They went down a rope in fine style into the first lifeboat lowered.

Although inexperienced in the work, the American soldiers proved handy men at launching and manning the lifeboats.

The Daily Record and Mail, 9 February 1918

The shock of the Great War has vibrated to the ends of the earth; and common suffering and sacrifice have made the whole world kin. Through one of the most melancholy and disastrous events of the war a link has been formed between our native island and the great Republic of the West which time will never efface.

On the night of 5th February, 1918, the SS *Tuscania*, conveying American Troops to this country, was torpedoed by a German submarine off the island of Islay, on the south west coast of Scotland. A shudder of horror went through the hearts of our fellow-islanders as in the grey dawn of the morning they found the shores strewn with the bodies of the unfortunate victims of the dastardly outrage. Sympathetic hearts and loving hands were not wanting to pay due honour to the gallant dead. The bodies were tenderly collected and every means taken to procure their identity. Large crowds gathered from all parts of the island to pay their tribute of respect to the memory of the fallen; and after solemn services, the bodies were reverently laid to rest in four different and specially selected cemeteries at Port Charlotte, Kilnaughton, Kinabus and Killeyan.

Souvenir Album of the *Tuscania* Disaster, Archibald Cameron, 1918

The sad fate of the troops and crew of the torpedoed troopship was forcibly impressed on the people of the district on the morning following, the 6th. A boat and crew of ten survivors landed at Port Charlotte and sought shelter in the early hours of the morning. They were kindly treated. Very soon news arrived that many dead bodies were being taken from the sea, and many being washed ashore. At Port Charlotte twenty-two bodies were landed and laid upon the pier. Near Easter Ellister fifteen bodies came ashore, and near Craigfad ten bodies were found. All were fine young men in military uniform and on Friday the bodies, to the number of 47, were collected at Port Charlotte Distillery. Coffins are being provided, and arrangements were being made for the internment to take place near Port Charlotte on Saturday. The sad proceedings have created great gloom and sorrow throughout the Rhinns district. Mr Hugh Morrison of Islay has taken a very kind interest both in the welfare of the survivors, who have been kindly treated at the Port Charlotte Hotel, and in the disposal of the dead. He personally chose a piece of ground near the village to form a burial-ground where the whole of the unfortunate young men are laid to rest.

The Oban Times, 1918

State of California
GOVERNOR'S OFFICE
SACRAMENTO

June 5, 1918

Mrs. Alexander Currie,
Port Ellen, Isle of Islay,
Scotland

Dear Madam:–

I have just heard from one of our California soldiers, who is with the U.S. Expeditionary Forces, and who was on the Tuscania when she was torpedoed, of the splendid treatment which you and your fellow-towns people accorded the survivors who were landed at Port Ellen.

I am told that you personally treated the boys with the same sympathy and tenderness that their own mother would have used. I deeply appreciate what you did for these boys under such trying circumstances. Such acts make us realize the strength of the bond that unites the people of this nation and Great Britian [sic] as Allies, and it is the spirit of which you have given evidence that is going to keep us fighting side by side until the victory is won.

Yours very truly,
Wm D Stephens
Governor.

Letter from the Governor of California, June, 1918

. . . upon the wild rocky coast of the Mull of Oa, at the south-west end of the island, there is a sense of sadness and gloom, even in calm sunny weather when the ocean is undisturbed by storms. Perhaps an echo remains here of that night during the Great War when disaster overtook the liner 'Tuscania' while she was convey-ing American troops to France. No more inhospitable shore for a wreck can be imagined. Great precipices overhang the sea. Jagged rocks project hungrily from the water's surface beyond the cliffs. It was little wonder that hundreds of American soldiers, and many British seamen also, met their deaths in that great disaster. Here and there, in rocky coves above the reach of the tide, the 'Tuscania's' life-boats lie, their wood bleached and splintered by rocks. Could they speak they might tell of a dark night of heavy seas and the black fangs of merciless rocks rising up in their path, to overwhelm them and those who crowded them. On the high ground looking over the sea here is a great tower, erected by the American Red Cross to the memory of those who had journeyed across the ocean to fight in France, and had lost their lives in that sea disaster before they had reached the land they had sailed overseas to defend. It was in keeping with the sadness of the place when a grey seal, lying on a skerry out to sea, lifted up his head and howled mournfully from time to time. His cries, sung as a *cronoch* or dirge, carried a full mile inland over the heather.

Seton Gordon, *Highways and Byways in the West Highlands*, 1936

It is believed that about 210 of the *Tuscania's* soldiers and crew lost their lives. Worse was to come. But this time it was not a German U-Boat to blame, but the eternal enemy of all those who navigate Islay's hazardous waters – the sea itself.

HMS *Otranto* was another British passenger ship that had been requisitioned by the Admiralty. It saw action as an armed merchant cruiser and was the flagship of Convoy HX-50, bringing young American soldiers to the war in Europe. But, on 6 October 1918 – just 36 days before the war ended – it collided in a terrible storm with another troopship.

As I stepped from the alley-way door to port my heart – I do believe – stood still. For there, on the crest of a huge wave, not twenty feet from the ship's side, was poised the axe-head bow of the Kashmir.

Archibald Bruce Campbell, *Otranto* survivor, *With the Corners Off*, 1937

Campbell, a paymaster-commander who would be the *Otranto's* senior surviving officer, never forgot the fatal impact as the *Kashmir* sliced into the *Otranto*, fatally wounding her.

The whole ship shuddered as if in the throes of death. With the grinding crashing of the steel plates as they were rent apart, the wrenching of fittings inside the stricken ship, amid the dreadful clamour, were mingled the shrieks of crushed and tortured men.

Miraculously, nearly 600 men were plucked from the stricken *Otranto*.

As the 12,124 ton *Otranto* wallowed helplessly in the storm, a 896-ton British destroyer approached. Its fearless (although ironically named) commander, Francis Craven, was attempting to pull alongside the stricken troopship to allow men to leap the 50 feet down onto the *Mounsey's* tiny deck. To the American troops it looked like salvation. To the *Otranto's* experienced officers and crew, it looked like madness.

> Now we got a close up view of the commander of the destroyer. A trim athletic looking officer who began waving two flags. Knowing the semaphore code, I read the message to the commander of the *Otranto:* 'I am coming alongside to take off the American troops.'
>
> The reply to the destroyer *Mounsey* from the captain of the *Otranto* was: 'Steer clear as you will lose your crew and your ship.'
>
> The reply to the Captain of the *Otranto*: 'I am coming alongside. If we go down, we shall go down together.'
>
> Memoir by Pvt. Edgar A.P. Sheppard, Museum of Islay Life

> The men started leaping across the yawning chasm between the ships. Some I saw reach their mark, but other missed and were drowned. I saw them down there drowning before my eyes . . .
>
> I jumped fully 15 feet. It was a horrible moment. My feet touched the edge of the deck of the destroyer. I thought I was going down, and I should have done so if I hadn't had my socks on. They gave me a moment's foothold and time to grasp a wire around the destroyer.
>
> Pvt. Harville Marsh, My Experience on the Troopship *Otranto*, papers of the American Legion Auxiliary

> The fate of those unfortunates who fell between the two ships was awful, for while a lucky few managed to climb aboard as the gap closed, the majority were crushed horridly to death as the waves forced the vessels together.
>
> Archibald Bruce Campbell, *With the Corners Off*, 1937

Commander Campbell's memoir tells of how he was one of the last to make the leap, landing 'on the destroyer's foredeck just as she was pulling clear.' Craven's little ship, repeatedly pounded against the huge *Otranto*, was severely damaged and was soon dangerously overladen with men who had survived the leap. He was forced to disengage and head for Belfast Harbour, leaving nearly 500 men aboard the stricken *Otranto*.

Her commander deserves a double Victoria Cross as I have spent my life at sea, but I have never seen such a magnificent piece of manoeuvring and ship handling in all my life. The destroyer was in danger of being dashed to pieces time and time again . . . it was a miracle how she got alongside.

> Survivor, quoted in 'Another Ocean Tragedy', unidentified contemporary newspaper cutting, Museum of Islay Life

Just off Kilchoman Bay on the north coast of Islay, the helpless *Otranto* struck *Botha na Caillieach* – the Old Woman's Reef. Almost instantly, her hull was ripped open.

When I saw that the boat was beginning to break up, I waited until it leaned almost over to the water, then I jumped over. I had on a good life belt, one that slipped on like a vest. The waves carried me away from the ship, then a wave as high as a house came over me and whirled me round like paper in a whirlwind. I went under about three of them, but then I got hold of a raft and drifted close to shore. Another big wave came and swept me off the raft close to the shore. I grabbed hold of a rock and hung on, and then I climbed. There was a Scots lad who got hold of me and took me to a cottage. All I had on was my underwear, pants and shirt and one sock. I had taken off the outer clothing before I left the ship. The wind was blowing as hard as I had ever seen it blow before. When we got to the cottage they gave us dry clothing and put us to bed. It was sure fine, two pairs of woollen blankets. The people there could not have treated us better.

> Letter to his mother from Pvt. David Roberts, *Otranto* Survivor, quoted in the *Lorain Times Herald*, Ohio, 4th November 1918

On shore, word of the wreck had got about. People from the fishing villages of Portnahaven and Port Wemyss hurried to the coast. Some managed to pull a handful of survivors to safety. Miraculously, 16 men pulled from the water survived. They were the lucky ones.

Sergt M'Neill, Bowmore received information that a shipwreck with serious loss of life had taken place earlier in the day at Machrie, Kilchoman Parish, Islay. He proceeded there with all possible speed, and was informed that H.M. Troopship "Otranto" carrying about 900

U.S. Troops and a crew of about 200 had been, about 9am that day, in collision with another ship of the same convoy some miles to the north west coast of Islay, and was so much disabled that she drifted on to the sunken rocks about a quarter of a mile from land, mid-way between Machrie strand and Kilchearan Bay, both in Kilchearan Parish, with the result that, owing to the severe gale of wind blowing and the heavy seas running, she broke in two and before night-fall completely broke up.

Over 30 bodies were picked up on the shore before dark, and 20 survivors were rescued and cared for at Kilchoman School and Kilchearan Farm.

Sergt. M'Neill immediately summoned the Constables at Ballygrant and Port Ellen to the assistance of Constable Clark and himself who were already on the spot.

From information received, it would appear that the total number of men on board H.M.S. "Otranto" were as follows:–

697 American soldiers of all ranks)
44 Naval Officers)
383 Naval ratings)
36 French sailors (rescued previously by "Otranto")
Total 1,160

and the numbers rescued by H.M.S. "Mounsey" were:-

318 American soldiers)
27 Naval Officers)
236 Naval ratings)
30 French sailors)
Total 611

Those who survived by coming ashore in Islay are 17 Americans, one Naval Officer and 2 naval ratings. One of the American soldiers, Pte. William J.P. Cooney, died of double pneumonia on 15th October.

The number of bodies recovered so far is 285. The Police had daily directed the work of recovering bodies washed ashore, identifying them and tabulating the property found on them.

The work of searching for bodies is being continued, and we have now the assistance of an officer and 30 men of a labour battalion, as the wreckage is piled up in some of the gullies along the shore to a depth of 10 to 15 feet. It is fairly certain that many bodies are buried underneath it. A full list of survivors on the island

and bodies washed ashore up to the night of nineteenth instant is enclosed herewith.

On 11th instant there was a burial service conducted by Clergymen resident on the island, when full military honours were accorded the victims; and the Americans held a similar service under the direction of their own Chaplain on 17th instant.

The number of graves dug is 9, 7 of which have been utilised for burying American soldiers, and the other two for burying naval ratings. A plan of the graves is attached.

All the bodies, American and British, have been coffined at the expense of the American Authorities.

Number 83 on the list has not been interred as the body is being conveyed by the Admiralty to Galashiels at the request of the relatives.

The names of the survivors at Kilchoman School and Kilchearan are as follows:–

(1)   Kilchoman School

719078   Pte. Charles Smithson, Fort Screven, Georgia, September
           Replacement Draft, 1002, R.Coast Artillery.

3372669   Pte. David Roberts   do.   do.   do.

720309   George S. Taylor   do.   do.   do.

2902652   Noah E. Taylor   do.   do.   do.

3239972   Earl Garvar   do.   do.   do.

2595863   Steward Early   do.   do.   do.

813640   Sergt. Chas. M'Donald   do.   do.   do.

3372671   Pte. Robt. F. Shand   do.   do.   do.

2595465   Wm. J. R. Cooney   do.   do.   do.

2595479   Thomas A. Kelly   do.   do.   do.

1278382   John E. Wean, 406 Casual Co.
           Lieut, W.B. Grandion, R.N.R.

(2)   Kilchearan Farm House

           A.E. Tilbrook, Junior Engineer, H.M.S. "Otranto"
           W. Holmes, Stoker, M.M.R.   do.   do.

2595522   Pte. Ben Smith, U.S.A

2595461   Robert Brown   do.

718854	Joseph Richards	do.
813672	Emil Petersen	do.
2595488	Joseph Tullock	do.

The following is a list of the bodies recovered with their identification number, name and note of their personal property. They are all to be buried in a spot by themselves in the vicinity of Kilchoman Parish Church, the date of burial being Friday 11th inst. at 1pm.

Argyllshire Constabulary report, Bowmore, 19 October, 1918

Rockside School was among the buildings used as a temporary morgue.

October 4th   Weather exceptionally stormy. Still attendance continues good. Percentage for week 96.3

October 11th   Owing to premises being occupied in connection with shipwrecked crew of Otranto no openings have been made from Oct 4th until October 14th. Otranto was shipwrecked Sunday 6th October

Extract from the Log Book of Rockside Public School

In the days that followed the shipwreck, the people of Islay scoured their rugged coast for bodies. Coordinating the search was Islay police sergeant, Malcolm MacNeill. It fell to him to painstakingly examine each mangled body in an attempt at identification. His notebook is displayed at the Museum of Islay Life, with the gracious permission of his grandson, Lord Robertson of Port Ellen, a former British Cabinet minister and Secretary General of NATO. They make grim reading.

304. A Midshipman. Letter and five ten-shilling notes. Body so much decayed that it is crumbling to pieces.

305. No disc. About 5' 11" and brown hair. Hair and teeth gone. Watch and one coin.

Sergeant MacNeill's notebook, February 1918

MacNeill paints a vivid picture of the efforts Islay people made to rescue and comfort survivors and give dignity to the dead.

Argyllshire Constabulary
Bowmore Station
22nd day of Nov 1918

Subject of Correspondence
Rescue of Survivors
"Otranto" Disaster

Sir

I beg to report in answer to your letter of 11th inst. re nature of services rendered by inhabitants of Islay on the occasion of wreck of HMS "Otranto" that I have ascertained that the following people took an active part in the rescue of survivors from the water and afterwards materially assisted them in recovering from the effect of their long and terrible exposure.

The disaster happened on 6th October about 11 am while the wind was blowing with terrific force from the south-west and a tremendous sea running on the shores. The oldest inhabitants in the neighbourhood of the wreck say that they never saw a heavier sea on the Machrie sands and very seldom a higher tide. The ship is said to have broken up in about half an hour after striking on the reef and immediately afterwards a tremendous lot of wood wreckage began to drift ashore. It is commonly believed that this driftwood following so closely after the men in the water and being dashed up against them is responsible to a great extent for so few men getting ashore alive as it is believed that many were struck by the floating wreckage and either stunned or perhaps killed outright.

The rocky nature of the coast was also very much against the chances of getting ashore alive with such a tremendous surf running.

To the ordinary observer it is a marvel how any at all escaped being dashed to pieces on the rocks. The first persons on the scene, so far as I am able to ascertain were David McTaggart, farmer, Kilchearan, who had previous to this dispatched a horse and van for life saving apparatus, and Donald McLachlan, ploughman, Machrie, Kilchoman. These two men brought three survivors out of the water with the aid of a long broom handle. McTaggart went in front as far into the water as he could while McLachlan held on to him by the jacket. McTaggart afterwards with the assistance of Donald Ferguson, shepherd, Kilchearan, both of them having to secure themselves with a rope were successful in rescuing another man who was in immediate danger of being drowned. This last survivor was named

Tillbrook. On arrival of the Life Saving apparatus it was found that it could not be used effectively and the horse and van was utilised to carry the survivors, some of whom were absolutely exhausted and unable to walk to Kilchearan Farm house where everything that was humanly possible was done for them by Mrs McTaggart and her staff of servants.

Donald McLachlan already mentioned seems to have been about the first person to notice the ship in distress and he lost no time in making his way to Kilchearan, a distance of between 4 and 5 miles to call out the Life Saving crew. It was on his way back after delivering his message that he assisted at considerable risk to himself in the rescue of the three survivors and afterwards accompanying them to Kilchearan and getting them into dry clothes etc.

Donald McPhee (18), Shepherd, Kilchoman and his brother John (17) also residing at Kilchoman with the help of a walking stick and reaching out as far as possible on the water and on top of the drift wood were successful at considerable risk to their own lives in rescuing 3 survivors.

John accompanied those survivors and assisted them along to his father's house where they were looked after in every possible way by Mrs McPhee and her daughter, Margaret. Donald McPhee afterwards with the assistance of Andrew Stevenson H.M.M.L 14 c/o HMS Sanges, Harwick, who was at Machrie on leave, rescued one man who was found among the drift wood with nothing but his head showing, his body absolutely jammed among the wreckage. After he was brought out his arm was found to be broken.

Peter Ferguson (aged 75) Machrie and Duncan McRae (70) Kilchoman were also doing brave work in assisting survivors from the shore after being got out of the water.

One girl, Katie McLellan, Coulererach, in my opinion deserves special mention. She happened to be on the rocks when the McPhee boys rescued the first 3 survivors, one of who was scantily clad. This girl at once in the midst of hail and sleet stripped off her own overcoat and wrapped it round the rescued soldier, and at once set off to Kilchoman Manse, the residence of the Rev M. D. Grant and informed Mrs Grant of what was happening.

Mrs Grant made coffee and tea and this girl along with Mrs McIntyre, Kilchoman school teacher, started on their errand of mercy to the shore. They met some of the survivors on the way and the coffee etc. they got from these two women greatly revived them.

There are also two soldiers belonging to Port Charlotte, Islay, who showed a great amount of courage, initiative and resourcefulness. Their names are 45469 Pt. Archd. Torrie, South Staffords and 25775 Pt. Donald McIndeor 1/6th Argylls.

These two young men who were on leave at the time saw an American soldier on a rock where he had been washed up by a huge wave but as there was a broad chasm between this rock and where they were it was impossible for the American soldier to get safely to land as the water was continually rushing through this gully. Torrie and McIndeor, determined to get to his assistance somehow and the only way was to jump across. This feat required a good deal of determination and courage owing to the gale of wind and the tremendous surf but it was accomplished by both young men, who at once got the American in hand and by the time they got back to this chasm others had procured some wood and formed a temporary bridge. The chasm will be about 6 or 7 feet broad but very deep and the least slip meant instant death.

So far as I am aware these are the names of the people who took an active part in the actual rescue work on the day of the wreck, and a short account of the actual work they did.

It is however to be remembered that the care and nursing of the survivors afterwards required as much devotion and self-sacrifice as the rescue from drowning and in this respect I do not think that too much praise can be given to Mrs Isabella McIntyre, school-teacher, Mrs Margaret McPhee and her daughter, and Mrs Elizabeth Grant, the Manse, all of Kilchoman, who were untiring in their efforts night and day to give comfort and rest to the survivors who were so tragically cast on their hospitality.

The Rev M Grant who was from home on the day of the disaster deserves a word of praise for his splendid work in connection with the recovery of bodies from among the wreckage for days afterwards.

Mrs James Clark, Rockside Farm, whose husband was also from home attending Sales at Oban, as also the Messrs Sam and Andrew Clark, Sunderland and A and W McEachern, Smaull, gave valuable services in labour and carting while bringing bodies from the beach to the burying ground.

There were a great many others who gave acceptable assistance in one way or another but as there is nothing of outstanding interest to record I think it would be superfluous to mention more names.

Letter from Sergeant Malcolm MacNeill, Museum of Islay Life

David MacTaggart, the Kilchiaran farmer who courageously waded out into the crashing surf to rescue men, was the best man to his brother, one of the bridegrooms who married the two Barr sisters in that joyful wedding of 1909.

Modesty prevented Sergeant MacNeill from mentioning his own enormous contribution, but it did not go unnoticed.

AMERICAN RED CROSS
DEPARTMENT OF MILITARY RELIEF
52 GROSVENOR GARDENS
LONDON SW1

November 6th, 1918

Sergeant Malcolm McNeill,
Bowmore,
Island of Islay

My dear Sergeant:–

I wish to take this opportunity of expressing my sincere thanks and appreciation for the loyal assistance you so generously gave me during the recent "OTRANTO" disaster and to assure you that your noble work in such a trying ordeal deserves the highest praise and consideration.

Without your work and assistance the work would have never been completed in such a satisfactory manner.

Again thanking you and with warm personal regards, I remain,

Yours very truly,
James Jeffers
1st Lieut
American Red Cross Commission to Great Britain.

Letter to Sergeant Malcolm MacNeill, November, 1918

Well after the disaster, letters from grieving parents were forwarded to him by James Jeffers of the American Red Cross.

James Jeffers
Manufacturer and Importer of Handkerchiefs
42 White Street
New York

June 2, 1920

Sergeant McNeal
Bowmore, Islay, Scotland
c/o Chief of the Argyll Constabulary

My dear Sergeant:

I received a letter this morning of which I am sending you a copy and I would ask you to look over your records of the disaster met by the ship Ortranto (sic) and see what you can do in identifying this boy and where his grave lies. This boy is one of the victims of the disaster of October 6, 1918 and I would like you to get the number of his grave and forward it on to me.

Send all mail addressed to my place of business,

42 White Street, New York City.

I hope to see you and your good people some time the latter part of the year. I hope to see your good wife and family and I hope to enjoy a good cup of tea and one of those scones which I still will not forget.

With kindest regards to you and your family, I am

Yours very sincerely,
James Jeffers

May 26, 1920

Lieut. James Jeffers

Kind Sir:

We lost a dear Boy on the ship Ortranto (Shellie L. Webb) and your name has been given to me as one who was there at the time and I am writing to you to see if I can get any information as to my dear Boy. We can't find where he was ever picked up. There are fifty-one unidentified buried there and my boy could be identified very well as his big toe on his left foot was off; also he had a scar on his left hand caused from a burn also he had a good watch that I would be so glad to get. It would be some relief to the heart broken family to know that he was buried. Now Kind Sir if you can help me in any way I assure you it will be appreciated.

Hoping to hear from you real soon I still remain a heart-broken mother,

Mrs J.T. Webb
Ray City, Ga.

We may never be certain as to how many died on the *Otranto*, but 470 seems the likely number – 315 Americans, 106 British crew, and six French fishermen who had previously been rescued by the *Otranto*. The scale of the loss shocked Islay. Charles MacNiven, one of the Kilchoman Bards, captured the feelings of his fellow islanders in verse.

> Air mios deireannach an fhoghair –
> An seathamh latha ma's maith mo chuimhne,
> Nuair a thainig an "Otranto"
> 'S iomadh gaisgeach a bha innte,
> Dhol a sheasamh saors' an t-saoghail,
> Chan e mhàin air raon na Frainge,
> Air gach uile chearn 'ga sgaoileadh,
> Bratach shaors' e dhaors' a naimdhean.
>
> Bu bheag a shaoil' nuair rinn iad fàgail,
> Seadh, gu'm bann air traigh an Ile
> A thachradh Righ Fuar a' bhais orr',
> Chum am fàgail ann 'nan sineadh;
> Is ged nach d' fhuair iad cùis air Nàmhaid,
> Fhuair iad bàs a cheart cho dileas:
> Fhuair gach aon dhiubh bàs mar ghaisgeach,
> Fad o dhachaidhean a shinnsear.
>
> Thiodhlaic sinne iad leis gach urram,
> A b'urrainn sinn a chur air saighdear;
> Chaidh am pasgadh mar bu mhiann leo,
> Anns a' Bhrataich Stiallaich Reultaich;
> Is am beagan a bha beo dhiubh,
> Nochdadh coibhneas mòr is bàidh dhoibh;
> Fhuair iad dion is blàthas is fasgadh,
> 'S tric a thaisbeanaich na Gàidheal.
>
> 'S iomadh màthair 's maith glé aosda,
> Chaill a h-aon mhac mùirneach gràdhach,
> 'S iomadh nighneag bhòidheach bhanail
> A chaill a leannan air an tràigh ud;
> Is O! cha till, cha till a h-aon dhiubh,
> Dh'ionnis' na dùthcha 'rinn iad fhàgail;
> Tha iad tosdach fuar, 'nan cadal,
> Fad o dhachaidhean an càirdean.

271

ISLAY VOICES

A-chaoidh bidh blàths gus 'n là mu dheireadh
Aig Ameireaga ri Ìle,
Oir tha còrr is ceithir cheud dhiubh,
Air an tiodhlaiceadh ann gu dìlinn,
Fo thulaichean gorma Chille Chomain
Tha na h-òganaich nan sìneadh,
'S los gun dùisgear o na mairbh iad,
Ghiùlan arm do dh'Ìosa Crìosda.

'Twas the latest month of Autumn –
The sixth day as I recall –
When we hailed the ship "Otranto"
With full freight, and heroes all:
They left home to fight for justice,
Liberty had heard the call;
And the Stripes were now unfurling,
On the war-torn fields of Gaul.

Little thought they when they parted,
From their friends beyond the main,
That upon the shores of Islay,
Soon that Death would make his claim;
Though they fought not in the battle,
Nor did to the strife descend,
Far from dear ones, home and kindred,
Still they met a hero's end.

On the peaceful sward full daisied,
Where the winds of ocean blow,
Shrouded in their own loved banner,
Tenderly we laid them low;
And the few that Death had spared us,
To the utmost love can know
They were tended well and bravely,
As our Gaels were wont to show.

Many are the loving mothers,
That now mourn the sons they bore;
Many are the winsome maidens,
Lost their loved ones on yon shore.

272

Never more with hearty greetings,
Will they meet them on the Strand,
For, alas, they now lie sleeping,
'Neath the flowers in distant land.

Till the last dread trump be sounded,
Never will Columba's Land,
Cease to think with pride, but sadly,
Of green Islay's distant land.
There full more than four hundred
Brave ones sleep beneath its sod,
Till they waken on yon morning,
In the skies to meet their God.

Charles MacNiven, *'In Memory of the Otranto Disaster'*

My Dear Sergeant MacNeil:–

I received the poem of Mr MacNeiven's and I think it is very good indeed. I am going to have it printed as soon as I reach the states. The people who have loved ones buried there in Islay will appreciate it very much. I am sending a little note to him thanking him for it. I hope it reaches him al-right.

Thanking you for your thoughtfulness in sending it to me and hoping that I may be privileged to come and see you again, I am,

Most Sincerely Yours
Earl H Weed
Chaplain 16th Inf
Am.E.F. Germany

Nearly six decades after the sinking, American veteran, David Roberts, who had been dragged ashore by 'a Scots lad', paid his own tribute to the Ileachs who sheltered him in their Kilchoman cottage.

"Gratefully After all these years . . . We meet again"

A Survivor
I, David Rhys Roberts
US Army SARD 7th Screven
Orville, Ohio, USA

Am a survivor of the Kashmir-Otranto disaster of October 6, 1918, and attest the fact by witnessed signatures of two surviving buddies.

In appreciation to the people of Islay, especially the McPhee family of Kilchoman who took me into their home after being helped from the wreckage by one of their sons.

Commemorative scroll, Museum of Islay Life

The heroic Captain Craven, who rescued 596 men from the *Otranto*, later joined the Auxiliary Division Royal Ulster Constabulary and was killed in 1922 in an IRA ambush. One of the men he rescued, *Otranto* officer Archibald Bruce Campbell, became a writer and radio broadcaster, appearing on more than 200 episodes of *The Brains Trust*. He often prefaced his comments on the programme with his famous catchphrase: 'When I was in Patagonia . . .' It is said that Campbell was sacked from the programme for suggesting that scientists, not animals, should be used as test subjects for the American atomic bomb tests on Bikini Atoll.

Sacred to the immortal memory of those American soldiers and sailors who gave their lives for their country in the wrecks of the transports Tuscania and Otranto February 5, 1918 – October 6, 1918. This monument was erected by the American Red Cross near the spot where so many of the victims of the disaster sleep in everlasting peace. "On fame's eternal camping ground, their silent tents are spread. While glory keeps with solemn round, the bivouac of the dead."

Plaque given by President Woodrow Wilson on the American Monument on the Oa.

The verse is the work of the Confederate soldier/poet Theodore O'Hara.

The 'war to end wars', did not.

In 1939, Islay men and women were called upon again to don Army khaki, the grey blue of the RAF, and Royal Navy blue. Men already serving in the Merchant Navy found themselves in the front line as Nazi Germany tried to blockade Britain into starvation and surrender.

The convoys that helped feed and arm Britain during World War Two sailed the same route as the ill-fated *Tuscania* and *Otranto* attempted during the First War – across the Atlantic, around the north of Ireland, and then south to the ports of Glasgow, Liverpool and Bristol.

The principal danger to shipping were the 'wolf packs' – groups of German U-Boats that would launch a concerted attack whenever they discovered a convoy. Islay was on the front line of the air war against submarines, with an RAF aerodrome at Glenedegale, a squadron of Sunderland flying boats on Lochindaal at Bowmore and an Air Sea Rescue unit at Port Ellen. Radar stations were built at Saligo and Kilchiaran. Islay had been 'invaded' – with between 1,500 and 3,000 allied service men and women stationed on the island throughout the war. Some never got home.

The graveyard of the Round Church, Bowmore, still bears witness to a tragic air crash, the story of which has been thoroughly researched by a retired Islay teacher.

The evening of Sunday 24th January 1943 was dark, wet and wild with a strong southerly wind that was freshening all the time and soon became gale force. Sunderland flying-boat MK111 DV of 246 Squadron Coastal command, based at Bowmore, was returning, low on fuel, from a lengthy patrol over the North Atlantic. It still had depth charges on board. There was a crew of twelve, commanded by 1st pilot Captain Eric 'Soapy' Lever of the South African Air Force.

Squadron 246 had been formed on 1st September 1942 but did not become operational until 12th December. It disbanded on 30th April 1943 and the aircraft were distributed amongst other units. A detachment of 442 Squadron from Oban arrived in May, but it became increasingly evident that a severe gale in the unsheltered mooring area would be disastrous, so it was moved to Northern Ireland in early November 1943. Bad weather was certainly partly responsible for the tragedy on 24th January.

Corporal Charlie MacMillan, a Bowmore man, was on one of the flarepath boats that night. A career airforce man, he had been posted to Islay on compassionate grounds because of his father's serious illness. He was the wireless operator at the RAF base in Bowmore, working in one of the distillery buildings where the mobile power unit was located. All Islay distilleries were closed down in wartime.

A buoy with a flashing light was permanently positioned in the centre of Lochindaal to aid landing, and when a flying-boat was expected three power boats went out. One tied to the buoy and the others took position on either side of it to form a line of illuminated boats about 200 yards apart. This was the 'flarepath', landings normally being into wind. Charlie was on the largest of the boats, a pinnace. I am told that the station had been closed that night for flying because of the weather and that the Sunderland was instructed to land at Oban instead, but for one reason or another, there was no reply from it. Wireless communication was of course not as reliable as it is today. One reason for the flying-boat not going to Oban may very well have been lack of fuel.

From eye-witness reports, it seems that on its approach to the loch, the Sunderland circled for some time – up to eight to ten times. Eventually it came in over the hill north of Blackrock, not over the low ground beyond Uisgeantsuidhe. Perhaps this was because of the wind direction and strength. The flying-boat's landing lights were on, then suddenly all its lights went out. This was witnessed by James MacColl from Shore Street in Bowmore. His sister Florrie was the girlfriend of Wally Johnson – Pilot Officer Wallace A. Johnson of the Royal Canadian Air Force (Co-pilot on the Sunderland). In the house on Shore Street, she waited anxiously for the return of the plane, along with her friend Mattie Winnard who was going out at the time with Captain Lever. The pilots were expected for a meal that evening.

James MacColl, who was in the Kilarrow section of the Home Guard, had spent most of the day on the Rifle Range. So too had Donald MacLeod, who with the Rhinns Section had been up at the range at Cnoc Donn. On their way home that evening their lorry, which had been lent by MacBrayne's, broke down several times, the final time at Bruichladdich. It was there that the group watched the Sunderland coming down. From where they were they didn't see the crash-landing, but they did not see the aircraft come down as expected on the Loch. As a report from the Air Historical Branch (RAF) of the Ministry of Defence, sent to David Woodrow, Bowmore, states, 'the aircraft undershot the landing area and struck the ground at the water's edge.' From several reports it seems that the plane's hull touched the hill above Blackrock – eye-witnesses saw the marks afterwards. It also probably hit the roof of Charlie Stevenson's joiner's workshop and caught the overhead telephone wires that ran alongside the road in those days. Certainly the next day the place was festooned with fallen wires and the workshop roof was destroyed, but this may have been because of the explosion that followed.

The aircraft came to a halt on the raised beach across the road from the joiner's workshop. Eleven of the crew were able to get out, the captain and the two others with injuries sustained on landing. This group of three escaped to the southwest of the craft, going down below the steep slopes of the raised beach. Eight of the crew, however, ran in the direction of the road, but then realised that one man, the rear gunner, was trapped in the gun turret. All eight returned to the aircraft to free him. At that moment the depth charges aboard exploded, killing all nine aboard.

The explosion blew the Sunderland to pieces, most of which scattered northwards towards Blackrock farm and even as far as Carrabus. The debris included one of the engines. A deep crater was blasted out on the spot where the crash had taken place, and this can still be seen.

The explosion was seen and heard and its consequences felt up to 20 miles away. In Bowmore's High Street, Mary MacMillan (now Dunford) Charlie's sister, knowing that her brother was out in the RAF pinnace, was looking over towards Blackrock when she saw the explosion, while in Shore Street the MacColls watched in horror as flames leapt from the wreckage. The young wife of one of the gunners was in despair as she realised what had happened, in the event one of the three survivors was her husband. In Kilmeny Church evening service was in progress, and Donald Bell, a young lad at the time, remembers the doors being blown in by the blast. But it was some time before the congregation discovered what had happened.

At Mid Carrabus, a mile from the crash site, Mary MacEachern (now Mary Merral) was sitting with her parents at the kitchen table above which a paraffin lamp was hanging. They had heard the drone of the Sunderland's engines, a sound to which they had become accustomed, and so they paid no attention until they heard a sudden almighty blast. Mary's father shouted 'Tha na Gearmailtich 'n seo!' for he had long feared a German invasion. Glass flew everywhere as the windows blew in and flames shot up from the wildly swinging lamp. It seemed, Mary says, like the end of the world to her. Her father, extremely concerned about Mrs Kate Stevenson whom he'd known since childhood, set off immediately for the Stevenson's house.

Because of the blaze, Mrs Stevenson had been unable to get out through her front door, and had made for the back, where there was a wooden lean-to scullery which collapsed around her. Her husband Charlie was along the road paying a visit to Glenburn, and hurried back home, as did his son Iain who was on his way home from visiting friends along the Lyrabus road. In a small house made of an old ship's cabin from a wreck near Blackrock farmhouse, lived Willie Dick, a young man at the time, and his mother. All their windows were blown in by the blast, and the old stone cottage beside the cabin was demolished by it. Nancy Gillespie (now Stevenson) tells how her uncle Angus was on his way across the fields from Carrabus to the postbox at Blackrock when the explosion occurred. He lay down till things had quietened down a bit and then went to see what he could do.

Meantime, the Rhinns Home Guard were on their way to the scene of the disaster, driver Neil Gillespie having commandeered a car at Bruichladdich. As they approached they found the wall blown across the road and as they drew to a halt they saw in the glow of the flames the figures of the three survivors. Donald MacLeod remembers the blood-soaked uniform of Captain Lever, whom he helped up to the car, and he also remembers how, dazed and in a state of shock, and unaware of what had happened, the man was saying 'they're all out!' the Rhinns section somehow got the three survivors into the RAF ambulance which eventually arrived, and they were revived with a cup of tea in Mrs Dick's small cabin before going home when they had done all they could.

The Kilarrow section of the Home Guard, under Lieutenant Bobby Hodkinson, were called out as were the men of the RAF regiment based at Glenegedale Airfield. The Bowmore local Fire Brigade, which then consisted of a distillery lorry pulling a pump, arrived soon. The fireboat which was usually out when a flying-boat was expected was not out that night. The road was closed and traffic diverted over the hill via Coullabus. Ammunition was still exploding among the flames of the wreckage.

When daybreak came, Bobby and his section found, lying face down at the water's edge, the body of Wally Johnson. Most of the others who died were blown to pieces and a gruesome task lay ahead for those who had to collect the shattered bodies and scattered debris during the following days. For many years bits of Perspex were found in a wide area around the crash site, and pieces of metal were embedded in the road surface and could be seen until quite recently. On a lighter note, one eye-witness recalls interest shown by some of the men in the dead hens lying around the Stevenson's ruined hen-house. In those days of austerity chicken was a rare delicacy.

Donald MacFadyen remembers how he and other pupils of Bowmore Secondary School watched from the school playground as the funeral procession wound its way to the sound of the pipes along Shore Street and up Main Street to the Round Church. The graves of Wally Johnson and two other men from overseas who were killed in the accident are in the graveyard at Bowmore: they were Sergeants Ernest Palmer and Roy Jabour, both Australians. Wally's brothers Jim and Keith came over from Canada several times to visit his grave and call on the MacColl family.

In 1986 Jim Johnson wrote to the late Iain Stevenson, whom he had missed during a visit to Islay, mentioning photographs which he had given to the Museum at Port Charlotte. These include pictures of flying-boats moored in Lochindaal. Jim Johnson died five years ago but his widow was over earlier this year, keeping up the family's links with Islay. Mrs Margaret Reid of Dunblane, who was friendly with another of the victims, Sergeant Walter Heath, at the time of the disaster, has also visited Islay and found comfort in doing so. She visited the Museum and saw the photographs.

This terrible accident, the worst tragedy of World War II in Islay, an event which seemed like the end of the world to one young witness, will never be forgotten by those who saw or heard it, or gave their assistance afterwards. Perhaps this short account of the events of the night of 24th January 1943 will ensure that the memory of the nine brave young men who died will not fade.

Rona MacKenzie, *Black Rock Tragedy*, 2002

Among the most moving documents in the Museum of Islay Life is a letter home from a 21-year-old Argyll and Sutherland Highlander serving in North Africa.

Dear Father and Mother,

I had hoped never to have to write in this strain. I did not expect to die in this war no one does. At first when I knew I was in danger I thought a lot about it. I worried frantically at the thought of all the happiness I would miss and of you dear Mums who loved me so wonderful, and built your lives around my health and happiness so successfully. I am deeply conscious of what I am fighting for and would not sit at home during this war. What I am fighting for is not any abstraction to me. It is not any vague idea of freedom or democracy. I reduce it to the most elemental of emotions, that of man's instinctive dominating intense desire to protect those individuals whom he holds dearest. So the fact that I may die while I am protecting you does not appal me in the least, if I do I shall be happy to have done what I have to preserve your lives and way of life. Do not grieve for me do not be bitter, remember me as the loveable cheerful boy, that loved you all, and was always content. I will go to meet my maker fearless undaunted and glorious and I will meet you all some day live out your lives to the fullest without loneliness or pain where ever I am I will be at peace. I have a clear conscience and a clean soul,

Farewell Father,
Farewell Mother
Farewell Sister and Brothers
Alisdair

Letter home, Corporal Alexander Williamson, April 1943

Corporal Williamson, who signed off with the Gaelic version of his name, Alisdair, was killed a few days later, on 17 April 1943. He is buried in the Medjez–el–Bab cemetery in Tunisia.

Towards Tomorrow

War as a rule does not benefit the ordinary man and woman, but Bowmore inhabitants and, in fact, all Islay benefited from the last war. A very handsome pier was built at Bowmore for the benefit of Coastal Command, a Squadron being stationed in Lochindaal and an R.A.F. Squadron in Bowmore, Glenegidale, and other parts of Islay. The pier was built so that barges could come in to discharge petrol etc. A pipe-line for petrol was laid from the pier to large tanks at the back of the church and also to Glenegidale. While the R.A.F. were here they kept the pier free from sand by dredging regularly, so that barges got in easily with supplies.

The R.A.F. also built a small power house near the school to supply electricity for their camps. After the war the North of Scotland Hydro-Electric Board bought the power house and since then have built a new one at Bunanuisge, which supplies the whole of Islay with electricity. Last year – 1965 – we were joined by cable to the mainland but with our gales the power house at Bowmore is still the sure supply. Eight men are employed regularly there and six or eight others on the maintenance side.

Mrs M. F. McQueen, Project in Local History, Islay Federation, Scottish Women's Rural Institute, 1966

Electricity for the island, a handsome pier for Bowmore, and an airport with a tarmac runway! The demands of war had valuable spin-offs for Islay, but the lack of opportunities for the young has meant that Islay's population has steadily declined.

In 1841 the island was home to nearly 15,000 people. Today, the population is a fraction of that – 3,457 in 2001, and down to 3,228 in 2011.

Despite being fewer in number, Islay's people remain energetic and enterprising. Their endeavours, and the work of the island's many clubs, societies, charities and committees, have been faithfully reported in the pages of the *Ileach*, the community newspaper. It began rolling off the press in 1973 and the first edition's lead story concerned a tourism initiative.

ISLAY VOICES

The Highlands and Islands Development Board has commissioned the making of a film "North Argyll and Islay in the Autumn", and this past week, a film unit from the company VIZ LTD., of Edinburgh, has been seen in various damp corners of the island. The film is planned to advertised the holiday opportunities in this area in the autumn, and birdwatching; and sea-angling will obviously figure in the Islay section.

VIZ LTD. is the company responsible for the highly acclaimed "Travelpath" and is now working on a major film about the Firth of Clyde. This Islay film, which is being shot by cameraman David Peat, is in 16mm colour, and should be of very high quality.

The Ileach, October 1973

Also on the front page of the first issue of the *Ileach* was an advert for the groundbreaking and radical play *The Cheviot, The Stag and the Black Black Oil*, which was being performed by the 7:84 Theatre Company in Portnahaven Hall.

Back in 1719, Islay's Stent Committee decided to raise £20, by local taxation, to build a schoolhouse for Kildalton parish. Two and a half centuries later education still preoccupied islanders. Until the mid-1970s, Islay children who wished to stay on at school beyond fourth year had to travel to schools on the mainland, and stay in lodgings during the week.

ISLAY COUNCILLORS HIT A SIX!

"In view of the overwhelming demands of the parents of Islay that Bowmore School provide 6-year Secondary courses and having regard to the Report of the Director of Education, this Committee recommend to the County Council that such provision be made and that Strathclyde Regional Council be requested to give urgent and favourable consideration to the matter."

Proposed by: F.T. Spears Esq.

Seconded by: Wing Commander D.D, McSwein.

This was the motion which Councillor Frank Spears proposed at the meeting of Argyll Education Committee in Campbeltown on September 18th.

In support of the motion Mr Spears pointed out that there had been a growing feeling that it would be to the educational advantage of the island children if education to Higher level were available on the island, where they would still be under the home influence.

He referred to the public meetings held in Bowmore and Port Ellen in May, and attended by the Director of Education, Dr Stewart, and the Chairman of the Education Committee, Mr E.T.F. Spence. At the Education Committee meeting in June, the *Oban Times* had quoted Mr Spence as saying that "the Bowmore meeting had unanimously favoured upgrading to 6th year status" while "at Port Ellen the majority had been in favour, but there had been a minority view".

The upgrading had the support of Argyll's MP, Mr Iain MacCormick, and of the Regional member, Mt Alastair Jackson, who was on the Regional Education Committee.

Indeed, the E.I.S. in a recent letter to all Education Committees, had recommended that all 4th Year schools should be made 6th Year.

The Director of Education had, at the Committee's request, produced a feasibility report which was "fair and factual". Mr Spears then proposed the motion.

Seconding it, Mr Donald McSwein referred particularly to the need for parental guidance throughout Secondary education. Islay children had the added difficulty of having to go into lodgings as no hostel places were available for them.

The good of the children came first, and to quote a recent remark of the Chairman, "Finance must not control education".

The Chairman emphasised to the Committee that if Bowmore School were upgraded, all Islay pupils would have to complete their education on the Island – there would be no freedom of choice. Furthermore, the building of a hostel at Campbeltown would have to be reconsidered.

The motion was then put to the Committee and carried unanimously.

The Ileach, September 1974

Islay children were soon leaving Bowmore School with Highers that equipped them for university, college or skilled jobs. But for many on the island, any sort of job was hard to find.

Dear Editor,

I am writing to complain about the way students get preference to local girls and get all the local jobs, whereas we are left jobless.

Another matter which makes my blood boil is married women working and they have husbands bringing in the weekly wage and they say, "I only work for the company" and we join the dole queue and they complain about teenagers being lazy layabouts.

I personally think it's a damned disgrace. What do other school leavers or even parents think about it?

Yours faithfully,
Angry Unemployed School Leaver.

(Although this letter was unsigned and unaddressed, we felt that it was so obviously sincere that it merited publication.) Ed.

Letter to *The Ileach*, July, 1976

That year, prominent economist Professor Kenneth Alexander became chairman of a development agency tasked with supporting the economy and communities in the Highlands and Islands. He visited Islay to see how things were for himself – and reported his findings to the *Ileach*.

Why have you come to Islay?
What are your impressions?
What happens next?

These are the questions I was asked on my recent whistle-stop tour of the island.

The Highlands and Islands Development Board recently reviewed its approach to developing the most difficult areas within its responsibility. Residents of Islay will know only too well the obstacles which check and prevent economic development and expanding prosperity. Transport costs and time spent in travel are clearly of very great importance. The limitations imposed by small numbers are also very great, restricting the level of local demand for products and keeping the scale of production well below the level necessary if the most up to date techniques of production are to be used. However the ten years' experience of the HIDB demonstrates that new developments are possible and that they can become commercially successful despite such difficulties.

Our review led us to decide that it was time to have a fresh look at the problems and opportunities of our most difficult and deserving areas. A four man team of specialists drawn from younger members of our staff was given the task of re-examining the problems and of making recommendations, and Islay and Jura were selected as the areas for study.

The team have been at work for nearly three months and will shortly be reporting to the board. My visit to Islay and Jura, along with two other senior colleagues, was to give me an opportunity to assess the situation for myself and to meet with as many of the local residents as possible, to hear their views and seek their advice.

Impressions gained from such a flying visit must not be adopted in too hard and fast a manner, and I will want time to digest my own views and qualify them with those of the team and the other colleagues who travelled with me. However, first impressions are often significant and I welcome this opportunity, offered by *Ileach*, to put a few on record.

Our team have a number of proposals to make which could take place in different localities, but they have concentrated their attention on the Rhinns and the district around Portnahaven. My visit has convinced me that this decision was correct, as we have an extremely fragile community, with a clear will to live, but facing great difficulties if healthy survival is to be achieved. The HIDB was created to improve such situations and we shall explore every possible way of helping that community, and through that, of making a contribution to improving the economic and social life of Islay. There are ideas to be followed up, possibilities to be probed, connections to be established. All of this takes time. The staff of the Board will spare no effort in trying to follow these through to success. But the only foundation on which such work can go forward is the enthusiasm of individuals and of the community concerned. The Development Board cannot make things work by itself.

In the last issue of *Ileach* there was a letter from an angry unemployed school-leaver. We all know that many school-leavers are forced to become "island leavers" by such unemployment. This, in the ultimate, is what the work of the HIDB is about and what my visit to Islay was about – the future of communities and in particular of the young within these communities. My visit to Islay has reinforced both my concern about the problems and my determination to find solutions.

Kenneth Alexander.

The Ileach, 30 July, 1976

But throughout the 1970s and '80s, 'difficult areas' like Islay, with their 'fragile' communities, continued to struggle with the problems brought about by a declining and aging population. Every job loss felt like a nail in the coffin.

Bitter Blow: Islay Loses 1 Distillery 25 Jobs

In the face of unacceptable bereavement we are hurt, disbelieving, uncomprehending – and these were the emotions evident last week as news spread of the imminent death of another distillery. Port Ellen Distillery, re-opened less than sixteen years ago after being closed in the recession of the '30s, will shut again on March 31. The official Distillers Company spokesman dealing, from London, with press enquiries would not predict its future.

Seventeen jobs will be lost at Port Ellen, some distillery workers, some office staff and an estimated six to eight between the other two Scottish Malt distilleries – Caol Ila and Lagavulin. Although all the workers at the three distilleries have been given option of voluntary redundancy, the terms are not yet known to them. Understandably the over-riding feeling is one of insecurity.

If the terms are good enough to attract men near retiring age to take voluntary redundancy then it is possible that the younger men at Caol Ila and Lagavulin will still have a job. If not they, like the workers at Port Ellen, will not know their fate until the compulsory redundancies (which take effect from March 31) are announced.

Workers still employed after March 31 will be on a rigid 4-day week with no extra work, but the London spokesman confirmed that the silent season will last 3 months as last year, and production will continue at the present level. Production at Lagavulin was cut back by 1 mash about 3 weeks ago.

The ripples from Port Ellen's demise will gradually spread to reach a wider community. There will be less draff so the farmers will suffer, as will Willie Currie's haulage business. Mundell's transport will lose half a day's work involved in taking malt from maltings to distillery, and two loads of whisky to the ferry per week. "We wouldn't have noticed a loss of that order two years ago" said manager Donnie Shaw, "but now every little counts". The loss of twenty distillery pay packets will be felt in the shops, pubs and service industries of Port Ellen.

Don Raitt, manager of Ardbeg, the first Islay distillery to stop production, was irate at the lack of attention the SMD closures have received from the media. "The whole of Scotland should realise that we are an old, established industry" he said, "Scottish politicians need to be ready to give the support we need whenever the good times return – for Islay that means getting the transport rates sorted out so that we can compete with mainland distilleries."

The Ileach, 25 February, 1983

Today, Port Ellen retains a whisky connection through its maltings, operated by Diageo. But the closure of the town's distillery was symptomatic of difficult times for the whisky industry and Islay. Producing the world class 'amber nectar' has not guaranteed Islay prosperity.

Towards the end of the book which served as the best guide to Islay for a decade or two, Norman Newton seeks to sum up the problems that have stopped Islay becoming the kind of Hebridean paradise that Martin Martin described around 1700.

A native of Skye, and a product of the culture he sought to describe, he saw the islanders in the following terms:

> 'If a man had a mind to retire to any of these isles there is no place of the known world where he may have products of land and sea cheaper, live more securely, or among more mild and tractable people . . . The islanders enjoy health above the average of mankind, and this is performed merely by temperance and the prudent use of simples . . . In religion and virtue they excel many thousands of others who have greater advantages of daily improvement.'

So, what went wrong? In a word, interference, or to use modern sociological jargon, cultural and economic imperialism. A vulnerable culture, its military resources broken by central government, situated in a fertile island which promised good economic return, its communal society under threat from leaseholders and estate surveyors, its language beaten out of its schoolchildren, and the scourge of overpopulation as the lairds' policies started to take effect – these were the ingredients which transformed the headquarters of the Lords of the Isles into the fragile island community we see today.

Norman Newton, *Islay*, 1988

The decline continued into the 1990s. In December 1993 Bruichladdich was mothballed. Following a hostile takeover of the distillery's parent company, the historic business was seen by the new owners as 'surplus to requirements'. Islay distilleries were increasingly perceived as disposable and tradeable assets in an increasingly globalised market.

Morrison Bowmore to sell to Suntory

Brian Morrison, Chairman and Managing Director of Morrison Bowmore Distillers Ltd., (MBD) announced on Thursday 21st July that he has decided to sell outright ownership of the company to Suntory Ltd., which has held a 35% interest in MBD since 1989.

Suntory is a private Japanese corporation and is one of the world's largest producers of spirits, wines and beers.

The Ileach, 23 July, 1994

Shock Job Losses in the Rhinns

On Monday 30th January, the employees of Bruichladdich Distillery were called to a meeting, to be informed that the distillery was closing down and the workforce was to be made redundant as from 3rd March 1995.

Mr Iain Allan, the Distillery Manager, said he was most upset at the news and was very concerned for the 8 members of staff, most of whom were young men who thought they had a job for life. He said that he understood that two of the workforce would be retained for care, maintenance and warehousing. "I am due to retire in April," he stated "and of course my post will not be filled." On behalf of those who were to lose their jobs he had contacted all the other distilleries on the island, for possible vacancies, to no avail.

Bruichladdich was one of the Invergordon Distillers Group which was acquired in a hostile takeover, just over a year ago, by Whyte and Mackay. Invergordon had fought the hostile bid 'tooth and nail' in order to prevent just such a scenario as is now happening. Two other Malt Distilleries bought over at that time are also to close, Tullibardine in Perthshire and Tamnavullin in Speyside.

The Ileach contacted Whyte and MacKay's Head Office and their spokeswoman, Ms Moira Pepper, explained that there were seven Malt Distilleries in the group and because of the surplus malt for blending throughout the whisky industry the difficult decision had been made to "mothball" three out of the seven, for a prolonged and indefinite period. A skeleton staff would be kept to operate a care and maintenance programme and for warehousing. As to the future of the popular Bruichladdich Single Malt Whisky this would still be available as there was enough stock to last fifteen to twenty years, she explained. "There were no plans in the foreseeable future" she stated, "to close down the 'Isle of Jura' distillery, which ranked 4th or 5th in the UK sales." The loss of 8 to 10 jobs in the Rhinns of Islay is a further blow to Islay's fragile economy and dulls somewhat the good news of new jobs at the nearly completed fish processing factory at Glenegedale. Eight job losses in an area like the Rhinns is akin to 800 job losses in a town like Paisley.

The Ileach, 4 February 1995

With the whisky industry in turmoil, the last thing Islay needed was disruption and uncertainty in farming and food production.

The Islay Cheese Company Falls on Its Sword

On a black day for the island, the Islay Cheese Company issued the following statement on Tuesday the 21st March.

The Islay Cheese Company took the decision on 21 March 2000, to cease production at their Port Charlotte Creamery.

Tony Archibald, chairman of the Company, said that the supermarkets, which dominate the retail side of the industry, demanded a huge profit margin which left it difficult for the manufacturer to cover costs.

The price of cheese on the open market had been driven so low by the strong pound that it was being sold at a loss. The combination of these factors meant that for the creamery to stay viable the price it could pay farmers would be below the cost of milk production.

Mr Archibald said, "All the dairy farmers are extremely disappointed we have had to take this decision and we would like to thank everyone who supported us over the last four years."

In the light of this tragic news, the question of the future of dairy farming on the island is answered: There isn't one. The fate of the farmers and of the cattle involved is still unclear, but cannot be other than bleak. The thoughts and the sympathies of this entire island are with them and with the workers at the Creamery and their families.

The Ileach, 25 March 2000

Islay cheese had an ancient pedigree. In 1263 tribute to King Haakon was paid partly in cheese, and in 1614 three thousand stone of cheese was part of the rent for Islay, paid to the Scottish Crown.

The Collapse of the Creamery: A Tragedy for Our Time

The dairy farmers face an immediate and catastrophic decline. One reckoned that 95% of his turnover had disappeared at a stroke while his assets are melting away 'like snow off a dyke'.

No wonder strong men have been reduced to tears. And there is no simple or speedy answer to their problems. Most of the 800+ dairy cows on the island are essentially worthless – £200 at most for the vast majority, who will end up (the ultimate indignity) in an incinerator. Even the relative handful that can be sold on the open market will be lucky to realise a third of their initial purchasing price. At the same time the island's milk quotas are ring-fenced, and until Ross Finnie changes the rules, unsaleable. When eventually the embargo is lifted, as it surely will be, what price the quota in this depressed market? Meanwhile the beef quota still stands at £200 a beast, if it's obtainable, and decent beef stock of breeding age changes hands for £400-£500. Dairy cows, besides attracting no subsidies, are unsuitable for beef breeding. Heifers take 18 months to two years to come 'on-line'.

Sheep are currently a very poor option – last year they were hard even to give away, and little improvement can be expected this year. No capital, no income, no future – there's no easy way out of this bind.

The knock-on doesn't end there. Dairy farmers are major consumers of cattle feed, wormers, chemicals, fertilisers . . . So hauliers will suffer, CalMac will be affected, the distilleries will face real difficulties in disposing of draff.

. . . And what will happen to the substantial dairy presence at the Islay Show? Gone and soon forgotten. In ten years' time, Islay children will not recognise an Ayrshire or a Friesian cow. And there lies a particular rub. Dairy farmers are a dedicated breed. Islay's farmers have generations of experience and knowledge behind them. When this is gone, it is gone for good. And it is simply unrealistic to think that it will ever reappear on the island. A thousand years or more of dairying has to all intents and purposes vanished into oblivion, mourned, but irretrievable.

Is it any wonder there is deep bitterness and deeper distress in the farming community on the island? Politicians may huff and puff, but here on the ground is disintegration, and no-one from on high seems to care. While whole lives are being destroyed, somehow the continuing humiliation, beyond even the irrational if natural feeling that past generations are being betrayed, is the ritual obscenity, in a world full of the starving, of enforced incineration. The milk of human kindness seems in remarkably short supply, as scarce and as quickly soured, as the milk of Islay's dairy cows.

Extracts from *The Ileach*, 8 April 2000

The Christmas edition of that year's *Ileach* had a piece of welcome news for the island.

Bruichladdich Revitalised

In a much anticipated move, the Murray McDavid group this week bought over the mothballed Bruichladdich Distillery with the aim of bringing the distillery back to full production as soon as is practicable. This is the group's first foray into the whisky industry. Bruichladdich Distillery has been closed for the past four years.

Taking over the job of Production Director and major shareholder in the project is former Morrison Bowmore manager, Jim McEwan, who has exciting plans in store for the distillery's resurgence. While he will have a 'hands on' role within the distillery's revitalisation, he will also continue to work as an international ambassador both for Islay and the product of Bruichladdich Distillery.

Plans in the coming years include the possibility of incorporating a hands-on teaching facility within the distillery as well as, uniquely, carrying out bottling on site. However, until a proper site visit has been carried out, Jim was unable to say how long it will take to have the distillery back to full production, but hoped it would be "as soon as possible in the New Year". The distillery will play an active part in this year's Islay Whisky Festival in May.

He was highly complimentary of the efforts made by John Rennie and Duncan MacFadzean to keep the distillery in excellent order, which should make the task of returning to full working capability all the easier.

The project to bring back the distillery from its sleep and to increase employment and faith in the Rhinns following the demise earlier this year of the Islay Cheese Company has the backing of major Islay landowners.

The Ileach, 23 December 2000

Opening of Kilchoman Distillery

Large crowds attended the opening of Kilchoman Farm Distillery at Rockside during Feis Ile. This inspirational project aims to produce small quantities of high-quality spirit employing a sustainable system in which all processes from the growing of the barley, through the entire distillation and maturation process, to the re-cycling of waste products, will be done on the farm.

The opening addresses were delivered by Managing Director Anthony Wills and well known whisky writer and journalist Charlie MacLean . . .

The Ileach is sure that everyone on Islay would like to join in wishing this remarkable new venture well. We look forward to reporting on the first run of spirit before long.

The Ileach, 11 June 2005

Today, Islay's economy has great strengths. Its single malt whiskies are enjoying worldwide recognition, and distilleries are expanding and upping production. Farmers are growing barley to feed the demand, while others are producing high quality beef and lamb. Tourism too is doing well. But while tourists come in droves, young islanders are leaving in alarming numbers.

Census figures show that, since 1981 when 3,792 people lived on Islay, the population as fallen every decade: 3,538 in 1991, 3,457 in 2001, and 3,228 in 2011.

Houses that once nurtured families are now holiday homes, and picturesque villages have entire streets where not a single light burns in a window throughout much of winter. Tourism is a double-edged sword – as it was more than a century ago.

> Stories of the salubrity of the climate, the splendid inns, its ozone-laden atmosphere, and its wealth of old world associations have reached the people of the cities, and they are coming, many and more, to test the truth. To those of us who knew Islay before, there comes a feeling – a selfish feeling – somewhat akin to fear lest the island may have to render up some of its charm in exchange for its popularity. Shall it be, as the years go on, we may have crowds of trippers, the strident pierrots, the raucous roaring of the side-show touts, and all the whirlwind uproar of an English seaside resort. Shall it come to pass that the Islayman shall lose that warm-hearted hospitality, that Celtic courtesy for which it is famous. But that time is not yet . . .

L. MacNeill Weir, *Guide to Islay*, 1911

The era of the Lordship of the Isles, when Islay was a centre of political and economic power, has long gone. But the island's history shows that it has always fostered people resilient and strong enough to adapt, survive and flourish. Nothing in the people of Islay's past suggests that mainland Scotland has much to worry about.

Old proverb

An uair a thrèigeas na dùtchasaich Ìle, beannachd le sìth na Alba!

When the natives forsake Islay, farewell to the peace of Scotland!

Epilogue

Islay's Ice Age Pioneers
Professor Steven Mithen

Whatever one is finding, archaeological excavation is a process of continuous discovery. That at Rubha Port an t-Seilich on the east coast of Islay just south of Port Askaig in August 2013 was particularly thrilling. It was here that we found the traces of the earliest known people to have set foot on Islay: Ileachs of 12,000 years ago.

We were digging a site that had been first found in 2009 when pigs foraging amongst bracken had unearthed a few flint artefacts. I immediately recognised them as coming from the Mesolithic period and we first explored the site in 2010. That confirmed there had been a 9,000-year-old Mesolithic camping site located on a terrace just above the straits of Islay. Many flint artefacts – arrowheads and barbs, knives, scrapers for cleaning skins – had been manufactured there. Wild boar, red deer and roe deer had been butchered, fish caught, hazelnuts roasted and no doubt many other activities that left no archaeological trace. There was a huge number of artefacts and bone fragments, suggesting the camping site had been used on many different occasions. Indeed, it appeared to be a Mesolithic Port Askaig, a landing place used by hunter-gatherers travelling between the islands in their skin boats.

In August 2013 we returned to undertake further excavation, seeking to establish the period of time over which the campsite had been used and gain further information about the settlement. A long trench was excavated through the middle of the terrace, which cut straight through a Mesolithic fireplace that must have been located in the middle of the camp. We were almost overwhelmed with the debris of Mesolithic life enabling us to readily imagine skin-clad hunter-gatherers, having paddled to Islay from the mainland perhaps by following the coastline of Jura, cooking fish over their fireplace while preparing their bows and arrows to go hunting for deer.

There was almost a metre of deposits, from which we were able to take fragments of charred hazelnut shell for radiocarbon dating. Some months later these told us that that the Mesolithic people had been using the campsite between at least 9,300 and 7,500 years ago, not necessarily every year but certainly on many occasions, with Rubha Port an t–Seilich as a key locality on their seasonal travels between the islands.

On the last day of the excavation we had reached the base of the Mesolithic deposits and were now cleaning the bottom of the trench onto the underlying geological deposits. I noticed that one of my diggers was still picking up flint tools. I jumped into the trench and asked to look, wiping the mud off them to reveal some particularly long blades of flint, delicately chipped into points. At that precise moment I knew we had found more than one of the best-preserved Mesolithic sites in Scotland. These tools were distinctive of an earlier time period, one of 12,000 years ago before the Ice Age had formally come to its end, when Islay was a tundra-like landscape with scattered birch and pine. So people wrapped in furs rather than skins had been the first to step onto the island. All we had were a small number of their discarded tools and the need to return to Rubha Port an t–Seilich for further excavation.

Acknowledgements

The compilation of this book would have foundered without the help and support of many people.

Malcolm Ogilvie and the Trustees of the Museum of Islay Life gave us free run of the museum's impressive library and unique collection of historic photographs. Malcolm, ornithologist extraordinaire, was also a staunch friend and sound adviser in an individual capacity.

Islay has been fortunate to have had its own community newspaper for more than forty years, and we are grateful to its Board of Directors for permission to include a number of articles from its pages. Thanks too to the *Ileach* staff for access to back copies and their photocopier.

Edinburgh University's Department of Celtic and Scottish Studies were kind enough to allow us to include folkloric material collected on Islay and published in *Tocher*, the magazine of the School of Scottish Studies.

Neil Woodrow and his team at Ionad Chaluim Chille Ìle, Islay's Columba Centre, also let us loose on their library, and Neil was liberal with his valuable advice. Hugh Smith's generosity with his time and knowledge helped shape our view of Islay's bardic tradition. As well as tea and shortbread, Etta Shaw shared with us her enthusiasm and knowledge of her talented uncles, the Kilchoman bards.

Anne MacGill did wonders in plugging the vast gap in our knowledge of Gaelic – but any mistakes are ours, not hers. And thanks to Meg Bateman for her bespoke translation of An-T-Oircean.

Pat Roy, Islay's great bookseller and bibliophile, has been a great advocate of all things written about Islay. Carl Reavy's knowledge of whisky, wildlife, and a gallimaufry of Islay lore learned during his years as *Ileach* editor, have been a rich source of inspiration. Grahame Allison gave us the freedom of his well-stocked private library.

Dr James Hunter's book, *For the People's Cause*, was a priceless source of writings by John Murdoch. John Marsden's *Somerled and the Emergence of Gaelic Scotland* was an invaluable guide to the early Middle Ages.

We would like to thank the authors of all the works still in copyright for permission to reproduce sections of their work. Thanks also to Duncan

Stewart Muir for permission to include his fine unpublished poem, *In Search of Magic, or, The Wizard's Apprentice*.

We were delighted to be able to end our book by going full circle in the story of Islay and its inhabitants by including a specially written piece by Professor Steve Mithen about his exciting new research on the island's earliest people – the Ileachs of 12,000 years ago.

Even before we undertook compiling this anthology, our understanding of Islay had been shaped by four important books: *Islay*, by Norman Newton; *Islay, The Land of the Lordship*, by Dr David Caldwell; *Islay, Biography of an Island* by Dr Margaret Storrie; and *Peat Smoke and Spirit* by Andrew Jefford. *Gun robh math agad* to all their authors.

Bibliography

Adomnán's Life of St Columba, edited by William Reeves, 1857

American Red Cross, Letter to Sergeant Malcolm MacNeill concerning *Otranto* victims, November 1918

George Anderson and Peter Anderson, *Guide to the Highlands and Western Islands of Scotland*, 1863

Iain F. Anderson, *Across Hebridean Seas*, 1937

Iain F. Anderson, *To Introduce the Hebrides*, 1933

Annals of Ulster 740, ed. W.M. Hennessy and B. McCarthy, 1887–1901

Argyllshire Constabulary report, Bowmore, 19 October, 1918

The Argyllshire Herald

Joseph Banks's Diary, 1st August 1772

John Bannerman, *The Beatons, A Medical Kindred in the Classical Gaelic Tradition*, 1998

Andrew Barr, Letter from Salonica front, 27 May 1917

John Barbour, *The Bruce*, translated and edited by A. A. H. Douglas, 1964

Alfred Barnard, *The Whisky Distilleries of the United Kingdom*, 1887

Mary Beith, *Healing Threads*, 1995

John Stuart Blackie, *Language and Literature of the Scottish Highlands*, 1876

Robert Blair, *William Livingston – A Memoir*, 1882

James Bramwell, *Highland View*, 1939

David Caldwell, *Islay: The Land of the Lordship*, 2008

David H. Caldwell, Mark A. Hall and Caroline Wilkinson, *The Lewis Chessmen Revealed*, 2010

Archibald Cameron, *Souvenir Album of the* Tuscania *Disaster*, 1918

Archibald Bruce Campbell, *With the Corners Off*, 1937

The Day Book of Daniel Campbell, edited by Freda Ramsay, 1991

John Francis Campbell, *Popular Tales of the West Highlands*, 1860–62

John Gregorson Campbell, *Witchcraft and Second Sight in the Highlands and Islands of Scotland*, 1902

Walter Frederick Campbell, *Transactions of the Highland and Agricultural Society of Scotland*. Mr Campbell on the Improvement of Waste Land of a District in the Island of Islay, 1834

Transactions of the Highland and Agricultural Society of Scotland, commentary on Walter Frederick Campbell's account, 1834

The Campbeltown Courier

Alexander Carmichael, *Carmina Gadelica*, 1900

Ceannaigh duain t'athar, a Aonghas (*Pay for Your Father's Poem, Aonghas*), in McLeod and Bateman, *Duanaire na Sracaire* (*Songbook of the Pillagers*), 2007

Sir Smith Child, *Three Weeks on Islay*, 1861

Chronicle of the Kings of Man and the Isles, edited and translated by G. Broderick, 1973

Sir Henry Craik, *A Century of Scottish History*, 1911

C. F. Gordon Cumming, *In the Hebrides*, 1901

The Daily Record and Mail

F. Fraser Darling, *Natural History in the Highlands and Islands*, 1947

Peggy Earl, *Tales of Islay*, 1980

Denis Fairfax, *Species History in Scotland: Man and the Basking Shark*, 1997

Alexander Fenton, *The Food of the Scots*, 2007

Interview for TV documentary 'The Lighthouse Stevensons', Billy Frazer, 2011

Anne Lorne Gillies, *Songs of Gaelic Scotland*, 2005

Glasgow Herald

Seton Gordon, *Highways and Byways in the West Highlands*, 1936

Governor of California, Letter to Mrs Alexander Currie and the towns-people of Port Ellen, 5 June 1918

Robert C. Graham, *The Carved Stones of Islay*, 1895

I. F. Grant, *Highland Folk Ways*, 1961

Alexander Gray, *The History of Islay Placenames*, 1940

Donald Gregory, *History of the Western Highlands and Island of Scotland: 1493–1625*, 1881

David Hamilton, *The Healers*, 2003

Robert Heron, *Scotland Delineated, or a Geographical Description of Every Shire in Scotland*, 1799

The Ileach

'Islay', by the Isle of Islay Federation, Scottish Women's Rural Institutes, 1968

Andrew Jefford, *Peat Smoke and Spirit*, 2004

Duncan Johnston, *Sine Bhàn* (song)

Thomas Johnston, *The History of the Working Classes in Scotland*, 1920

Clifford N. Jupp, *The History of Islay*, 1994

Lebor Gabála Érenn (The Book of the Taking of Ireland), edited and translated by R. A. Stewart Macalister, 1941

William Livingston, *A Message to the Bard (Duncan's Wife's Song)*, 1863

William Livingston, *Blàr Traigh Ghruineart, Cumha Mhic Ill'eathain (The Battle of Traigh Ghruineart, Lament for MacLean)*, 1882

William Livingston, *Blar Shumadail*, 1882

William Livingston, *Na Lochlannaich An Ile (The Danes in Islay)*, 1882

Poems of William Livingston, edited by Robert Blair, 1882

London Gazette, Victoria Cross citation, 25 October, 1918

Angus MacDonald, *Renunciation of the Lands of Islay, 1st January 1612* in *The Book of Islay*, 1895

Colin M. MacDonald, *The History of Argyll*, 1950

Hugh MacDonald, *History of the MacDonalds*, c. 1660

William MacDonald, *Sketches of Islay*, 1850

Reverend Donald Macintosh, *A Collection of Gaelic Proverbs and Familiar Phrases*, 1785, added to and republished by Alexander Nicolson, 1882

Rona MacKenzie, *Black Rock Tragedy*, 2002

Edgar Stanton Maclay, *A History of American Privateers*, 1899

J.G. MacNeill, Islay, 1899

Sergeant Malcolm MacNeill's notebook concerning *Otranto* victims, February 1918

Sergeant Malcolm MacNeill, letter concerning *Otranto* victims, 22 November 1918

Nigel MacNeil, *The Literature of the Highlanders*, 1892

MacNìmhein C. agus MacNìmhein D. – Poets of Place, Bòrd na Gàidhlig leaflet, 2012

Alan MacNiven, *The Vikings in Islay*, 2015

Pvt. Harville Marsh, My Experience on the Troopship *Otranto*, papers of the American Legion Auxiliary

Martin Martin, *A Description of the Western Islands of Scotland*, 2nd edition 1716

R. Andrew McDonald, *The Kingdom of the Isles*, 1998

John McNab, Letter from the trenches, 4 Oct 1915

Mrs M. F. McQueen, Project in Local History, Islay Federation, Scottish Women's Rural Institute, 1966

Donald Meek, *A Land That Lies Westward*, 2009

William Milliken and Sam Bridgewater, *Flora Celtica*, 2004

Miniugud Senchusa Fher n-Alban (Explanation of the History of the Men of Scotland), seventh century. Translated by John Bannerman, *Studies in the History of Dalriada*, 1974

Steven Mithen, *To the Islands,* 2010

John Monipennie (ed.), *Certayne Matters concerning the Realme of Scotland*, 1603

Donald Monro, *Description of the Western Isles of Scotland*, written around 1563

Duncan Stewart Muir, *In Search of Magic*, or *The Wizard's Apprentice (In Memoriam Edmund Cusick)*, unpublished poem, 2014

John Murdoch, unpublished autobiography, 1889–1898 (National Library of Scotland)

Norman Newton, *Islay*, 1988

Oban Times

Malcolm Ogilvie, *The Birds of Islay*, 1992

Robert Oliphant, *The Tourist's Guide to Islay, The Queen of the Hebrides*, 1881

Abraham Ortelius, 1527–1598

Thomas Pattison, *Captain Gorrie's Ride*, 1890

Thomas Pattison, *Fair Day, Gaelic Bards*, 1890

Thomas Pattison, *Sir Lachlan Mor*, 1890

Thomas Pennant, *A Tour in Scotland and Voyage to the Hebrides*, 1772

Report from the Committee upon the Distilleries of Scotland, House of Commons, 1798

Report of Her Majesty's Commissioners of Inquiry into the Condition of the

Crofters (Napier Commission), 1884

Report of the Select Committee on Emigration, 1826

Rockside Public School, extract from school logbook concerning *Otranto* disaster

Letter to his mother from Pvt. David Roberts, *Otranto* Survivor, quoted in the *Lorain Times Herald*, Ohio, 4 November 1918

School of Scottish Studies Archives, University of Edinburgh, from Donald Dewar, labourer, Port Charlotte, Islay. Published in *Tocher* 24, p. 327, 1976 (Maclagan Mss p. 277)

School of Scottish Studies Archives, University of Edinburgh, recorded from Mr A. Maclachlan, Braico, Islay, about 1893, published in *Tocher* 28, p. 259, 1978 (Maclagan Mss p. 6209)

School of Scottish Studies Archives, University of Edinburgh, from John Gillespie, Port Charlotte, Islay, published in *Tocher* 14, 1974 (Maclagan Mss p. 277)

School of Scottish Studies Archives, University of Edinburgh, Mrs D. Brown, Port Charlotte, Islay, published in *Tocher* 22, p. 243, 1976 (Maclagan Mss pp. 5003-5)

School of Scottish Studies Archives, University of Edinburgh, recorded from Donald Ferguson, Port Wemyss, Islay by D. A. MacDonald and Alan Bruford, published in *Tocher* 28, 1978 (SA 1968/95 A3)

School of Scottish Studies Archives, University of Edinburgh, from Dugald Bell, Port Charlotte, Islay, published in *Tocher* 23, p. 284, 1976 (Maclagan Mss pp. 5083-4)

School of Scottish Studies Archives, University of Edinburgh, recorded from Mrs Earl, Port Ellen, Islay by Mary MacDonald, 1969, published in *Tocher* 11, p. 99, 1973 (SA 1969/27/A16)

School of Scottish Studies Archives, University of Edinburgh, recorded from Calum MacLachlan, a native of Kilchoman, Islay by Morag MacLeod and John MacLean, 16 February 1971, published in *Tocher* 1, p. 27 (SA1971/17 A6)

School of Scottish Studies Archives, University of Edinburgh, recorded from Gilbert Clark, Port Charlotte, Islay, by Ian A. Fraser, on 20 November 1970, published in *Tocher* 6, p. 179, 1972 (PN 1970/39)

School of Scottish Studies Archives, University of Edinburgh, recorded from Alasdair Hay, Portnahaven, Islay, by Mary MacDonald in November 1969, published in *Tocher* 4, p. 101, 1971 (SA 1969/144/A)

Scots Magazine, Emigration of 500 People from Islay, Summer 1771

Seanchas Ìle, Islay's Folklore Project, List of Old Proverbs, 1988

Memoir of surviving the *Otranto* disaster by Pvt. Edgar A.P. Sheppard, Museum of Islay Life

William Forbes Skene, *The Highlanders of Scotland*, 1837

Robert Smith, Letter to Andrew Barr on the Salonica front, 5 May 1918

W.A. Smith, *Off the Chain*, 1868

Statistical Account, 1791–1799

The Stent Book and Acts of the Balliary of Islay, 1718–1843

Robert Louis Stevenson, *Memoirs of Himself* (written in 1880, published in 1912)

Robert Stevenson, *An Account of the Bell Rock Light-House*, 1824

Major-General David Stewart, *Sketches of the Character, Manners and Present State of the Highlanders of Scotland*, 3rd edition 1825

Magnus Barefoot's Saga, 1220, from the Icelandic of Snorri Sturleson, trans. Samuel Laing, 1844

Lord Teignmouth, *Reminiscences of Many Years*, 1878

James Thomson, *Transactions of the Geological Society of Glasgow*, 1875

Robert Thomson, *A Cruise in the Western Hebrides or a Week on Board the SS* Hebridean, 1891

The Rev. John Walker, *Report on the Hebrides*, 1764

William J. Watson, *The History of the Celtic Place Names of Scotland*, 1926

Earl H. Weed, US Army Chaplain, Letter concerning *Otranto* victims

L. MacNeill Weir, *Guide to Islay*, 1911

Tom Weir, *The Western Highlands*, 1973

The Whisky Exchange blog, 1 April 2015

S. B. Wilkinson, *The Geology of Islay, Memoirs of the Geological Survey*, 1907

Corporal Alexander Williamson, Letter home from North African front, April 1943

James Wilson, *A Voyage Round the Coast of Scotland*, 1842

President Woodrow Wilson, commemorative plaque to the *Tuscania* and *Otranto* victims on the American Monument on the Oa

Leo V. Zimmerman, *Tuscania* Survivor, National *Tuscania* Survivors' Association pamphlet